ON MAKING SENSE

Stanford Studies in
　　　　COMPARATIVE RACE AND ETHNICITY

ON MAKING SENSE

Queer Race Narratives of Intelligibility

Ernesto Javier Martínez

Stanford University Press
Stanford, California

Stanford University Press
Stanford, California

© 2013 by the Board of Trustees of the Leland Stanford Junior University.
All rights reserved.

No part of this book may be reproduced or transmitted in any form or by any means, electronic or mechanical, including photocopying and recording, or in any information storage or retrieval system without the prior written permission of Stanford University Press.

Printed in the United States of America on acid-free, archival-quality paper.

Library of Congress Cataloging-in-Publication Data

Martínez, Ernesto Javier, author.
 On making sense : queer race narratives of intelligibility / Ernesto Javier Martínez.
  pages cm. -- (Stanford studies in comparative race and ethnicity)
 Includes bibliographical references and index.
 ISBN 978-0-8047-8339-2 (cloth : alk. paper) -- ISBN 978-0-8047-8340-8 (pbk. : alk. paper)
 1. Sexual minorities' writings, American--History and criticism. 2. Gays' writings, American--History and criticism. 3. American literature--Minority authors--History and criticism. 4. Sexual minorities in literature. 5. Homosexuality in literature. 6. Race in literature. I. Title. II. Series: Stanford studies in comparative race and ethnicity.
  PS153.S39M37 2012
  810.9'920664--dc23
                        2012019389

Typeset by Bruce Lundquist in 10.5/15 Adobe Garamond

For my family
Marcolina Feliciano, Jorge Martínez Cardenas,
and Jorge Gabriel Martínez Feliciano
and for
Michael Hames-García

You think your pain and your heartbreak are unprecedented in the history of the world, but then you read. It was books that taught me that the things that tormented me most were the very things that connected me with all the people who were alive, or who had ever been alive.

James Baldwin

TABLE OF CONTENTS

	Acknowledgments	xi
	Introduction: On the Practice and Politics of Intelligibility	1
1.	Morrison and Butler on Language and Knowledge	23
2.	Dying to Know in Baldwin's *Another Country*	45
3.	Queer Latina/o Migrant Labor	77
4.	Shifting the Site of Queer Enunciation	112
5.	Cho's Faggot Pageantry	137
	Notes	161
	Bibliography	183
	Index	195

ACKNOWLEDGMENTS

I owe a heartfelt thank you to Michael Hames-García, foremost for being a loving friend and partner (a companion in the true sense of the word) for so many years. He also read more drafts of this book than I care to admit. But the manuscript is better for it, and I am grateful to him for sharing his intellectual and editorial support. I also want to thank my mother and father, Marcolina Feliciano and Jorge Martínez Cardenas, who always share what they know about balancing work and family, and who I hope understand that my career (even though it has taken me so far away from home) never means more to me than they do. My education and the writing of this book would not have been possible without their tireless support. I also want to thank my brother, Jorge Gabriel, who has always been for me proof that intellectual life is not limited to the academy. I have always hoped to write this book in a manner that he would be able to appreciate. Last, but certainly not least, I want to thank Kevin. He helped me to understand that designing my workspace could "feed" my writing (and it did!). He also cared for me, in a manner altogether his own, during the last stages of the writing process. I thank him for his love and patience.

Paula Moya, Satya Mohanty, and María Lugones deserve special recognition. For very different reasons, each of them has played a crucial role in the development of my ideas, and their close mentorship and friendship has meant a great deal to me. This book would not have gone to press without Paula's discerning eye and unfaltering support. Satya (generous with his time and always encouraging me to clarify) gave me invaluable criticism and advice throughout.

Lynn Fujiwara has been a generous reader and accountability partner through various stages of the writing process. I thank her, along with several other friends and colleagues whose support and feedback on various stages of my writing was invaluable: Linda Martín Alcoff, Ulka Anjaria, Bernadette Marie Calafel, Pedro Di Peitro, Michele Elam, Sangita Gopal, Dorothy Hale, Jennifer Hartford Vargas, Ellen Herman, Kathleen Karlyn, Jodi Kim, David Lee, Amy Macdonald, Bonnie Mann, Julie Minich, Dayo Mitchel, José Esteban Muñoz, Priscilla Ovalle, Peggy Pascoe, John "Rio" Riofrio, Irmary Reyes-Santos, Shireen Roshanravan, Ramon Saldívar, Carmen San Juán-Pastor, Susan Sánchez-Casal, Tze-Lan Sang, Carole Stabile, Lynn Stephen, John Su, Anita Tijerina Revilla, Tania Triana David Vazquez, Alex Woloch, Yvonne Yabro-Bejarano. Ellen Scott and Lynn Fujiwara (in their capacity as department chairs) were generous in ensuring I had time to write this book, and I thank them kindly for doing so. Yvonne Braun, Charise Cheney, Linda Fuller, Dan Martinez Hosang, Shari Hundorf, Brian Klopotek, Judith Raiskin, and Lizzie Reiss have made departmental citizenship during the long process of finalizing the book a unique pleasure.

My time studying, living, and working in upstate New York laid the early groundwork for this book. I am grateful to Mary Pat Brady, Roger Gilbert, Biodun Jeyifo, Nilsa Maldonado Méndez, Ken McClane, Kate McCullough, Satya Mohanty, Paula Moya, Hortense Spillers, and Helena María Viramontes for their advice on the earliest drafts of this work. Falu Bakrania, Deborah Elliston, Thomas Glave, Leslie Heywood, Joseph Keith, Ricardo Laremont, Joshua Price, Gabriela Sandoval, Oktay Sekercisoy, Susan Strehle, Carol Tushabe, and Lisa Yun played a special role early on as well.

The Future of Minority Studies (FMS) research project has been indispensible in my intellectual development, and there are many people to thank. I thank Stephanie Fryberg for being a constant intellectual partner and collaborator, and for inspiring me to dream bigger and accomplish more. Linda Martín Alcoff, Chandra Talpade Mohanty, and Paula Moya were the first to invite me to share my work-in-progress. I thank them for their commitment to mentorship, and for helping my scholarship through their example. Tobin

Siebers and Beverly Guy-Sheftall, in ways that are unique to their intellectual training, temperament, and areas of expertise, have gifted me insights that I continue to work through in my scholarship. M. Jacqui Alexander and Minnie Bruce Pratt took me on a two-week intellectual journey in the summer of 2010 that was, in every sense of the word, decolonizing in its praxis and impact. Tiffany Willoughby-Herard writes in a way that makes me listen, and I thank her for modeling courage and good humor in an academy that often does not have our best interests in mind.

As with most research projects, financial support is crucial. I received generous financial support and mentorship from the Center for Race, Ethnicity, and Sexuality Studies, the Center for the Study of Women in Society, the Oregon Humanities Center, and the College of Arts and Sciences at the University of Oregon. I also received mentorship and support from the Ford Foundation, the National Woodrow Wilson Career Enhancement Fellowship, the Mellon Mays Undergraduate Fellowship, and the Future of Minority Studies (FMS) research project.

ON MAKING SENSE

INTRODUCTION
On the Practice and Politics of Intelligibility

"AGAINST OBSESSIVE FUCK COUNTING"

In 2003, one of the largest nonprofit AIDS services organizations in the United States, AIDS Project Los Angeles (APLA), placed itself in a precarious position regarding conservative funding streams by departing from HIV prevention models grounded solely in the empirical social sciences and launching a provocative, sex-positive cultural journal as an alternative method of HIV prevention. This journal, called *Corpus*, focused on writings and artwork devoted to gay sex primarily from the perspectives of men of color, and it was spearheaded by three gay Latino intellectuals: a trained clinical psychologist (George Ayala), a writer (Jaime Cortez), and an artist (Patrick "Pato" Hebert). Rather than understand gay sex from the perspective of epidemiologists and government officials as "a problem to be solved or behavior to be quantified," *Corpus* understood gay sex (and gay male life) as a "platform from which to launch more sophisticated and nuanced explorations of desire, pleasure, culture, HIV and the challenges of living with multiplicity."[1] Ayala, APLA's then director of education, notes that the motivation behind this shift was to address the decreasing salience of HIV prevention campaigns at the turn of the twenty-first century for gay men. This decrease was attributable not only to an outreach agenda that was overly generic and didactic—unable, as Ayala notes, to address "the subjective experiences of gay men in visible and affirming ways"—but also to methods of analysis that were reliant on presumably objective, but ill-conceived empirical measures.² Ayala explains, "We continuously ask gay men to report how often condoms were not used during anal sex with how many sex partners of which gender in what positions in a given window of time, as if this would teach us how to reduce the risk of HIV infection. Our obsessive fuck counting, however, yields only an impoverished understanding of what gay men think and feel when we have sex. In the end, we learn little about pleasure and desire, the place each occupies in our lives, and the meaning that we bring to each."³

What Ayala understands as problematic, and what *Corpus*, in turn, is designed to correct, is an HIV/AIDS industry's self-induced myopia regarding gay men, a reduction of gay men's complex lived reality under the pretense of objective epidemiological and scientific analysis. In addition to addressing what previous models of HIV prevention did not fully understand (or care to know) about gay men—namely, that gay men's sexual lives are not problems to be solved nor behaviors to be quantified—Ayala brings attention to the cumulative effect this knowledge gap has *on* gay men. The HIV/AIDS industry accumulates information about MSM ("men who have sex with men") in an effort to curb and end the spread of HIV and AIDS. But this information, as it filters down to gay men (as information about the category "men who have sex with men") reproduces the process by which gay men become, yet again, alienated from themselves, rarely serving as reference points for knowledge unless they are a population to be studied. The adage "information is power," gets flipped here, not because gay men can do without knowing such things as how HIV is transmitted, but because the abstraction employed in collecting and disseminating "facts" about "MSM" coheres with forces that systematically rob gay men of their ability to interpret their own lives and deny them credibility as knowers.

APLA's decision to foreground the subjective experiences of gay men (and in particular gay men of color), to do so through literature and the telling of personal and cultural stories (rather than through sociological data only), and to claim that better knowledge could be gained about gay men and the spread of HIV, raises important questions. With what notion of identity, subjectivity, and experience, and with what critical understanding of stories, of literature and culture, does APLA claim to be accessing not just new, but better knowledge about gay men and the world in which gay men carve out an existence? What kind of claim to knowledge is APLA making with this journal? What might count as its proof? What bodies of theoretical work might substantiate its practice?

"PEOPLE CANNOT BE HANDLED THAT WAY"

In 1962, about forty years before *Corpus* was inaugurated, the gay African American writer James Baldwin published a provocative novel—reviewed by his contemporaries with limited acclaim, referenced as a paradigmatic example of Baldwin's racial self-hatred, and banned domestically and abroad for its sexually "obscene" nature. Panic aside, the novel arguably explores a set of emotional states previously undocumented in the racial and sexual discourse of the American mid-twentieth century—states of profound confusion and unacknowledged incoherence that accompany a group of "well-meaning" friends and lovers as they negotiate cross-racial tensions and queer desires. Implicit in this novel is Baldwin's own theory of the role literature can play in politics and social analysis. For Baldwin, the novel has the opportunity to exceed the didactic limits of political pamphleteering as well as the presumed (detached) objectivity of the social sciences, and to tell a different story altogether. The novel, for Baldwin, has the opportunity not simply to chronicle crimes against humanity, shocking and shaming people into social action, but to explore another narrative with a different question: What motivates people to commit those crimes in the first place? Likewise, the novel—when dedicated to providing an account of *what it feels like* to negotiate knowledge in oppressive contexts, rather than to simply tell people what to think—presents a confrontation and rebuttal with the logic of the mid-twentieth century social sciences as unbiased mediators of "truth" (about minority populations) through "facts." Baldwin captures this critique of the establishmentarian social sciences by reminding us of the difference between the knowledge we need (in order to live and survive the contradictions of a racist and homophobic America) and the knowledge that we often get (which is so frequently alienating): "We think that once one has discovered that thirty thousand, let us say, Negroes, Chinese, or Puerto Ricans have syphilis or don't, or are unemployed or not, that we've discovered something about the Negroes, Chinese, or Puerto Ricans. But in fact, this is not so. In fact, we've discovered nothing very useful because people cannot be handled in that way."[4]

Baldwin is unconvinced by the truth effect produced about minority "populations" through empirical methods; more so, he is passionate and unequivocal about the role literature can play in providing alternative stories, accounts that contain liberatory insight otherwise minimized, misread, or never accessed.

A DECOLONIZING POLITICS, A REALIST PRACTICE

The critical turn toward literature and cultural stories promoted by Baldwin in the early part of his career and redeployed by APLA at the turn of the twenty-first century represents more than critique of the empirical social sciences. Indeed, it echoes an ambitious vision promoted by an overlapping cohort of intellectuals, cultural producers, and activists (among them several social scientists) about the necessity of decolonizing our knowledge-generating practices.[5] Cherríe Moraga's call to theorize from the "flesh and blood experiences of women of color" and Gloria Anzaldúa's theory of "la facultad" to explain the ability of marginalized groups to "see in surface phenomena the meaning of deeper realities" are luminary Chicana lesbian feminist instantiations of epistemic decolonization.[6] They share with theorists of decolonization like Paolo Freire and Rodolfo Kusch, or Walter Mignolo and María Lugones, a radical commitment to *think from* the position of suppressed knowledges and marginalized subjectivities, rather than about them. This commitment amounts to purposeful epistemic insubordination within Western paradigms of knowledge production because it engages ways of thinking and ways of being that have been considered, as Laura Pérez notes with regard to Chicana art and spirituality, illegitimate starting points for knowing, and also because it calls critical attention to the proclivity in Eurocentric disciplines to hide, or remain unconcerned by, the geo-historical and class locations of their own theorizing.[7] Roderick Ferguson, in his articulation of "queer of color critique," has argued similarly for a type of decolonizing reading practice, anchored in African American literature as a complex archive of social analysis that challenges canonical sociology's account of African American lived reality. The decolonizing challenge in Ferguson's approach is not grounded in the illusion that African American literature is free from contradictions and ideological mystifications. The challenge, instead, is that queer of color critique deliberates about the world from the "underside" of modernity/coloniality, by attending to ways of knowing and acting that have emerged from subjugation or distortion, and that have the potential to raise new insights about the social world. Critical race theorists might similarly be thought of as decolonizing the field of legal studies, if only by challenging the "implied objectivity, neutrality, and impersonal voice of mainstream scholarship" through an explicit and rigorous engagement with the "material, aesthetic, emotional and spiritual experiences of people of color."[8]

The decolonizing imperative in this body of work should not be confused with an embrace of antirealism or relativism. Rather, embedded within the efforts of APLA, Baldwin, Anzaldúa, and Moraga, among others, are a set of recurring and underappreciated "realist" arguments regarding the epistemic status of social identities and minority experiences.[9] Part of my effort in this book is to unearth and clarify these arguments, showing that through a greater attention to the subjective levels of reality—particularly through the careful study of stories and narratives that arise from the experiences of queers of color and other marginalized people—we can gain better knowledge about our shared social world.[10] Realist arguments manifest themselves frequently in the assertions queers of color make about how they acquire better and more accurate knowledge, and about how they make sense of their experiences. The full impact of these arguments, however, remains potentially unrecognized by contemporary critics because of the excessive skepticism that has dominated academic discourse regarding the relationship between identities, experiences, and objectivity. This skepticism often derives from an antirealist or subjectivist belief that there is no truth of the matter—that all we can talk about is how "truth" and "identity" are constructed, and how they are ultimately no more than fictions.[11] Although how "truth" and "identity" are constructed is of great concern to me, I want to argue against the skepticism that presents this as the only interesting question to be asked of "truth" and "identity." I aim to show how the rich and meaningful experiences of racial and sexual minorities can be best gleaned if we assume that there is indeed an objective reality, and that reference to that reality is possible. This inclination can lead us to other questions, like whether a given truth claim is valid or whether a given identity is useful—and for what end.

Few scholars in literary and cultural studies today are inclined to speak of "objective reality" and "objectivity" without some degree of cynicism. While many good reasons for this cynicism exist, one undergirding justification is poorly conceived. Critics too often spar with the static and easily dismissible notion of objectivity as certainty, as knowledge that is presumably context transcendent and free from bias. This is not the notion of objectivity to which I refer in this book. I understand objectivity as a process of approximation necessarily tied to social and historical conditions, a process that requires the analysis of different kinds of subjective and theoretical bias, as well as an understanding that knowledge claims are fallible, open to revision and critique.[12] This less totalizing and more useful understanding of objectivity is frequently at play in the way that queers of color deploy literature and cultural stories. Related to this understanding of objectivity is an equally substantive understanding of the epistemic status of identities and experiences.

Returning to *Corpus*, for example, we notice that the editors' decision to *think from* the position of gay men of color implies an understanding of identity and experience as useful resources for the acquisition of better, more accurate knowledge. This perspective diverges from understandings of identities as imposed impediments, as limiting constructions that are politically unreliable and which we would do best to critically distrust rather than believe in.[13] Similarly, the knowledge that Ayala understands he can generate about the lives of gay men through cultural production and personal experience is not simply *different* from that produced by empirical studies; it is also in some crucial ways *better*. Explaining the richness of this evaluative claim entails, at least in part, an account of the utility of social identities that goes beyond rote understandings of them as only "strategically" important. Instead of understanding identities as *arbitrary* social constructs, as *fictions* which impose meaning rather than provide access to an existing reality, *Corpus* understands identities less negatively and rigidly. *Corpus* shares with US minority realist critics the belief that identities, precisely because they are mediated (constructed) and causally related to the social world, are crucial avenues for deep social literacy. While *Corpus* does not naively rely on identity-based knowledge as a given, it remains optimistic about identity at a historical moment where optimism pushes up against the limits of established frameworks of credibility. This optimism, far from signaling a lack of judgment and sophistication, employs Linda Alcoff and Satya Mohanty's more nuanced assessment of identities as social constructs, an assessment that shows how identity claims can be not only "specious, narrow, and incorrectly described," but also "plausibly formulated and accurate."[14] Alcoff and Mohanty clarify, "We contend that identities can be no less real for being socially and historically situated, and for being relational, dynamic, and at times, ideological entrapments. Moreover, we believe that identity-based knowledge can achieve objectivity, not by the (unachievable) ideal of the disinterested, passive observer, but through a more workable approach to inquiry that aims to accurately describe the features of our complex, shared social world."[15]

This realist perspective on the relationship between identity and knowledge is implied in James Baldwin's work as well. Throughout his career Baldwin was emphatic about the constructedness of black and white identities, showing us how profoundly and inelegantly these identities produce opacity in the lives of everyday Americans. But he was equally attuned to the tangible reality of living in a world organized so predictably and systematically on the subjugation and distortion of what black people feel and know. Additionally, Baldwin provocatively reminds us that although the *reality* of antiblack racism certainly has negative consequences for "black" communities (that is, for how they can live, where they can go, and who they can imagine themselves to be), it most peculiarly and negatively leaves "white" communities epistemically compromised and damaged. He tells us in his 1963 speech "A Talk to Teachers" that curricular change in America's K-12 education system is necessary not only in order to teach blacks "their history," but also to teach white US Americans theirs. Baldwin writes:

If [...] one managed to change the curriculum in all the schools so that Negroes learned more about themselves and their real contributions to this culture, you would be liberating not only Negroes, you'd be liberating white people who know nothing about their own history. And the reason is that if you are compelled to lie about one aspect of anybody's history, you must lie about it all. If you have to lie about my real role here, if you have to pretend that I hoed all that cotton just because I loved you, then you have done something to yourself.[16]

For Baldwin *better* knowledge about oppression can be achieved through a comparative analysis of identities and their cognitive, material, and relational consequences. These methods are *realist* because they recognize the ideal of objective knowledge as the constant evaluative touchstone guiding social justice movements. Objective knowledge about black and white relationships is possible, Baldwin would add, but not as definite certainty. It is available in degrees, through attention to error, and through the patient effort it takes to reconsider, revise, and own up to mistakes. What matters is not whether identities are constructed but "what difference different kinds of construction make."[17] Against the tendency to associate the constructedness of identities and experiences with epistemic unreliability, realists have sought a more complex and supple account of how identities make possible better and worse knowledge about the world.

TOWARD A DECOLONIZING REALISM

On Making Sense, in the broadest terms, speaks to the prospects of acquiring reliable knowledge about the social world through literary and cultural production and from an embodied perspective. The arguments in this book build upon close readings of literary and cultural texts in order to examine how genres other than critical theory and political practices other than direct activism contribute uniquely to social theorizing and to the thriving of minority communities, particularly by paying attention to ways of knowing and acting in the social world that have emerged from subjugation and distortion and that too often have escaped the purview of systematic theorizing. On the whole, this study is motivated by questions regarding the usefulness of literature and cultural production for engaging historically subjugated knowledge and marginalized subjectivities. Additionally, however, it seeks to understand the role minority identities and experiences—mediated as they may be through language, historical context, and ideology—can play in achieving better, more objective knowledge about key features of our social world.

Literature, culture production, social identity, and subjective experience are all mediated social phenomena. What we understand each to mean depends on a variety of shifting social, historical, geopolitical, and linguistic determinants. In this sense, they are unruly, some might even say questionable, places for developing truth claims about the social world. And yet queers of color, like many other marginalized groups attempting to give meaning to their lives in oppressive contexts, have found rich epistemic and political recourse in them.[18] Some of the best literary and cultural studies criticism on race and sexuality grapples with this complexity, but perhaps too often by underemphasizing the dual challenge queer writers and artists of color pose, both to Eurocentered epistemologies in the US academy and to the antirealism that has influenced theoretical discourse in the humanities for the last twenty years.

Eurocentric epistemologies tend to conceal or remain indifferent to the geo-historical locations of their theorizing. The world and its phenomena are up for interpretation and explanation, sometimes in progressive ways and toward liberatory ends, but always with a return to those thinkers and those intellectual traditions grounded in the production of "the West." Queer writers and artists of color pose a threat to this logic, not by claiming to be outside of Eurocentric thinking regiments, but by exploring their own geopolitics of knowledge production. This is different than acknowledging the "situatedness" and "constructedness" of experience and identity, Walter Mignolo reminds us, for it involves a critical *decolonial* emphasis.[19] It entails an attention to the experiences, contradictions, and minutia of thinking and feeling within what has been called the *colonial matrix of power*, a matrix that has oppressed and dominated at a global scale not only through racism and the control of labor, but through the control of subjectivities and the regulation of knowledge production.[20] The decolonizing challenge posed by queer writers and artists of color regarding knowledge production deserves further attention, especially at the level of textual meaning and cultural interpretation. What we understand certain texts to mean, and how we might endorse certain understandings of the social world over others, demands mindfulness about habits of reading and attention to communities of readers who justify certain forms of social literacy over others.

With respect to reading habits in the academy, an additional assessment is warranted regarding the challenge queer writers and artists of color pose to antirealist schools of thought first popularized by poststructuralist and postmodernist thinking in the late 1980s and 1990s. Antirealist standpoints are rarely named "antirealist." Still, they are recognizable by the lingering afterlife of their iconic claims: identities are fictions, normative claims are violent, linguistic reference is indeterminate, subjecthood is only and always a form of subjection, intelligibility (if desired) is a normative yearning to be recognized as a legitimate subject. Antirealist frameworks share, among other things, a propensity for skepticism toward identity categories. They also endorse suspicion regarding the possibility of accurately referencing an objective reality. On the surface, none of these claims is necessarily objectionable, and it is certainly true that these approaches have been useful as a critique of Western universalism, foundationalist methodologies, and poorly conceived identity politics. But they have left too many critics eager to find fault with a notion of identity- and experience-based human inquiry that conflates the desire to produce *better* knowledge about minority groups and about social injustice with the naive quest for error-free certainty about the social world. The importance one might attribute to the initial iterations of antirealist perspectives becomes difficult to substantiate when these perspectives are taken as dogma in their extreme, unqualified form. When too much emphasis is laid on the elusiveness of identity, knowledge, and experience, scholars can be left with too few tools for recognizing the real substance of the contributions made by artists and activists.

Antirealist frameworks have been uniquely dominant in literary and cultural studies. As a consequence, identity-based knowledge claims made by minority writers and artists of color have often risked distortion and underappreciation. For example, critics informed by antirealist frameworks have tended to rehearse a teleological narrative that characterizes experience-based knowledge and identity-based projects not only as theoretically naive, exclusionary, and politically pernicious but also as antiquated remnants of the past. A number of critics have challenged this implicit teleology. In the field of queer studies, Michael Hames-García has criticized the notion that queer theory solved the pernicious essentialisms of feminist and lesbian and gay politics in the 1970s and 1980s.[21] He notes that queer declarations of theoretical originality and political progress presuppose genealogies that misrepresent, when they do not completely ignore, the contributions of writers and intellectuals of color. He reminds us that in 1981, Cherríe Moraga collaborated with Amber Hollibaugh and then with Gloria Anzaldúa, publishing paradigm-shifting feminist intersectional social analysis before Gayle Rubin argued in 1984 that feminism had not and could not articulate a radical theory of sexuality because it had only been a theory of gender oppression.[22] Hames-García goes on to show that a range of black feminists were producing antiessentialist work in anthologies like the 1982 *All the Women Are White, All the Blacks Are Men, But Some of Us Are Brave* and in essay collections like Audre Lorde's 1984 *Sister Outsider*, long before Diana Fuss argued in 1989 that black women theorists had shown a preference for essentialist modes of theorizing rather than embracing poststructuralist critiques of identity.[23] In her full-length study of lesbian feminism and queer theory, Linda Garber similarly notes that any careful engagement with the cultural and literary production of working-class lesbians and queer people of color of the 1970s and 1980s shows no overwhelming evidence of crude thinking or a naive reliance on identity and experience.²⁴ Likewise, Sharon Holland, E. Patrick Johnson, Ann Pelligrini, Judith Halberstam, and Hiram Pérez, among others, argue that the continued vilification of sophisticated forms of identity politics practiced by working-class lesbians and queer people of color calls into question queer theory's status as an ethical discourse. Indeed, they suggest that queer theory's claims of sophistication and originality coexist uncomfortably with its erasure of people of color and working-class white women as critical thinkers.²⁵

Scholars eager to make space for experiential knowledge and minority political perspectives have had to contend with the normative pressures of antirealist thinking, most recognizably in the 1990s by conceding "essentialism" and arguing instead for its "strategic" deployment. Chicana feminist theorist Emma Pérez is frequently associated with this careful maneuvering in her much cited 1994 essay "Irigaray's Female Symbolic in the Making of Chicana Lesbian *Sitios y Lenguas* (Sites and Discourses)." She writes, "I essentialize myself strategically within a Chicana lesbian countersite as a historical materialist from the Southwest who dares to have a feminist vision of the future. My essentializing positions are often attacked by a sophisticated carload of postmodern, post-Enlightenment, Eurocentric men and by women who ride in the back seat, who scream epithets at those of us who have no choice but to essentialize ourselves strategically and politically against dominant ideologies that serve only to disempower and depoliticize marginalized minorities."²⁶ Here we see Pérez courageously confronting, on the frontlines of the postmodern theory debates, Eurocentric antirealist doctrine. Since then, similar battles have been fought, with the result of "strategic essentialism" circulating and continuing to serve as a rhetorical touchstone for rationalizing the analysis of queer racialized identities. Cindy Patton and Benigno Sánchez-Eppler, for example, gesture toward this sentiment in 2000 when they state that the debate over identity in gay and lesbian studies has been "well-rehearsed," and that "now, identity is viewed as strategic, rather than essential."²⁷ Eight years later, Latino literary critic Lázaro Lima reaffirms the political expediency that motivates the deployment of Latino identities as "real," while simultaneously acknowledging the theoretical incoherence that accompanies this necessity. He writes, "I am interested here in invoking Gayatri Spivak's well-known recourse to 'strategy' and its necessary interests in praxis value over theoretical use value. . . . Latino identity is therefore strategic . . . , grounded in the knowledge that it is a necessary fiction."²⁸

What we see here is a kind of subversive ambivalence. With few exceptions, identities first get framed in the language of antirealism (as "fictions"), but these framings are then neatly set aside or obfuscated in practice. This is accomplished in ways that suggest not only hesitancy in embracing antirealist standpoints, but also a much different and nuanced alternative understanding of what identities might actually be, and what relationship their "constructedness" may have to the production of reliable knowledge.[29] Far from being idiosyncratic deviations, these predictable shifts have served a function in the wake of antirealist theorizing: preventing experience-based knowledge and minority cultural production from being easily dismissed as theoretically naive and simplistic. But this tactic has come with a price. It has enticed scholars to embrace an unjustifiably high level of incoherence between theoretical commitments and political practices.[30] Indeed, with remarkable predictability, identities are often framed in these studies as arbitrary illusions of homogeneity utilized pragmatically from political necessity, but they are then treated less cynically in the practice of interpreting particular case studies. It would seem, then, that a less hyperbolic notion of identity as "constructed" has been available in minority literature and cultural production, and in the body of criticism that takes it seriously, for quite a long time now. This understanding of identity seems closer to the one minority realist critics have advocated for, an understanding of identities, not as essences or fictions, but as bits of social theory. Identities, from a realist perspective, are "socially significant and context specific ideological constructs that nevertheless refer in non-arbitrary (if partial) ways to verifiable aspects of the social world."[31]

One might argue that the tendency to invoke identities from a strategic essentialist perspective (as "necessary fictions") has run its course, and that my summary, while applicable perhaps to the 1990s and with a few key examples in the early twenty-first century, is overstated with respect to contemporary criticism. I agree that fewer scholars today feel the need to explicitly make such claims. The tapering of strategic essentialist rhetoric, however, feels more like an arrived-at consensus of what we presumably already know to be true than a revised understanding of certain inconsistencies and underjustified theoretical assumptions. Not enough attention, I think, has been given to the incommensurability between schools of thought that prioritize and accentuate the *instability* of meaning in texts, identities, and experiences, or that dismiss accurate reference to an objective reality, and those queer writers, artists, and intellectuals of color who—despite attending to the deeply mediated quality of experiential knowledge and creative cultural production—still make claims to understanding real features of their social world.[32]

In the context of discussions over minority identity, cultural production, and social theory, a realist framework aids the process of epistemic decolonization. Realism offers theoretical justification for the disposition to *think from* the locus of suppressed knowledges and subaltern subjectivities. Realism understands the complexity of engaging identity- and experience-based knowledge (and theory-mediated knowledge broadly speaking) but does not give up on the ideal of objectivity so central to the evaluative claims of antiracist, antihomophobic feminist projects. Realism is not simply an *alternative* theoretical framework for contemporary criticism. It is one of the implicit decolonizing assumptions at work in much queer ethnic literature and cultural production. It is worth noting that the realism functioning in this body of work has less to do with achieving error- or presupposition-free certainty about oppression, and more to do with tackling the complex epistemic issues at stake in resistance and survival for queer of color communities, as well as understanding the unique role literary and cultural production might play in articulating knowledge that has emerged from subjugation, distortion, and attempts at erasure.

TO KNOW AND BE KNOWN

The more than fifty-year period between Baldwin's reflections on literature and social justice and APLA's bold inauguration of *Corpus* represents an eclectic and vibrant outpouring of queer ethnic cultural production in the United States. More important than this exponential output, however, is the recurrence and redeployment of an argument—about the importance of cultural production and identity-based knowledge in addressing profound forms of injustice affecting queers of color, particularly affecting them in their capacity to know and be known. In this book I juxtapose key texts produced by black, Latino, and Asian queer writers and artists to argue that, across ethnic groups and genres, and over an extended period of time, queers of color have been developing a decolonial realist understanding of knowledge acquisition in oppressive contexts, one distinguished by a recurring preoccupation with intelligibility. This preoccupation is best understood as a concern with the everyday labor of *making sense of oneself* and of *making sense to others* in contexts of intense ideological violence and interpersonal conflict. The necessity of making sense in these texts should be understood less as a desire to be recognized or accepted by society on society's terms, and more as a desire to confront specific forms of, what philosopher Miranda Fricker has termed, "epistemic injustice"—injustice that affects people in their capacity as knowers and as community members worthy of being known.[33] In their capacity as knowers, queers of color often experience a peculiar set of difficulties. These come in hermeneutic and testimonial forms, as queers of color often struggle not only to interpret their lives accurately, but to be seen as legitimate bearers of knowledge. In their capacity as community members worthy of being known, queers of color often experience challenges, due in large part to the systematic erasure of queer people of color from the social imaginary (i.e., they are simply *not* represented and therefore rarely thought of as important) or through the experience of distorted or diminutive incorporation (i.e., coerced into visibility, but only so long as they remain entertaining, marginal, witty, and benign).

When societies work against queer people of color, they do so not only by ascribing incoherence to their desire and gender expression, not only by making them vulnerable to racism and homophobia (and delegitimizing their experience of it), but also by making it difficult and painful to find community backup and solidarity. This compounded form of oppression induces confusion and fear with respect to burgeoning identities, imposes social isolation and displacement, and naturalizes ridicule and violence. In response to these circumstances, queer writers and artists of color have explored provocative ways of living and resistant forms of consciousness worthy of further critical attention. Chapters 3 and 4 in this book highlight two innovative routes of social theorizing, one having to do with the ways queers of color have represented the process of knowledge acquisition about oppression *spatially*, often as a process of "migrating" in and out of different collectivities, and the other having to do with strategic shifts in narrative perspective, direct confrontations with *where* one reasonably should expect to hear queer stories of resistance and resilience. In both cases, we witness a decolonial realism in practice, particularly as these forms of social theory help us to reframe communities of color as locations from which to elaborate liberatory possibilities.

Chapter 3—"Queer Latina/o Migrant Labor"—turns to queer Latina/o writings of the 1980s and 1990s, particularly essays, short stories, and poetry exploring the "migratory" nature of certain forms of queer social resistance (e.g., moving away from home in order to be queer) in order to understand how coming to consciousness for queers of color is not simply a matter of thinking differently about oneself and one's interests, but a matter of moving into (and creating) spaces where the status quo can be reimagined. This spatial attentiveness is important to note, not solely as a feature of queer ethnic cultural production, not only as a method of knowledge acquisition, but as a critical index of the way societies are structured spatially to control knowledge production and behavior. Rather than catalogue multiple spatial practices of queer Latina/o resistance, this chapter is concerned with making a conceptual distinction between two types: practices that explicitly address spatiality, like queer exodus, and practices more often conceived purely as identity practices that have an undertheorized and/or underacknowledged spatialization. The goal in both of these cases is to foreground the epistemic consequences and challenges of such practices, understanding how an examination of the spatiality of such strategies highlights the knowledge acquisition process for queers of color in contexts of multiple oppressions.

To maintain, as I do, that a meaningful set of questions can be foregrounded and answered when understanding queer ethnic literature and cultural production *as* social theory is not an attempt to disregard formal specificities distinguishing literary and cultural texts from conventional scholarship. On the contrary, such juxtaposition is intended to be suggestive of the distinctiveness of creative cultural production and, more importantly, suggestive of how that distinctiveness might matter for a methodological reconceptualization of social theory. I show in Chapter 4—"Shifting the Site of Queer Enunciation"—how queer writers of color mine profound social insights in their writings not only thematically but also through experimentations with narrative perspective. Drawing on the work of contemporary writers Manuel Muñoz and Randall Kenan, I explore the significance of writing queer stories from nonqueer perspectives. If the literary history of oppressed groups is, in essence, the history of first-person narratives, of providing testimony from personal experience, what is the significance when queers of color begin narrating queer stories through the eyes of others? I argue that these stories, precisely because they shift the anticipated site of queer enunciation—moving it from the queer subject proper to the queer subject's siblings, friends, parents, and neighbors—produce a fundamental break with the logic of social fragmentation, the logic of community purity that refuses intersectional subjects their social girth, their relationship to various people, histories, and ways of thinking. This narrative-theoretical approach, which I describe as "shifting the site of queer enunciation," emphasizes the intersubjective and social contexts in which queers of color come into being. "Shifting the site of queer enunciation," as a narrative practice, helps us to see that queer experiences are actually *coproduced and shared* by larger collectives (even though these collectives often deny their own implicatedness in queer sociality). It also provides an unusually in-depth reminder that some nonqueer people actually work to resist the logic of social fragmentation mandated by homophobic societies and that they do so, at times, by bearing "faithful witness" to acts of queer social resistance—even when it is dangerous to do so.

A very important, but relatively recent critical body of scholarship has proliferated around questions of race and sexuality, and has challenged a longstanding pattern of rendering questions of race, intersectionality, and queer people of color marginal within contemporary theory. This body of scholarship—often grouped under the term "queer of color critique"—has enriched our understandings with respect to the everyday lives and political perspectives of queers of color, but it has also developed new theoretical approaches, with interventions tailored to specific schools of thought. Ferguson's version of "queer of color critique" commits itself as a challenge to liberalism and Marxism. Another version of queer of color critique has taken on queer theory. This latter version is the body of work I am particularly interested in, since it has made a point of addressing (with varying degrees of discomfort and disillusionment) a palpable Eurocentric queer scholarly indifference to the knowledge produced by racial minorities broadly speaking, and by queer people of color specifically.

This version of queer of color critique might be said to have three related formulations. These formulations overlap and are coextensive, but I separate them here for analytic purposes. The first formulation expresses little or no concern with the theoretical frameworks employed by Eurocentric queer theorist (in fact, it often applauds those frameworks). However, it does question the lack of *thematic* engagement in this body of work with questions of race, ethnicity, and nation.[34] The problem, according to this perspective, is racial "blind-spots"; the error is in failing to attend to "other" foci of interest. The second critique concerns itself with the absence of people of color as interlocutors as well as with the lack of thematic attention to questions of race, but it places critical emphasis on the ways that mainstream queer theorists falsely universalize their theories of sexuality and gender by failing to name their own Eurocentric grounding.[35] The third formulation, which we might want to name "suppression through citational incorporation," points out the ways that some queer theorists actually disengage with the work of people of color by rendering them innocuous through brief citation and footnote. In this last instance, queer theorists are critiqued for conveying interest in, as well as general knowledge of, this body of work, in a manner that ultimately renders it topical, particular, and more generally irrelevant to the theorization of "sexuality" and "gender."[36] Mariana Ortega, drawing on the work of María Lugones and Marilyn Frye, has named one version of this form of incorporation within white feminist theory "loving, knowing ignorance."[37] Ortega considers this phenomenon acutely pernicious because it "produce[s] ignorance about women of color and their work at the same time that it proclaims to have both knowledge about and loving perception toward them."[38] Through this purported engagement, women of color become "important" in theoretical debates, but only because white scholars have distorted their critiques and perspectives through sanitized citation.[39] Sharon Holland addresses a more caustic version of this sanitizing process as a "criticision—somewhere between an intellectual statement and a bris—a critic's way of pronouncing the death knell for a particular intellectual line of inquiry by managing it."[40]

I am interested in all three manifestations of this critique, but particularly in the way that scholars like Omise'eke Natasha Tinsley have characterized the issue as one of decolonizing the academy. For Tinsley, decolonization hinges on how carefully the academy *"listens to other kinds of theorists."*[41] This claim may sound overly simplistic to some, eerily close to the version of "identity politics" vilified in antirealist theoretical circles. But here Hiram Perez's reflections on how "identity politics" gets invoked by white queer theorists as policing epithet with regulatory consequences needs to be heeded: "It is entirely possible that I am revisiting already exhausted arguments, but it is also possible that queer theory quite opportunely resists engaging particular types of inquiry. The field needs to ascertain how any such resistance is rewarded. After a decade (or longer) of hearing 'the same thing,' it might be time for queer theory to start listening."[42] Along these lines, I think a stronger critique—oriented toward theoretical presuppositions rather than solely toward white ethnocentrism—can be made. The repeated lack of engagement with intellectuals of color and with questions of race in contemporary queer theory might be tackled differently, in other words. Locating problems with background assumptions and philosophical standpoints might help us to deepen what Tinsley and Perez mean by "listening," disputing the claim that this body of work simply needs to introduce new objects of study.

Chapters 1 and 2 in this book bring further attention to this issue by foregrounding the ways that antirealist theories of language and identity become overlooked liabilities in contemporary criticism, particularly around the inclusion of, and engagement with, minority cultural production. Chapter 1—"Morrison and Butler on Language and Knowledge"—argues that the contemporary study of queer ethnic literature and cultural production requires, as a point of clarification and as a new, critical point of departure, an overdue assessment of the role writers of color more generally have played in key antirealist studies. Specifically, I examine a disjuncture between the ways writers of color have tended to conceptualize knowledge acquisition in oppressive contexts and the ways that antirealist Eurocentric critics have understood that process. This chapter draws on Toni Morrison's theory of narrative (as generative and referential) and links it to the practice and politics of epistemic decolonization at the root of queer ethnic literature and cultural production. This chapter also points out the racial logic and racist significance by which Morrison's theory becomes valued (only because it is misread) in Judith Butler's study *Excitable Speech: A Politics of the Performative*. In Butler's study, Morrison's lecture is selectively cited in order to support claims about the indeterminacy of language that are curiously at odds with Morrison's own understanding of language and social reference. This chapter raises questions about Butler's use of Morrison not only to point to discrepancies but also to pose broader decolonial observations about the perfunctory and instrumental presence of writers of color as evidence in critical projects employing antirealist presuppositions.

Chapter 2—"Dying to Know in Baldwin's *Another Country*"—builds on the previous discussion by examining an important text in queer ethnic literary history, James Baldwin's idiosyncratic 1962 novel *Another Country*, arguing that the novel's peculiar emphasis on the near impossibility of acquiring reliable knowledge in oppressive contexts actually challenges antirealist articulations of the "indeterminacy" of linguistic reference and the "social construction" of identities. The difficulty that Baldwin explores in this novel refers to the difficulty of living in resistance to oppression. Baldwin shows how living differently in oppressive contexts (living against oppressive "common sense") frequently involves making extreme, nonarbitrary shifts in self-conception—of who one is in relation to society. These shifts, however, are often experienced as dangerous, confusing, and self-menacing because they register the complexity of opposing a social order in which one is implicated. Baldwin implies that shifts in self-conception hold liberatory promise because these shifts have implications for how we act, think, and feel in relation to oppressive social orders. But not all shifts in self-conception, according to Baldwin, lead to the acquisition of reliable knowledge or produce social change. Rather than understand identities as mere "social constructs" we would do better to *undermine* or be better without, Baldwin understands identities as nonarbitrary and yet malleable "theories" that have a complex, causal relationship to the social world. Identities, according to Baldwin, can be limiting, but they can also be rethought to explain aspects of the social world and our experiences in it. Rather than simply assert this fact, Baldwin writes a novel that helps us to better understand why such potentially important shifts in self-conception are so rarely achieved.

Both Chapter 1 and 2 of this book point to a hegemonic antirealism, often barely recognizable in its regulatory effects but for the frequency with which the identity- and experience-based claims of writers and intellectuals of color are misread or dismissed. Critical race theorists have noted the complicities (unwitting at times) between antirealism and white ethnocentrism for several decades now.[43] No longer dismissible as simple "identity politics," these critiques now spanning more than three decades, carry with them lasting indictments, not the least because the scholars deploying these critiques actually share some constructivist commitments.

As noted by Mohanty, the "return to realism" among minority literary critics and philosophers in recent years can best be understood as a corrective response to the authority postmodern skepticism has received as an epistemological position in the academy.[44] Realists are committed to the idea of social construction, but are less pessimistic about the attainability of objective knowledge.[45] This revised constructivism makes possible new avenues for understanding what role identity- and experienced-based knowledge might play in decolonizing social inquiry.

However, this revised constructivism might still be refuted on the grounds that "identity politics" (read as *reductive* politics) is still alive and well; marginalized groups are still susceptible to liberal humanist "over-idealizations," their perspectives too often taken as unquestionably factual and too frequently deployed as ideologically untainted.[46] The realist argument for granting "epistemic privilege" to marginalized groups, however, does not come from sidestepping complexity, but from carefully interrogating the social and epistemic consequences of social location.[47] Writing on the idea that people who experience oppression might know something important about how it functions, Moya explains that "the key to claiming epistemic privilege for people who have been oppressed in a particular way stems from an acknowledgment that they have experiences—experiences that people who are not oppressed in the same way usually lack—that *can* provide them with information we all need to understand how hierarchies of race, class, gender, and sexuality operate to uphold existing regimes of power in our society."[48] Moya's account of epistemic privilege insists on the value of experiences, without claiming that experiences have, in and of themselves, inherent meaning. There is no one-to-one correspondence between experiences of oppression and accurate knowledge of how oppression works, but neither is the relationship between the two random.[49]

The kind of objectivity to which realists refer is inextricably tied to social and historical conditions, and it is the product "*not of disinterested theoretical inquiry so much as of particular kinds of social practice.*"[50] Drawing on Sandra Harding and Richard Boyd, Mohanty reminds us that oppositional social struggles are precisely the kind of activity that fosters greater objectivity. Mohanty writes:

> In the case of social phenomena such as sexism and racism, whose distorted representation benefits the powerful and established groups and institutions, an attempt at an objective explanation is necessarily continuous with oppositional political struggles. Objective knowledge of such social phenomena is in fact often dependent on the theoretical knowledge that activism creates, for without these alternative constructions and accounts . . . our capacity to interpret and understand the dominant ideologies and institutions is limited to those created or sanctioned by these very ideologies and institutions.[51]

Oppositional social struggles, however, are not objective simply because they are oppositional in the abstract, but because they are oppositional within certain social and political contexts and with certain theoretical and political commitments in mind. Realists are not arguing that objective knowledge is achieved by context-blind acts of oppositionality, or, for that matter, by error-free oppositional practices, but that oppositional struggles have the possibility for contributing to objective knowledge given their ability to "reference" key aspects of the social world that would otherwise remain invisible. In other words, the kinds of practices that may yield objective knowledge, although plural, are not infinite and do obey some epistemological and social constraints. These "constraints" should not be conceived as arising from a reality unfettered by ideology and language, but neither should they be understood as entirely contingent.[52]

I conclude this book, in Chapter 5, by reconsidering a realist claim regarding oppositional social struggles and objectivity—that knowledge about oppression is not the product of "disinterested theoretical inquiry, so much as of a particular kind of social practice." For many radical queers, an epistemically disobedient social practice is to refuse being in the position of defending the humanity of gays and lesbians (as if one could simply mitigate homophobic violence by pointing to queer people's "true humanity" and "essential value"), and instead assert, with provocative pleasure and irreverence, queerness as a way of life to be desired and modeled after. This practice refuses to participate in the politics of explanation, which necessarily centers homophobic logics. From a realist standpoint, any claim to objectivity on behalf of this practice (that is, any claim that this practice points to something true in the social world) relies less on whether it is conventionally "balanced" and "fair," and more on what its provocation makes possible, its "objectivity" resting on the fact that it points to a social world that actively thwarts the queer imagination. Chapter 5—"Cho's Faggot Pageantry"—turns to the work of comedian Margaret Cho and engages her stand-up comedy as an entry into this irreverent practice of "making queerness desirable." Her highly acclaimed performances of identification with gay male subculture are unique locations from which to theorize oppositional struggle and objectivity, not because she claims to represent gay men accurately or in their full complexity and diversity, but because she highlights the fractured (compromised) locus from within which gay men negotiate active subjectivities, and from which she herself negotiates survival as a racialized, queer woman. This fractured locus is not "shared" in any conventional sense of being experienced or understood similarly, but it is collectively discerned through defiant acts of witnessing and coimplication, of valuing and creating connection to what would otherwise be marginalized and shamed. Cho celebrates gay men, not as an act of detached empathy or diffident longing, but as a way to recreate her own sense of agency in the face of racial, gender, and sexual oppression. Notably, an important mechanism through which she performs this appreciation of gay men is through *racialized conduits*—through performances that signify "black gay men/black drag queens" and through her caricature of her Korean immigrant mother. These racialized conduits, or what Kathryn Bond Stockton has recently theorized as "switchpoints," powerfully transmit the idea of the gay community as alluring (in their resistant and crafted perversity) and empowered (through a redeployment of their presumed marginality) by evoking the specific meanings and emotions usually attached to "black gay men/black drag queens" and Asian immigrant women. The *queer* impact of her show also rests on her hallmark "disidentification" with heterosexuality, a complex balancing act of critique that allows her to be perceived as heterosexual for her audiences even as she works to demystify heterosexual masculinity and heterosexual desires as idealized and natural.

As I try to show in this book, queers of color have been developing unique and often theoretically rich forms social and political literacy that deserve further attention. They have become acute readers of their circumstances. But how they have gone about cultivating these robust literacies and why these might be important for contemporary theory remain questions to be carefully answered. Examining these forms of literacy, and becoming fluent in them, does not imply that they explain everything about the social world, or that they explain the social world well in every instance. However, engaging these literacies and coming to understand them as creative and hopeful attempts to make sense of a world often hostile at every turn, initiates a process with decolonizing and realist implications. My goal has been to trace and explore the ways queers of color have been grappling with epistemic forms injustice in their lives, forms of injustice that affect them most insidiously in their capacity to know and be known. Rather than understand this epistemic injustice as functioning solely at the level of everyday life, I address it at as a palpable, albeit ironic reality at the level of contemporary theory and criticism.

CHAPTER 1

MORRISON AND BUTLER ON LANGUAGE AND KNOWLEDGE

> Language remains alive when it refuses to "encapsulate" or "capture" the events and lives it describes. . . . The violence of language consists in its effort to capture the ineffable and, hence, to destroy it, to seize hold of that which must remain elusive for language to operate as a living thing.
>
> Judith Butler, *Excitable Speech*

> Your answer is artful, but its artfulness embarrasses us and ought to embarrass you.
>
> Toni Morrison, *The Nobel Prize Lecture in Literature*

BEYOND "RACE FATIGUE":
A PROLOGUE ABOUT OUR TIMES

"*Everything that I am about to say in this essay has already been said.*" This is the strategic concession deployed by the literary critic Hiram Perez in his courageous 2005 critique of Euro-American queer theory, a subversively bifid acquiescence gesturing toward what we may want to call the phenomenon of "race fatigue" operating within feminist and queer theory circles today. This race fatigue comes in at least two forms. On the one hand, there is the fatigue of a certain kind of feminist or queer academic who feels, as Perez notes, "disgruntled" about the persistent appeal to be in conversation with intellectuals and writers of color, to not misuse their ideas, and more importantly to elaborate antiracist, non-Eurocentric scholarship. This disgruntlement can have various manifestations, as is the case when queer theorists like John Champagne dismiss such perceived injunctions as theoretically naive and emotionally manipulative or when early feminist scholars like Mary Daly simply do not respond to the perception that women of color have been misused.[1] On the other hand, there is the fatigue of primarily intellectuals and writers of color who, faced with a laundry list of erasures and distortions, express grief and anger at the persistent lack of reciprocity, not to mention a profound sense of exhaustion at having to perform, time and time again, the spectacle of the angry person of color obsessed with questions of race and racism.

What is striking about Perez's performative utterance is that it registers a record of exhaustion for which there are at least two seemingly incommensurable understandings. Yet, how do we resolve the problem for which "race fatigue" is, perhaps, only a symptom? If scholars are indeed tired (albeit for significantly different reasons) of concerns being raised about race and racism in the work of white feminist and white queer scholars, how do we move productively through such differently justified exhaustion? What tools are at our disposal in order to address a problem that is as pervasive (according to many scholars) as it is unsubstantiated (according to many others)? Will "theory" remain a "racialized" domain, with the obvious privileges of Eurocentric whiteness in American society limiting our capacity to say what we mean and to be heard clearly?

Feminist theorists of race have been especially conscious of these questions, reminding us that if assertions of advancement (with regard to race and racism) often rest on the "inclusion of racial difference," then as a matter of critical assessment the methods and circumstances of incorporation "need to be carefully scrutinized."[2] In the context of struggle over the role of minority intellectual production in feminist and queer theory, I argue that closer attention should be paid to the use of writers of color in projects that employ antirealist assumptions regarding language, identity, and knowledge.[3] I utilize as a primary case study a prominent scholar who straddles feminist and queer theory, Judith Butler, and reflect upon her peculiar misuse of Toni Morrison's *Nobel Lecture in Literature*. By contrasting the theories of language and narrative developed by Morrison in her Nobel lecture with their misappropriation by Butler in *Excitable Speech: A Politics of the Performative*, I show how Butler selectively cites Morrison to support claims about the indeterminacy of language that are curiously at odds with Morrison's understanding of language and social reference. In fact, as I argue, Butler's use of Morrison is a form of aggressive theoretical misappropriation that is symptomatic of a certain antirealist tendency in contemporary scholarly culture.

My discussion of Morrison and Butler builds on Roderick Ferguson's "queer of color critique" as a critical reading practice—turning toward African American literature as a crucial archive of negotiation and launching from that nexus a new interrogation, not of liberalism and Marxism, as Ferguson does, nor of canonical sociology and the distortions of African American lived reality that Ferguson argues it accomplished, but of some of the most taken-for-granted approaches in feminist and queer theory today, antirealist approaches that proclaim antiracist intent and applicability, but converge with racist logics. Deploying queer of color critique in this manner suggests a recalibration of our most basic presuppositions regarding identity and language, not the least because we can now point to several ways in which antirealists distort, in the most predictable manner, some of our writer's most important and nuanced decolonial contributions.

Echoing an extensive record of apprehension and critique expressed by feminists of color such as Barbara Christian and Deborah McDowell, bell hooks and María Lugones, Chandra Mohanty and M. Jacqui Alexander, and Linda Martín Alcoff and Paula Moya, I raise questions with respect to how racialized minorities are represented in antirealist projects, especially those projects informed both by poststructuralist theories of linguistic reference (particularly the belief in the radical indeterminacy of language) and by postmodernist skepticism toward identity categories. I argue, drawing on feminist theorists Paula Moya and Shari Stone-Mediatore, that these projects have recurring interpretive limitations (not to mention regulatory effects) that cannot be overcome without relinquishing some core antirealist commitments. Moya has pointed out that "women of color are often called on in postmodernist feminist accounts of identity to delegitimate any theoretical project that attends to the linkages between identity (with its experiential and epistemic components) and social location."[4] To demonstrate her point, she examines the work of Butler and of Donna Haraway, showing not only how these two theorists misuse Cherríe Moraga's words "without attending to her theoretical insights," but also how they "employ her work at key moments in their arguments to legitimate their respective theoretical projects."[5] Similarly, Shari Stone-Mediatore has engaged Joan W. Scott's influential 1991 essay "The Evidence of Experience"—an essay that advocates a rigid, a priori skepticism toward experience-based knowledge—to reveal its reliance on a series of telling misreadings of Samuel Delany's 1988 memoir, *The Motion of Light in Water*.[6] According to Stone-Mediatore, Scott lodges an unfounded accusation of naive empiricism against Delany, a charge that selectively misreads his words in order to manufacture proof of poststructuralism's timely and unique importance. Far from being a minor example for Scott's argument, Delany becomes what Janet Halley recently referred to as "Scott's 'set text'—the text that she reads and rereads at least three times in the course of the essay."[7] Set up through a series of close readings as the earnest but ultimately naive subaltern who deploys experience in uncomplicated ways, Delany's presence becomes functional—his blackness, gayness, and use of personal experience come together to form the decisive evidence for Scott's avant-garde critique of experience. The academic ripple effects of Scott's argument, rooted in such a misreading, should be cause for concern, in part because white queer scholars like John Champagne have been, in effect, authorized by it to cast doubt on and minimize the identity-based knowledge generated by people of color,[8] but also because scholars of color writing on race in the wake of antirealism have been placed in the awkward position of genuflecting to a body of work that has, in several instances, undermined the importance of ethnic minority intellectual production.

The antirealist theorists mentioned here (e.g., Butler, Haraway, Scott, Champagne) are all white scholars engaged in promoting theoretical propositions based in traditions of scholarship that have not taken the lives and experiences of people of color or the legacies of colonialism as core concerns. By contrast, the writers of color they have misread (e.g., Delany, Moraga, Morrison, Hemphill, Riggs) emerge from cultural and intellectual traditions predicated on the tenet that race and colonialism are constitutive of the categories of modern knowledge production. Rather than imputing racist motives to these well-respected white scholars, however, I suggest that there is a recurring racial logic and racist significance to these erasures that requires further investigation. Quite independent of (white) identities or any presumed (racial) motives, these patterns of erasure and misappropriation reflect a racial logic grounded in the supposition that writers of color are less theoretically astute. Independent of any intentional motives, these misappropriations also carry a powerful racist significance: the ideas of thinkers of color are suppressed and subordinated to the ideas of white theorists. Tacit presuppositions that reflect a larger cultural economy of race are embedded in the claims of leftist scholars who are quick to find fault with, impute naiveté to, dismiss, or subsume under their own views the ideas of people of color. In fact, these precedents have a history and a geography, described by Mignolo, Grosfoguel, and others by the phrases "coloniality of knowledge" and "geopolitics of knowledge." Knowledge claims, including the antirealist claims of queer theory, are based in traditions and practices that as a matter of course take Europe, the West, and the unmarked categories of white existence as an unacknowledged starting point, dismissing as naive or crude anything that departs from that familiar terrain. The result is a necessary misreading, misappropriation, or dismissal of traditions taking off from incompatible points of origin. The examples set by Butler, Haraway, and Scott are illustrative, pointing to the propensity of certain theoretical projects to undermine the insights of writers of color, even as they proclaim a desire to think complexly alongside their work.

A focus on antirealist presuppositions and the interpretive skepticism toward identity and experience that they encourage affords a more capacious account of the pervasiveness of this racial logic. As Moya has argued, scholars across a range of identities can find themselves ill prepared to engage insights produced by writers of color when those insights are grounded in claims concerning identity and experience.[9] Presumed to be always already naive and essentialist, any claims based in identity and experience must be aggressively justified, if not immediately rejected. Interrogating background beliefs and theoretical assumptions, then, may offer new ways to explore relations between Eurocentrism and racism by excavating pernicious presuppositions informing even the most seemingly progressive modes of thought.[10]

If certain theoretical projects consistently invoke people of color in ways that suppress their insights, that isn't just an interpretive misfire (one scholar misreading another), for it influences what and whom we value. To explore the racist significance and racial logic of such misappropriations, I turn to Morrison's realist and decolonial observations concerning language and social reference and then trace how these views are misleadingly appropriated, enlisted into Butler's theoretical project through a series of partial readings. The nature of the misreading is important to note, for it is not simply an interpretive error in need of revision. On the contrary, Butler's misreading obscures the challenge that Morrison's ideas pose to Butler's antirealism. The misreading also has the effect of discrediting scholars of color working within the field of critical race theory, since Butler justifies her framework (through Morrison) in order to critique critical race theory's purportedly dangerous naivete. Reading Morrison's theory of language and reference against Butler's antirealism helps us to understand the significance of knowledge grounded outside the traditions of colonial modernity, and it illustrates the forms of talking past each other that can result when such traditions encounter Euro-centered theoretical projects.

MORRISON ON LANGUAGE AND SOCIAL KNOWLEDGE

In the introductory remarks to her *Nobel Lecture in Literature*, Morrison asserts that narrative has never been "merely entertainment" for her, that in fact she conceives of narrative in a much more robust fashion, as "one of the principal ways" in which knowledge about our shared social world is pursued and acquired.[11] To illustrate and add nuance to this point, Morrison proceeds to address her audience not in a traditional lecture format but by telling a story. The story Morrison begins to tell, however, is not the same one she ends up narrating at the end of her lecture, and it is precisely the staged relationship between these two stories, the seamless rendering of one into the other, that appears central to what Morrison wants to communicate about the dialogic work and indexical nature of telling stories.

The story Morrison begins to narrate as part of her lecture is of an old, black woman whose "reputation for wisdom is without peer" and who is visited one day by young people who "seem to be bent on disproving her clairvoyance and showing her up for the fraud they believe she is."[12] Knowing that she is blind, the children enter her home with malicious intent and ask a question, the answer to which, we are told, "rides solely on her difference from them."[13] One of the children asks, "Old woman, I hold in my hand a bird. Tell me whether it is living or dead."[14] The blind woman—assessing the encounter to be one born of hostility, precisely because "she is blind and cannot see her visitors, let alone what is in their hands"—responds by recasting the cruel question as a problem for the children, themselves, to remain accountable for: "I don't know whether the bird you are holding is dead or alive, but what I do know is that it is in your hands. It is in your hands."[15] Such is the initial parable that provides Morrison with an occasion to reflect on "what (other than its own frail body) that bird in the hands might signify."[16] Choosing to read the bird as language and the woman as a practiced writer, Morrison considers the significance of understanding language as "a living thing over which one has control" and for which all human beings can be said to be responsible (through their own practices of narration).[17]

Among the claims Morrison makes based on this parable, the overwhelming emphasis is on the misuse and abuse of language. Morrison goes on, for example, to speak candidly about the misuse of language by the state in order to censor or by the powerful in order to demean and control.[18] In fact, she comments on various methods of misusing language. She writes, "Whether it is obscuring state language or the faux language of mindless media; whether it is the proud but calcified language of the academy or the commodity-driven language of science; whether it is the malign language of law-without-ethics, or language designed for the estrangement of minorities, hiding its racist plunder in its literary cheek—it must be rejected, altered and exposed. . . . Sexist language, racist language, theistic language—all are typical of the policing languages of mastery, and cannot, do not, permit new knowledge or encourage the mutual exchange of ideas."[19] This emphasis on various misuses of language is not, of course, intended as a description of the totality of what language can be. For Morrison, language can also be put to more productive purposes. Still, the emphasis on the entrenched misuse of language in this first half of her lecture does have enhanced thematic salience precisely because of its relationship to the parable on which it is based and the way the children in that parable have viciously used language in order to assail and insult the blind woman.

Midway through Morrison's lecture, however, a crucial and unexpected shift in perception is dramatized for her audience, and it is done in a way that fundamentally inflects all of Morrison's previous comments about language and violence. In short, Morrison asks her audience to question the veracity of the initial parable—the tone in which it was narrated, the feelings it invoked, the perspective from which it was told. She does so by staging a dialogic encounter between a new group of visitors, in an undisclosed place and time, visitors who—"once upon a time," after having listened to the story of the children and the old woman—ask the following set of challenging and provocative questions:

Who are they, these children? What did they make of the encounter? . . . Suppose nothing was in their hands. Suppose the visit was only a ruse, a trick to get to be spoken to, taken seriously as they have not been before. A chance to interrupt, to violate the adult world, its miasma of discourse about them. Urgent questions are at stake, including the one they have asked: "Is the bird we hold living or dead?" Perhaps the question meant: "Could someone tell us what is life? What is death?" No trick at all, no silliness. A straightforward question worthy of the attention of a wise one. An old one. And if the old and wise who have lived life and faced death cannot describe either, who can?[20]

Such an encounter requires that Morrison's audience reconsider the initial attribution of malice to the children and the question they have ventured. The significance of Morrison's perspectival shift, the importance of her retelling halfway through her lecture, cannot be overstated. The act of questioning the parable's assumptions and, similarly, the process of providing alternative accounts for why the young people asked the question that they did set in motion certain qualities of language and narrative that Morrison wants to emphasize.

By staging the communal process through which an accepted interpretation of a common story can be challenged, Morrison effectively emphasizes the dialogic aspects of producing meaning.[21] She demonstrates that, as part of a collective effort, the interpreters support one another through the risky process of proposing an alternative explanation for a story that is being used to create knowledge. Implied in the staging of the dialogic encounter is a basic presupposition, namely, that the power of language and narration arises, in large part, because we share a common social world and because that world is populated by others who use language similarly. In a characteristically moving and prophetic tone, Morrison compresses such a sentiment of universality in the following manner: "We die. That may be the meaning of life. But we do language. That may be the measure of our lives."[22] According to Morrison, we "do" language not alone, but together—as a social and political activity, a relational one. This point is most eloquently elaborated in Morrison's lecture through her redeployment of the Tower of Babel parable, which she recasts to account for language as an indeed messy but nonetheless dialogic and relational activity with great possibilities:

> The conventional wisdom of the Tower of Babel story is that the collapse was a misfortune. That it was the distraction or the weight of many languages that precipitated the tower's failed architecture. That one monolithic language would have expedited the building, and heaven would have been reached. Whose heaven, she wonders? And what kind? Perhaps the achievement of Paradise was premature, a little hasty if no one could take the time to understand other languages, other views, other narratives. Had they, the heaven they imagined might have been found at their feet. Complicated, demanding, yes, but a view of heaven as life; not heaven as post-life.[23]

The complexity Morrison ultimately attributes to language (what she calls its "nuanced, complex, mid-wifery properties")[24] comes from her explicit acknowledgment that we share a common (albeit diverse and deeply stratified) social world and that our world is populated by others who (despite significant disparities and tangible incommensurability) use language similarly—to communicate, grieve, love, chastise, imagine, assault. According to Morrison and her creative gloss on the Tower of Babel, language will never function as a vibrant possibility for self- and community actualization in any static or easily surmised form. This is so precisely because language is carried out among a plurality of people and interests, and those people and interests, even if at odds, are precisely the catalyst for the vitality of language.

Furthermore, this doing of language, which is a communal doing, has—as a consequence of the people involved, the ideologies at work, and the realities at stake—an indexical dimension.[25] Here I am drawing on Morrison's own implicit assertion that while language can be radically generative ("creating us at the very moment it is being created"),[26] it is also subject to significant constraints. To argue for the indexicality of language is to suggest, on a very basic level, that any utterance (as in the simple phrase "I want this") makes reference to a context, so that its meaning is completed by that context. In other words, any purposeful use of language gets its significance, in part, through its reference to a situation or set of circumstances. With the use of the parable form of communication, however, Morrison intimates another related feature of the indexicality of language. If parables are not indexical in any standard way—because they seem either to have a very general meaning that makes sense in many different contexts or at least to have an unusual freedom from the context of utterance, not requiring that we complete their meaning by reference to that context—the peculiar indexical dimension highlighted with parables, then, is the context of reception and interpretation. For instance, we will never know what exactly the children wanted from the old woman—whether they were there to molest or whether they were there for the possibility of conversation or something in between. The question of indexicality at stake in the parable is not surmised by having access to some true incident that may have happened once. What we do know, however, is that what is there to be understood about this scenario—about how narratives can be used and misused, engaged with, and perhaps even contested—can only be accounted for as we risk providing readings, initiating the process whereby our biases and dispositions, our cultural training and values, come into view as lenses through which we interpret and make sense of our world. This is not simply risking or venturing postulates in the abstract or on one's own, but risking together, affirming, qualifying, and challenging one another to see what can be found there.

The indexicality of language, then, is a necessary complement to the generative power of language previously mentioned and can be summarized in the following way: we are responsible to (and constrained by) what the world is like, what the world is like as far as we know, and what others say about the world and how they act in it. The generative power of language complements its indexicality, reminding us of our ability to shape the world, to influence the terms on which it is understood and experienced. Morrison is not making the extreme claim, regarding the radical, generative power of language, that shifts in how we account for the world can fundamentally change that world. She is making the more qualified and astute claim that the stories we are capable of generating about our shared social world do indeed affect what we can ever know about it. This is the case if the blind woman continues to believe in the unqualified, unforgivable maliciousness of the children and therefore refuses the kind of interaction and compassion on which the children's livelihood and sense of self perhaps depend. A corollary to this claim is also being intimated in Morrison's lecture: our stories, our narrative accounts of our lives, even if they can influence the world, will not entirely constitute the world (in the same way that the children may still remain good children, even if the blind woman perceives them to be malicious and sends them home).

All of this is, admittedly, a preliminary gloss on Morrison's rich lecture. Still, her speech contains a complex set of claims about language and how we make use of language through narrative, claims that hinge fundamentally on the progression from the initial parable to the one she ends up staging as a communal by-product of many people's perspectives. The syncretic and strategic merging of these narratives toward the end of Morrison's lecture cannot be overstated. It is from here that the new visitors question the old woman, and it is from this new vantage point that the children have the opportunity to account for themselves and their question, to say more than they originally wanted or were allowed to. The second part of the lecture does not so much resolve the questions of fault and intentional malice as it begins to narrate a story about the possibilities of communication and trust that arise out of communities of people taking responsibility for language and making use of it in ethical ways. With this staging of responsibility and cooperation, Morrison braids a beautiful narrative that proves, ever so subtly and successfully, that the stories we tell about the world and the creativity that we invest in the telling do not have to invalidate their truth value, their reference to the real world. The children, at the very end of Morrison's lecture, do not, for example, ask the old woman to simply create fictional stories from thin air. Their goal is not to be entertained or distracted but to be moved by stories that reflect the history that they share. They ask, "Tell us about ships turned away from shorelines at Easter, placenta in the field. Tell us about a wagonload of slaves, how they sang so softly their breath was indistinguishable from the falling snow. How they knew from the hunch of the nearest shoulder that the next stop would be their last. How, with hands prayered in their sex, they thought of heat, then sun. Lifting their faces as though it was there for the taking."[27] What is peculiarly moving about this request for stories is that these children invest so much care in the process of requesting them that they themselves actually begin the storytelling process, morphing the necessity of knowing with the responsibility of narrating. In this way, Morrison once again stages the power of collaborating in the storytelling process, ending her lecture with the prophetic voice of the woman who has remained momentarily silent but not aloof, a woman blind and wise: "Look. How lovely it is, this thing we have done together."[28]

BUTLER ON MORRISON AND LANGUAGE

When Judith Butler enlists Morrison's *Nobel Lecture in Literature* to support her thesis on "linguistic vulnerability"—a compound thesis arguing, among other things, that language is always somehow out of our control, that agency (or a certain kind of agency) arises in language rather than in people, and that any attempt at asserting control over language and its effects is pernicious and violent—we get a distorted, partial sense of Morrison's own theory of language and narrative.[29] To accomplish this distortion, Butler must not only ignore the second half of Morrison's lecture but must also fundamentally misread significant portions of Morrison's theory of oppressive language. For instance, at the structural level, Butler's disregard for the second half of Morrison's lecture affords her the opportunity to theorize as if she is learning from Morrison's work, but without having to deal with the political and theoretical imperative of Morrison's ideas taken as a whole. Butler asserts a theory not of language that can be violent (when put to poor use) but of language as acquiring "its own violent force" when it attempts to accurately represent the world.[30] Butler develops a theory not of language that has the potential to exploit the social vulnerabilities of historically marginalized communities but of language as producing an inherent condition of vulnerability in all people; this is a result of language's "interpellative power" and of interpellation's function in "introduc[ing] a reality rather than report[ing] on an existing one."[31]

Making use of Morrison's initial parable, with the children's maliciousness never in question, Butler makes claims about language that overemphasize the abusive purposes to which it is often put to use—"The hate speech that the children perform seeks to capture the blind woman in the moment of humiliation"—in order to lend credibility to her own theoretical emphasis on language and its effects: "The children's question is cruel not because it is certain that they have killed the bird, but because the use of language to force the choice from the blind woman is itself a seizing hold of language, one whose force is drawn from the conjured destruction of the bird."[32] Neglecting to theorize with Morrison's revised parable in mind—where the motivations of the children are recontextualized, where the children take more responsibility for what they are saying—Butler in effect distorts Morrison's own approach to language, an approach interested in the misuses of language, especially to the extent that they serve as instructive possibilities for understanding its more ethical and productive uses. Despite restricting the importance of Morrison's ideas to the claims she makes in the first half of her lecture, Butler is still unable to make Morrison's words mean what she wants them to. This is evident when Butler moves too quickly from Morrison's specific claim that "oppressive language does more than represent violence; it is violence" to her own,[33] very different, claim that all language is violence and that language has the possibility of reducing its violence when "it refuses to 'encapsulate' or 'capture' the events and lives it describes."[34] Butler reaffirms this thesis on language when she paraphrases Morrison a second time, saying that "the violence of language consists in its effort to capture the ineffable and, hence, to destroy it, to seize hold of that which must remain elusive for language to operate as a living thing."[35]

To many readers, Butler's use of Morrison may not seem entirely inappropriate. In fact, Morrison at times appears not only to make the claim that language is somehow always out of our control but also to argue for the more extreme assertion that when language attempts to accurately represent reality it "acquires its own violent force."[36] This is what Butler has us believe, anyway, when she cites Morrison as saying that "the vitality of language" rests in its capacity not to represent (or aspire to represent) reality accurately but to merely and modestly "limn the actual, imagined and possible lives of its speakers, readers, writers . . . , [to arc] toward the place where meaning may lie."[37] There are at least two important reasons to question Butler's framing here. One has to do with literariness in Morrison's work, and the other has to do with differences in the way that Morrison and Butler conceptualize agency and social reference. If we remind ourselves of the speech context in which Morrison initially presented her reflections on the "vitality of language" (that is, the *Nobel Prize Lecture in Literature*) and we pay close attention to her lecture as a whole, we note that her use of the term "language" is repeatedly (if, perhaps, unevenly) in dialogue with literary discourse and not simply with language writ large. Signs of this preoccupation are everywhere in the text, not the least because Morrison explicitly reads the blind woman in the parable as a "practiced writer."[38] This emphasis on literary discourse is also evident when one compares Morrison's original speech delivered for the Swedish Academy in 1993 to the published version in 1994. Whereas the print version of her speech begins with the phrase "Narrative has never been merely entertainment for me,"[39] the original recorded version begins "Fiction has never been merely entertainment for me."[40] The original emphasis on "fiction," rather than "narrative," should not be overly stressed because it is not clear on what grounds Morrison decided to move from referencing a specific genre to referencing the act of telling stories more broadly. However, it should be one important reminder that literariness is in large part what Morrison's lecture is about.[41]

My point is that the claims Morrison makes about language in her lecture need to be contextualized as, in part, reflections on literature. Any claims based on Morrison's lecture—especially with regard to the "vitality of language" resting on a steadfast rejection of simple, one-to-one correspondences between language and reality—need to remain accountable to what Rey Chow, in another context, reminds us is the defining feature of literariness: that it "specializes in indirection."[42] Chow is clear on this point: "Theoretical and literary discourses are distinguished from each other by an essential articulatory difference."[43] She goes on to write, "In literature, the modus operandi is not to speak about something expressly even when one feels one must."[44] Butler's use of Morrison elides this distinction and lends false credibility to her implicit claim that Morrison shares her extreme antirealist philosophical commitments.

Evidence that Morrison differs with Butler on more than questions of (literary) language can be found in the sentences immediately following the one Butler initially quotes, where Morrison offers the following reading of Abraham Lincoln's Gettysburg Address:

> When the President of the United States thought about the graveyard his country had become, and said, "The world will little note nor long remember what we say here. But it will never forget what they did here," his simple words were exhilarating in their life-sustaining properties because they refused to encapsulate the reality of 600,000 dead men in a cataclysmic race war. Refusing to monumentalize, . . . his words signal deference to the uncapturability of the life it mourns. It is the deference that moves [the wise woman], that recognition that language can never live up to life once and for all. . . . Language can never "pin down" slavery, genocide, or war. Nor should it yearn for the arrogance to be able to do so.[45]

That the power of Lincoln's words comes from "refus[ing] to encapsulate" the atrocities that have transpired may seem, at first glance, to support Butler's argument. However, what is being referenced here is the agency and creativity inherent in all language users with respect to the circumstances of their lives. To put it differently, some realities—perhaps especially the most terrible ones—cannot be fully captured through literal language, and the wise speaker will know when not to attempt to do so. Accurate representation, however, is still a legitimate goal and a necessity, especially for marginalized and oppressed communities. For example, it is only through an understanding of language as referentially accurate that future generations can ever know that roughly six hundred thousand people died in the Civil War. Morrison is unapologetic about her concern with the realities that people face (terrible at times) that matter to what they can and cannot say.

And this is where an understanding of Morrison's reflections on literariness (as a specialization in indirection) is especially pertinent. When Morrison argues that language can never "pin down" slavery and that it should not "yearn for the arrogance to be able to do so," her claim is not that we should, for example, abandon historical efforts to document the lives of slaves or relinquish the ability to make moral judgments regarding the enslavement of human beings, but rather that literary language, perhaps more than any other kind of language, has the possibility of doing more than pinning down and representing literally. Her claim is that literary language—precisely because we give it the opportunity to somehow, always, be out of our control—holds important ethical, emotional, and political possibilities for all who value the importance of seeing the world in new ways and learning to think differently. Morrison's implicit claim here sounds closely related to the work of another important African American literary figure, James Baldwin, whose understanding of literature as an open-ended form of social analysis was significantly developed throughout his career. For Baldwin, literary work is not a thesis-driven enterprise, and yet it holds the promise of powerful social insight and impact. He writes, "Let's pretend I want to write a novel. . . . I want to impose myself on these people as little as possible. That means that I do not want to tell them or the reader what principle their lives illustrate, or what principle is activating their lives, but by examining their lives I hope to be able to make them convey to me and to the reader what their lives mean."[46] Baldwin's sentiment—about the power of literary language to communicate not via facts and theses but via description and exploration—is echoed in Morrison's lecture with a new urgency.

Near the end of her lecture, Morrison returns to the story with which she began. This time, however, she suggests that the children, rather than acting maliciously, are instead trying to muster the courage to hold the blind woman accountable for her ability to share with them some sense of what the world is like and what the world can be. They ask this of her with a desire not only to hear stories that speak truths in the face of power and violence but also to hear stories that might help them to tell their own in the future: "For our sake and yours forget your name in the street; tell us what the world has been to you in the dark places and in the light. Don't tell us what to believe, what to fear. Show us belief's wide skirt and the stitch that unravels fear's caul."[47]

As problematic as what Butler decides to quote (and misread) from Morrison's lecture is what Butler refuses to emphasize about Morrison's own work: namely, that Morrison has a completely different understanding of language and violence, narrative and knowledge. For Morrison, there is no ambiguity about oppressive language: "Oppressive language does more than represent violence; it is violence; does more than represent the limits of knowledge; it limits knowledge."[48] Additionally, Morrison writes, "Sexist language, racist language, theistic language—all are typical of the policing languages of mastery, and cannot, do not, permit new knowledge or encourage the mutual exchange of ideas."[49]

This uncompromising account of the effects of oppressive language is exactly what Butler, in her study, sets out to critique. Drawing on J. L. Austin's speech act theory, Butler develops an understanding of the "gap" between speech acts and their potential effects in order to encourage progressive scholars to understand why seeking government intervention on issues of linguistic violence is conceptually flawed. She is thinking here of acts of linguistic violence such as hate speech, and she is critical of progressive thinkers (critical race theorists in particular) who argue that offensive, abusive language directed at historically oppressed communities may constitute punishable action and is not protected free speech. In fact, Butler suggests that if we develop an understanding of offensive language as never able to fully achieve what it portends—as never having the accuracy and verifiability of physical violence—then we can come to understand that racist and sexist language does not have to constitute injury, if we do not let it. She writes:

The firmer the link is made between speech and conduct, however, and the more fully occluded the distinction between felicitous and infelicitous acts, the stronger the grounds for claiming that speech not only produces injury as one of its consequences, but constitutes an injury in itself, thus becoming an unequivocal form of conduct.

The collapse of speech into conduct, and the concomitant occlusion of the gap between them, tends to support the case for state intervention, for if "speech" in any of the above cases can be fully subsumed under conduct, then the First Amendment is circumvented. To insist on the gap between speech and conduct, however, is to lend support for the role of nonjuridical forms of opposition, ways of restaging and resignifying speech in contexts that exceed those determined by the courts.[50]

A working toward this possibility—a possibility of, for example, racist slurs not having to constitute an injury comparable to racist physical violence—is part of the substance of Butler's argument that we can resist racist speech without having to involve the government, particularly on account of the government's ability to punish action, but not speech, and on account of the necessary gap between speech acts and their effects.

Butler's goal of encouraging nonjuridical forms of opposition to racism is, admittedly, thought provoking. On first glance, it even seems to share rough similarities with contemporary social movements like INCITE! Women of Color against Violence and Critical Resistance, both of which point to the role of the state in continuing the criminalization of minority communities and criticize the tendency in liberal thinking to see the state as an unbiased mediator of social conflict.[51] Unfortunately, Butler's argument is grounded in a number of elisions and false assertions, placing the justifiability of her claims, and her possible affinities with these movements, in doubt. That she misreads Morrison for strategic purposes has already been argued. According to feminist philosopher Lisa Schwartzman, however, Butler's work is also laden with other misreadings, from misappropriating Austin's distinction between perlocutionary and illocutionary speech acts to then deploying that misreading against critical race theorists and, in the process, mischaracterizing critical race theory's rationale for how speech acts have the possibility of wounding.[52] These arguments are carefully laid out by Schwartzman, but what bears emphasis (and has relevance to Butler's reading of Morrison) is Butler's remarkable skepticism with respect to understanding the effects of a speech act through an analysis of context. According to Schwartzman, Butler is resistant to the claim that, "in order to know what makes the force of an utterance effective . . . one must locate the utterance within a 'total speech situation.'"[53] In fact, the possibility of defining the "total speech situation" presents, for Butler, a series of problems.[54] More than problems, it leads Butler to make a series of underdemonstrated accusations: "Butler implies that any attempt to define the 'total speech situation,' or to describe the social context in which a speech act occurs, will automatically suggest that there are enduring structures that are permanent and 'static.' More specifically, Butler suggests that the particular accounts that are offered by these hate speech theorists are themselves 'static' accounts of power."[55]

Schwartzman is helpful in identifying the errors in Butler's arguments. First, she shows how hate speech theorists do not, in fact, view social structures as static and unchanging; they actually "attempt to call attention to the context itself as something that desperately needs to be changed."[56] Second, she reminds us that it is Butler's own implicit obsession with certainty—her extreme antirealist fixation on the impossibility of ever achieving error-free, unmediated truth—that renders her a perpetual skeptic, incapable of understanding that attempts to describe social and historical contexts do not automatically lead to impositions of coherence and stability on processes that are always changing and unfixed. Elaborating on this point, Schwartzman writes:

> To say that the context can be given any particular description right at this moment only means that there is some way that the context can be characterized at this point in time. To the extent that an action that occurs within that context (such as an utterance) has any meaning at all, its meaning must be located in some understanding of the context, conventions, or "total speech situation." If future actions or events change the understanding we have of this particular context, we may come to understand the "speech acts" that occurred within this context differently. This is not to say that the speech act has no meaning, but it does suggest that meaning can shift over time and that what we once thought meant one thing can actually later be discovered to have meant something else.[57]

Explicit in Schwartzman's defense of the possibility of interpreting our social world accurately (of identifying key features of any given "speech situation") is a flexible understanding of objectivity, one that is not obsessed with the illusion of error-free, unmediated certainty but is attentive to knowledge as that which arises contextually and through an examination not only of claims and outcomes but also of basic background beliefs and presuppositions. Importantly, Schwartzman's understanding of objectivity anticipates error as part of a methodology of self-reflection and revisability.

For Butler, the fact that a total speech situation is never fully definable presents damning evidence against those who would propose to study social circumstances to assess the ability of speech acts to cause harm. Schwartzman poses two succinct responses to this notion, challenges that I think help to summarize the way that Butler's background beliefs constrain her form of theorizing and, ultimately, her way of reading Morrison. For Schwartzman, the anything-short-of-absolute-certainty-is-not-knowledge framework that Butler employs against critical race theorists is underjustified, if not in fact deeply mistaken. It presumes to be concerned with complexity but works to mask the actual processes necessary to acquire understandings of the world that are more or less reliable or more likely than not correct. Related to this critique is Schwartzman's final claim: that anyone seriously interested in the effects of oppressive language would turn to empirical studies and examine political, historical, and social movements rather than follow Butler's "far more dubious plan of resistance," which is to rely on conjecture, on "the *possibility* that speech could be 'restaged' or 'resignified' by the recipient responding in unanticipated ways."[58] As Schwartzman notes, critical race theorists actually agree with Butler that "language does not *always* succeed, but they do not agree that the way that language fails is as random or arbitrary as Butler suggests."[59] This understanding of the predictable ways that language misfires has to do with who has the power in society to make their words mean what they say. This insight is garnered not through philosophical speculation but through empirical examination and study. To be sure, Schwartzman's critique of Butler is not antitheoretical; it is simply less skeptical with regard to the knowledge generated by other disciplines and less suspicious of the communities and social movements that have worked collectively to end injustice.

The relevance of Schwartzman's work to my discussion of Butler on Morrison on language is important to clarify. Butler's misreadings seem to be linked to her theoretical presuppositions. Central among these is the belief in the radical indeterminacy and arbitrariness of linguistic reference. This background assumption, among others, leads her to make strange claims, not the least of which is that Morrison shares her philosophical commitments. Butler's use of Morrison to support her claims relies on an extreme misrepresentation of Morrison's work. Such an engagement conveys a sense of being in conversation where no conversation exists; it employs an acclaimed and well-respected woman of color's writing as a source of profound theoretical insights on language but only in ways that prove strategic and functional.

That Butler mines Morrison's writing for postmodernist phrases and thoughts, ignoring those that stand in the way of her own thesis, is not an exaggeration. Nor is it an isolated incident that can be easily dismissed as careless scholarship.[60] Butler's use of Morrison is instructive, I think, not as the isolated error of a single theorist but as symptomatic of a larger theoretical project whose methods and background presuppositions are proving to be a liability. The practice of indiscriminately deploying a radically skeptical disposition toward language, identity, and experience comes into crisis when it refuses to fully account for its implication in an intellectual history hostile to the lives and experiences of minorities. Such a crisis comes into focus when theorists employing an extreme antirealism work their way through the cultural production of racialized minorities, claiming (often by brief citational practice) an interest in their lives and theoretical perspectives but ultimately remaining unable to challenge their own most basic methods and presuppositions in the process.

TURNING TO MORRISON WITHOUT BUTLER

Serious questions are at stake here about how to interpret minority texts, about the relationship between language and reality, and about miscommunication and genuine dialogue. All of these get explored with uncompromising clarity and courage in Morrison's work, but they do not find themselves accurately represented in Butler's writing. The misrepresentation produces confusion with regard to Morrison's own ideas and ultimately limits our ability to substantively engage with Morrison's work. Turning to Morrison without Butler is necessary, if only because it allows us some space to read Morrison without Butler's particular shadow of influence. It also represents an opportunity to annul that ever-so-old contract (of gratefulness?) between the people who get mentioned and the people who have the authority to mention, between the people who express themselves, often with extraordinary courage in the face of hostility, and the people who tell us what to think and feel about those people and their expressions. The bird that is undoubtedly in Morrison's hands feels different without Butler; its restless flutter motivates us to discern a different story.

Turning to Morrison without Butler, we find ourselves with an opportunity to evaluate our responsibilities, as language users, to the world we find ourselves in and to the world that we think we want. Morrison walks a fine line between asserting the importance of describing the world as it is and reimagining the world, through language and action, for a better future. "Word work," to borrow a phrase from Morrison, is indeed "sublime."[61] But it is perhaps most inspiring when it also entails a healthy regimen of accountability or, at minimum, a principle of reciprocity. This reciprocity, or what we might want to call *coimplicatedness*, can be thought of in different ways: as reciprocity between the word and the world; as reciprocity among communities that need to communicate better in order to survive; as reciprocity among people who, ultimately, need each other in order to know. Morrison makes this claim by staging it—through the dialogic encounter with young children who have urgent, if only misunderstood, questions and through the courage of active listeners who, "once upon a time," challenge the wise woman's basic assumptions. The staging of conflict, revision, and collaboration is powerful. Language for Morrison has the possibility to injure and misrepresent, but also the power to heal and speak truths. We learn through Morrison that there are important possibilities that we are likely to ignore when listening to one another. More importantly, we learn that it is through the act of rereading, of courageously risking new interpretations, that better knowledge can be achieved.

A FINAL NOTE

Reading Morrison and Butler on language may seem like a peculiar way to begin a book dedicated to the study of queer writers and artists of color. Not so odd, however, if one takes Morrison seriously as a theorist of language and race, even less strange if one understands a legacy and continuity in thinking between communities of color and their queer folk. If there was such a thing as a "house of Morrison" (to borrow the language of drag families in ballroom culture) this book might belong to it; this book's readings of queer ethnic literature and cultural production would be the house of Morrison's "up-and-coming" children. In the next chapter, I build on Morrison's exploration of language and reference to reality, addressing specifically the question of agency, of what it might take (in disposition, in effort, and in self-reflexivity) to produce better, more accurate knowledge about oneself and one's relationship to oppressive circumstances. Instead of focusing solely on theorizing language, however, I focus also on identity. I explore through James Baldwin's writing how identities (and identity shifts) play a powerful, but difficult to understand role in knowledge acquisition and knowledge production.

CHAPTER 2

DYING TO KNOW IN BALDWIN'S *ANOTHER COUNTRY*

> Because I am an American writer my subject and my material inevitably has to be a handful of incoherent people in an incoherent country. And I don't mean incoherent in any light sense. . . . It's a kind of incoherence that occurs, let us say, when I am frightened, I am absolutely frightened to death, and there's something which is happening or about to happen that I don't want to face.
>
> James Baldwin, "Notes for a Hypothetical Novel"

> Acquiring an understanding of systemic injustice is sometimes personally threatening in a way probably avoided in the acquisition of other kinds of understanding. . . . Investigating systemic injustice requires in the first place the imaginative capacity to make specific personal commitments, often to a sort of identity or to the loss of it.
>
> Susan Babbitt, "Moral Risk and Dark Waters"

One of the most unsettling features of James Baldwin's 1962 novel *Another Country* is that while it emphasizes the need to challenge the racist and homophobic status quo of the American 1950s, it simultaneously presents a series of characters who are rarely successful in bringing about any kind of change.[1] The characters who would most benefit from a revamping of social norms find themselves confused and unable to actualize even minor changes in their own lives. Those involved in interracial relationships frequently mistrust and hurt one another; the men in same-sex relationships are perpetually troubled by a fear of fleetingness, if not utter untenability; and the ghostly protagonist, Rufus Scott, positioned at the intersection of these two lines of social conflict, ominously commits suicide because of his deep-seated loneliness and desperation. Confusion and incoherence are thus thematically central to Baldwin's vision, but it is their chronic presence that makes *Another Country* a particularly difficult novel to read. Early critics of Baldwin's fiction dismissed such an emphasis as symptomatic of Baldwin's own "incoherent" identity.[2] Recent critics have been prompted to impose narrative and thematic resolutions.[3] But just about every reader is left with questions about the logic of a novel that so consistently depicts its major characters in states of deep confusion, incapable of reaching even preliminary conclusions about the nature of their predicaments.[4]

Another Country is preoccupied with incoherence and confusion as epistemically significant states and needs to be read as an extended meditation on the peculiar difficulty of gaining self-knowledge in oppressive social contexts. The difficulty that Baldwin explores is not just intellectual or cognitive in nature, for it refers to the difficulty of living differently, living in ways that either imply or lead to new self-knowledge. Baldwin shows how self-knowledge frequently involves more than simply "opening one's eyes" and how it often requires complex acts that themselves have significant social, psychological, and epistemic effects. The novel's preoccupation with confusion and incoherence can be understood, then, as having both epistemological and ethical dimensions. What Baldwin's characters can *know* about themselves and their social contexts is intimately related to what they are willing to *do* in the social domain.

I explore this epistemological and ethical feature of *Another Country* by interrogating what I call the novel's suicidal sensibility.[5] This sensibility involves an attentiveness to imminent action that is deliberate, seemingly irrevocable, and self-menacing, and it lies at the conceptual center of Baldwin's novel. Through it Baldwin examines how self-knowledge in oppressive contexts often depends on people making extreme shifts in their conception of self—of who they are in relation to their society. These shifts are experienced as states of what Baldwin in the epigraph above calls incoherence, as destabilizing and dangerous, because they register the complexity of opposing a social order in which one is implicated and enmeshed. Baldwin understands this incoherence to be a distinctly American affliction and compares it to the terror associated with purposeful evasiveness and impending doom ("when . . . I am absolutely frightened to death, and there's something which is happening or about to happen that I don't want to face").[6]

Another Country is motivated less by the tragedy of Rufus's suicide early in the novel than by the ethical imperative faced by all the characters to risk their sense of self (to figuratively commit suicide) in order to better understand their lives. They need to be willing to die, as it were, to come to know more fully.[7] Ironically, *Another Country* rarely depicts successful instances of this figurative suicide. Indeed, it boldly foregrounds characters who seem unable or unwilling to risk their sense of self. This emphasis in Baldwin's text is uncompromising testimony to the often deeply menacing process of acquiring self-knowledge in oppressive contexts.

Baldwin's view on self-knowledge is supported by an implicit thesis about identities and their epistemic value. In the novel, identities are often depicted as impediments that one would do best to discard. But if discarding them appears self-menacing, it is because Baldwin also understands identities as necessary for making sense of the world. Identities, for Baldwin, entail not only multiple ways of life but also multiple modes of knowing. Instead of simply thinking of identities as impediments (as social constructs we would do better without), Baldwin thinks of them as practices of interpretation and interaction for which we need to be increasingly more responsible and through which we might better understand our social world. Thus the novel focuses on the fear of shedding identities only as testimony to the difficulty of taking responsibility for one's identity in oppressive contexts; Baldwin's novel ultimately argues that something new and epistemically more adequate must be worked toward and put in their place.[8]

This nuanced emphasis in Baldwin's novel shares affinities with the recent work of philosophers and literary theorists developing realist approaches to identity, experience, and knowledge.[9] Like Baldwin, contemporary realist theorists understand identities as potential resources that, to lesser and greater degrees of accuracy, offer us access to aspects of the social world. The access that identities offer us is not self-evident, but it is, as realists argue, achievable because identities are neither arbitrary fictions nor inexplicable essences. Identities are more like lived theories that have a complex, causal relation to the social world and its organization. They can be limiting, but they can also be rethought and redeployed to explain aspects of the social world and our experiences in it. Baldwin not only anticipates basic realist theoretical principles but also provides a provocative version of realist ideas. If, as realists argue, identities are like theories and can be evaluated (examined for degrees of epistemic value), Baldwin provides indispensable phenomenological detail regarding the enormous difficulty of actualizing that potential in oppressive contexts.[10]

SUICIDAL RUMINATIONS ON "RESPONSIBILITY"

Rufus Scott's unexpected suicide ninety pages into Baldwin's novel is the narrative premise that sets in motion the tense interracial and homosexual relationships in the novel. However, Rufus's suicide also insinuates itself into the novel's epistemology and ethics, becoming one of its conceptual frames. A suicidal sensibility forms a central part of the novel, since how and what the characters know is intimately tied to the manner in which they come to terms with the moral and mortal risks of acting outside the normative codes of conduct. Rufus's decision to kill himself—an act of desperation arising out of a compelling identity crisis and loneliness—looms heavily over attempts in the novel to explore more figural, but no less dangerous, losses of self. These attempts are often cast in terms of what it might mean to take responsibility for one's self (and one's identity) in contexts of intense ideological violence and interpersonal conflict, particularly when the possibility of unscripted action (action that transcends and challenges the norms of one's community) is obstructed by self-doubt, confusion, and fear.

The characters in *Another Country* face constitutive difficulties in understanding their emotions and articulating their motivations.[11] These perceptual and communicative entanglements, I want to suggest, should be understood in the way that philosophical realists like Susan Babbitt and Satya Mohanty have outlined, as typical of activities where the acquisition of knowledge about oppressions—and one's place in relation to them—are central.[12] Coming to better understand systemic forms of oppression, Babbitt argues, deserves recognition as a particular kind of learning process, one that is often disorienting because it stresses who people understand themselves to be, where and among whom they find themselves located, and what they see from that location. Because their interactions are socially unsanctioned (sexual encounters with the same gender, interracial relationships) and intimate, Baldwin's characters are on the verge of knowing something fundamental about how oppression in the United States functions in their lives. Assimilating such knowledge, however, is particularly difficult for these characters not simply because they are learning about previously unfathomed networks of power but because the prospect of acquiring knowledge about their lives is fundamentally tied to who they understand themselves to be and, more important, whom they are willing to risk losing and becoming.

One of the main African American characters of the novel, Ida Scott, exemplifies the complexity of such a suicidal sensibility. For instance, Ida finds it hard to grasp how she can be in love with a white man (Vivaldo, the "sweetest man" she's ever known)[13] and still feel a sense of impossibility at the thought of making a life together with him. While her anxiety is partly explained as the inability to clearly foresee what their life together, as an interracial couple, might be like, it is also accounted for as a consequence of her ability to *correctly* discern constitutive features of her social world. Ida understands that Vivaldo's dismissive disposition toward questions of racist oppression (i.e., his all-too-anxious persistence that race should not matter) prevented him from coming to the aid of her brother, Rufus, when he was most in need. Even though Ida cannot see, or is simply unwilling to see, some factors (like Vivaldo's queer sexuality) that kept him from treating Rufus with integrity, she is able to perceive that Vivaldo's underexamined attitude toward questions of race made him act irresponsibly with Rufus. Ida intimates as much when she states to one of Vivaldo's friends, "Well, you know, Vivaldo was his best friend—and Rufus was *dying*, but Vivaldo didn't know it. And I was miles away, and I *did*!" From her vantage point, Ida concludes that she could never marry Vivaldo. A partnership with him would be a contract of mutual self-destruction: "It would be the end of him and the end of me."[14]

The idea that committing to spending her life with Vivaldo is, in essence, committing suicide is a provocative declaration. It not only undermines the liberal humanist notion that love can transcend all obstacles but also reinscribes the trauma of Rufus's suicide into the way Ida conceptualizes her actions and circumstances.[15] Ida's association of interracial marriage with suicide might be understood, by some, as a consequence of her inability to think and behave in ways unscripted by the racialized tensions of the 1950s. Such a perspective, however, mischaracterizes the predicament that Ida seems to be in, especially in terms of the multiple structures of domination she is running up against and the distinctly praxical and deeply personal manner in which they are coming to light. An alternative account of Ida's suicidal reflections would interpret them less as an effect of racialized tensions and more as the thoughts of a conflicted agent in the midst of negotiating these tensions. From this perspective, Ida is relatively clear about her abilities to act in an unprecedented fashion, but she deeply fears the consequences. That is to say, Ida discerns correctly that a "true" commitment to staying with Vivaldo may not mean a literal death but would require Vivaldo and Ida to rethink their relationship significantly, thereby challenging the sociopolitical circumstances that undergird it. To the extent that these circumstances form key aspects of their own self-conceptions and interpretive horizons, committing to a life together in this radical way would imply, in certain instances and to certain degrees, ending their former ideas of self. Suicide, in this sense, is not so much hyperbole as it is the mark of integrity and responsibility for themselves (and for their identities) in an interracial relationship.

Taking responsibility for one's self and one's identity in this suicidal manner constitutes a monumental difficulty for the characters in Baldwin's novel, in terms of what they see themselves capable of knowing and how they conceptualize their possibilities for action. This is so, in part, because taking responsibility for one's self and one's identity often consists, as the literary theorist Paula Moya notes, of a commitment not only to exploring the correlations between what one knows and where and who one is but also to distinguishing between "better" and "worse" frameworks for understanding the self.[16] For characters like Ida, however, the ability to discern how some frameworks are more significant than others lies in the adoption of, and responsibility for, new ones. One cannot, in other words, simply imagine the value, efficacy, or durability of an identity but must manifest that identity in the world and "stand behind it," as Babbitt (drawing on the work of Claudia Card) puts it, in such a way that its possibilities in the social can have consequences.[17] Here, it is important to note what Ida's identity would be if, as an African American woman in the 1950s, she were married to a white man and also to consider the speculation one could make about what constitutes the psychology, emotions, and epistemic consequences of that positionality—something one might never fully know without inhabiting that social location. To take up a stigmatized identity and lifestyle in this way, one must develop a disposition toward the self that is, on the one hand, experimental (challenging oppressive norms) and, on the other, relatively stable (not easily swayed from counterhegemonic stances). The difficulty inherent in developing such a disposition, the novel seems to suggest, is that identities are not simply lenses through which one sees the world, nor are they easily acquired or discarded. As the example of Rufus and his suicide illustrates so poignantly, identities often structure how we are emplaced in the world and what we experience from that location. Our identities, in other words, are intimately connected to our knowledge *and* sociality, not only influencing our values but, more precisely, determining whom we find ourselves living, learning, and loving among. Consequently, as the novel shows, taking responsibility for one's self and one's identity implies reconceptualizing one's relation not only to one's self but also to one's community and belief systems. Taking responsibility in this way means that to know the world and one's relation to it—to know them better—one might have to adopt new senses of one's self, new identities that, in any given circumstance, might contradict former self-conceptions and community values.

In repressive societies where bodies and resources, ideas and behaviors, are carefully monitored and often punitively controlled, there are no guarantees that taking responsibility for one's self and one's identity will lead to positive outcomes. Taking responsibility against the grain of oppression may in fact result in isolation rather than insight, in social stigma and violence rather than community. This sobering reality deserves further attention. As Rufus's case proves so poignantly, men having sex with men in a homophobic society and whites becoming romantically involved with blacks in a racist society does not, in and of itself, produce insight and social change. In fact, unsanctioned intimacies of this sort can easily accommodate the logic of heternormativity, misogyny, and racism. Rufus subjects his white girlfriend (Leona) to mental and physical abuse; he also disavows his attraction to Eric, his former male lover. Clearly, Rufus moves against the grain by becoming involved in interracial and homosexual relationships. Yet, he very rarely takes responsibility for his identity in the process. Lest we too quickly judge Rufus out of hand, it is important to note that every character in the novel has difficulty taking responsibility for their identity, but only Rufus kills himself because of it. It behooves us, therefore, to ask what Rufus's horizon of possibility is, given his social location. What does he see and know from where he stands—from how he moves in the social world—that others cannot see and know? What, in other words, are the implications of his actions, given his precarious position as a black man negotiating his ambiguous sexual desires and social standing in a racist and homophobic society? In the next section, I want to spend some time thinking about Rufus. Ultimately, however, I will return to the question of "taking responsibility" for one's identity and what the novel as a whole seems to be saying that is intimately tied to Rufus's suicide.

NOMADISM AS CRITIQUE: RUFUS'S QUEER PLACELESSNESS

Rufus's frequent movement and self-reflection in spaces of impermanence and transit (i.e., the city street, the subway, the movie theater)—particularly on the day he commits suicide—underscores his inability to participate fully in the communities of meaning he migrates between. There are at least three identifiable "regions" that Rufus can be said to be at once fleeing and remaining near—these are Harlem, the interracial jazz club scene, and the much more amorphous space of queer sociality and hustling, each of which is a "location" where aspects of Rufus's identity are emphasized while others are occluded.

Harlem is figured as a dangerously predetermined location—a confined setting, as Rufus's father puts it, where "A nigger . . . lives his whole life, lives and dies according to a beat."[18] Rufus's exodus away from this fated "beat," away from Harlem's restrictive concrete urban geography ("on the stoop . . . , behind the stairs . . . , on the roofs . . . , on the streets . . . , leaning out of windows . . . , above the pavements"), is an attempt to overcome, for himself and his family, not only a seemingly "regional" deprivation but also the ossified behaviors that are thought to be indigenous to that location. What he finds in the world outside of Harlem, however, is not the opportunity of transcendence. For example, Rufus first leaves Harlem for a navy boot camp located in the South. Instead of experiencing, through this boot camp, an opportunity to break free from what he sees in Harlem as racially determined cycles of deprivation, Rufus experiences a reinscription of his racial confinement. While in

Harlem, Rufus encounters "the white policeman who . . . taught him how to hate," outside of Harlem, in the South, Rufus encounters "the shoe of a white officer against his mouth."[19]

From this experience in boot camp and a brief navy stint overseas, Rufus returns to New York City and begins a career as a musician in the increasingly interracial jazz club circuit. This is a "region" where an unprecedented cross-cultural community can be witnessed, but where genuine communication and kinship is only tenuously achieved. The novel's first poignant description of the jazz joint paradox bifurcates the setting between "the frantic black people on the stand" (the musicians) and the "oblivious, mixed crowd at the bar."[20] This is the emotionally stratified context where the music, "loud and empty," is said to be "hurled at the crowd like a malediction in which not even those who hated most deeply any longer believed."[21] Cognizant of the tenuous links connecting this group of people in this particular location, the musicians "participate" in this community in the only form expected of them: "So they blew what everyone had heard before, they reassured everyone that nothing terrible was happening, and the people at the tables found it pleasant to shout over this stunning corroboration and the people at the bar, under cover of the noise they could scarcely have lived without, pursued whatever it was they were after."[22] Despite Rufus's ability (as one of the cognizant black musicians on stage) to more or less perceive correctly the lack of commitment, integrity, and responsibility holding this group of people together, he nonetheless attempts to make a viable place for himself among the white patrons outside of his role as entertainer. Unfortunately for Rufus, his practice of interracial cohabitation and belonging proves idealistic. In every public instance of interracial intimacy, Rufus is the only person aware of potential dangers. The night Rufus and his white lover Leona first meet, for example, his "blackness" and her "whiteness" fundamentally influence the way they experience the hailing of a cab outside of a jazz club. While the interracial crowd of people who pour out of the club along with them are still enjoying themselves ("talking and laughing . . . [with] much sexual confusion"), for Rufus this experience in public is much more troubling. He sees the policemen in the area "carefully and in fact rather mysteriously conveying their awareness that these particular Negroes, though they were out so late, and mostly drunk, were not to be treated in the usual fashion."[23] Rufus's fear is not appeased by the police officers' conditional restraint. Observing the lessening of the crowd on the street as they all begin piling into cabs, and fearing the impending reality that "Leona would soon be the only white person left," Rufus becomes uneasy and angry at his inability to influence the circumstances to which he might soon be subjected. Leona is eventually successful in hailing a cab, but there is no intimation that Leona has felt any of the anxiety and anger that Rufus has just experienced. And this, perhaps, is what makes Rufus's perception of social dangers so unbearable; his frequent experience of feeling ill at ease and on alert when in public is not shared or acknowledged by the people who put him at risk.

"Ain't nothing wrong in being colored" is Leona's utterly ineffectual way of "reassuring" Rufus—"time and again"—that she at least is not racist.[24] But for Rufus, such statements further prove Leona's deep lack of understanding, not only of his particular social predicament but also of her implicatedness in the logic of that predicament, in the loneliness of it. Her statements seem to be founded on an ignorance of racism's impact on Rufus's everyday life, suggesting that even as they share a household and life together—even as Leona herself is adversely affected by racism—they live and know the world in substantially different ways. Despite Rufus and Leona's shared emotional intimacy and physical proximity, the *difference* in the way they have come to be affected by racism seems to determine what aspects of racism they become aware of, if they become aware of them at all. Rufus is aware of particular racial interactions because he is more likely to be subjected to racial violence in particular ways. Part of being white in a racist society, even white with the best of intentions, is exercising the privilege to not see or know this.

The difference in Rufus's and Leona's consciousness about racism is not accounted for through the logic of individual maliciousness or indifference. The discrepancy, rather, is accounted for as a perceptual gap (a cognitive liability) constitutive of Leona's identity as a white Southern woman in a racist US context. However, whiteness is not invoked to place blame. Whiteness is interrogated as a way of exploring responsibility, for even as the novel explores interactions among individuals it is concerned with phenomena at the group level. Among these is the idea of whiteness as a perceptual barrier—a roadblock in understanding how life experiences are determined by race.

Whiteness as a perceptual barrier is most evident in those instances of public interaction where Rufus's lovers and friends make decisions that put him and themselves (although they do not acknowledge it) at risk of scrutiny and attack. For example, a walk in the park with his girlfriend Leona and his close friend Vivaldo is an endeavor that Rufus takes up with apprehension. Rufus sees, for example, the way the Villagers "look them over as though where they stood were an auction block or a stud farm."[25] Leona and Vivaldo, however, do not share his experience of being scrutinized, nor do they share in a historical memory where such a scrutiny, of slaves in particular, determined worth. Consequently, they act as if they live under circumstances utterly under their control, "oblivious to everything and everyone." Leona, for example, publicly manifests the nature of her relationship to Rufus in her gestures and looks ("if there had been any doubt concerning their relationship," Rufus notes, "her eyes were enough to dispel it").[26] For Leona, there is no reason to think that this moment between lovers is anything out of the ordinary. And, for one moment, Rufus begins to believe this might be the case: "If she noticed nothing, what was the matter with him? Maybe he was making it all up, maybe nobody gave a damn."[27] Unfortunately for Rufus, holding out for this possibility is quickly undercut as he discerns disapproval in the way a young Italian adolescent looks at them when passing by: "The boy looked at him with hatred; his glance flicked over Leona as though she were a whore; he dropped his eyes slowly and swaggered on—having registered his protest, his backside seemed to snarl, having made his point."[28] The indignity of being diminished in this manner repeats itself several times that day, but does not manifest itself into physical violence. This experience, however, especially due to the liberty that Vivaldo and Leona exhibit in public, reminds Rufus of an occasion where his friend's inattention to highly racialized contexts actually resulted in violence.

He remembers the rainy day he agreed to meet Vivaldo and his girlfriend Jane for a drink at a white working-class bar. Upon entering, Rufus is acutely aware that his presence, as a black man, is resented by the regular patrons. As a consequence, all Rufus can think about is leaving once the rain lets up. While waiting for an opportune time to leave, Rufus finds himself caught up in an escalating argument with Jane. While he indeed instigates part of the argument by maliciously mocking her, he very quickly becomes aware "that they were beginning to attract attention . . . saying to himself. Okay, Rufus, behave yourself. And he leaned back in the booth, where he sat facing Jane and Vivaldo."[29] But

Jane, having little awareness that this argument might be perceived by white patrons as offensive, continues the quarrel. As soon as Jane fathoms the type of scrutiny that they are all under, a danger that Rufus has been sensing all along, she attempts to change the tone of their interaction. The subdued struggle between Jane and Rufus that immediately ensues, however, demonstrates how fundamentally different their awareness is of the impending violence: "She leaned forward and grabbed Rufus's hand. 'I didn't mean it the way it sounded.' He tried to pull his hand away; she held on. He relaxed, not wanting to seem to struggle with her. Now she was being Joan Fontaine. 'Please, you *must* believe me, Rufus!'"[30] Jane is unaware of the significance of body comportment in scenarios of racial hypervisibility. She is not accustomed to having her behavior policed, at least not racially. Consequently, she not only continues to interact with Rufus in a manner that conveys a patronizing intimacy, but more specifically, places her hands on his in a manner that does not allow him to move away. This contributes to their interaction as a racialized spectacle, a literal embodiment of white America's racialized anxieties: black men struggling with America's white women. Jane, like many of Rufus's friends, behaves in a manner that is altogether consistent with taking one's racial identity in a racist environment for granted. The privileges of whiteness, some of which include a perpetually reaffirmed sense of individuality and social invisibility (the ability to blend into society), crystallize for Rufus in Jane's behavior that day and in the beating that they receive from the Irish working-class patrons for their perceived racial transgressions. As for the majority of white characters in the novel, there is a palpable desire to achieve some form of interracial "harmony," but the sorts of changes this might entail for their own behavior is rarely fully assimilated. The vision of interracial cohabitation that the novel constructs through its characters, in other words, is never a felicitous one. This "region" of interracial relationships, much like Rufus's vision of Harlem, is populated by a group of people similarly "living and dying" to "a beat" that influences even their most noble attempts at compassion and solidarity.

The lack of ease Rufus feels among whites (in the interracial jazz club community) and among blacks (in Harlem) seems to be the novel's way of critiquing a lack of responsibility for dominant identities, on the one hand, and the enormous difficulty of sustaining against-the-grain subordinated identities, on the other. In the jazz club context, for example, there is only a superficial commitment to act responsibly—a real desire, ultimately, for the festivities and enticements of inhabiting social spaces with black people and "their" music, while not wanting to get too involved or too changed by the perceived exchange. In Harlem, there is a fundamental crisis in the lived experience of the du Boisian "double consciousness"—of how black people know they are seen (by whites) and how they struggle (often to no avail) to see themselves otherwise. Harlem, as remembered by Rufus, is the space where taking responsibility for one's self and one's identity seems trumped by the weight of history, or as his sister Ida describes it, responsibility in Harlem is overshadowed by the day-to-day reality of needing to hustle and get by.[31]

Rufus's dissatisfaction in these communities becomes manifested not only in the way he experiences these places, but also in the way he uses locations of impermanence as locations in which to dwell. The novel, for example, opens by describing Rufus in a movie theater: "It was past midnight and he had been sitting in the movies, in the top row of the balcony, since two o'clock in the afternoon. Twice he had been awakened by caterpillar fingers between his thighs."[32] Rufus uses the transient space of the movie theater in ways it was not meant to be used; in its most explicit manner, as a place to rest and retreat. Notably, his use of it as respite coincides with queer uses of it as a cover for illicit sexual activity. Locations of impermanence, as the novel frequently points out, are the very in-between spaces that facilitate queer sexual encounters: "In an empty locker room, on an empty stairway or . . . in the shadow of a wall in the park . . . , they surrendered to the hands, to the stroking and fondling and kissing of the despised and anonymous sex."[33] In a homophobic world, places of impermanence become the "region" for a transient queer sociality. For this reason, it is compelling that in some form or another Rufus continuously finds himself "there."

This is not a location where Rufus finds fulfillment, however, in part because the sex he has with other men in these spaces is depersonalized, most explicitly by the scenario of hustling. While it is important not to trivialize the possibility that Rufus prostitutes himself with men solely out of material necessity, it is also crucial to acknowledge that hustling provides an excuse for his presence in queer locales. Similar to the way in which Rufus first refused to admit and verbalize his desire for Eric—but nonetheless pursued an affair with him—Rufus once again seems to refuse homosexual identification through hustling. Such a decision to defer the question of sexual identity, in both of these instances, leaves Rufus even more isolated from the men he has sex with. Without opportunities to nurture genuine intimacy and trust, Rufus is forced to participate in activities (and communities) that further buttress his loneliness and insecurity. In this case, locations of queer sociality emphasize his sense of himself as not being able to love or be loved. "I don't want no more hands on me, no more, no more, no more" is what Rufus states to himself as a "rough-looking" white man propositions him on the street.[34] One notes in this interaction, that Rufus's overwrought response to the particular hustling scenario is not explicitly articulating a lack of desire for men, but a rejection of another "bleakly physical exchange."[35] This focus on degradation is emphasized when Rufus loiters in an area frequented by hustlers and their tricks and the novel comments on the people Rufus sees there:

Some laughed together, the young, with dead eyes set in yellow faces, the slackness of their bodies making vivid the history of their degradation. They were the prey that was no longer hunted, though they were scarcely aware of this new condition and could not bear to leave the place where they had first been spoiled. And the hunters were there, far more assured and patient than the prey. In any of the world's cities, on a winter night, a boy can be bought for the price of a beer and the promise of warm blankets.[36]

There is a distinct attribution of the pathological and diseased in this description. These attributions, however, have less to do with homosexuality per se and more with the power dynamics and dehumanization of the specific hustling scenarios he describes. That a young man's body and company can be purchased "for the price of a beer and the promise of warm blankets" suggests that the young, with "dead eyes set in yellow faces," are degraded by the exchange, not by their desires.

If Rufus's dwelling in locations of impermanence is to be understood in the three ways I have tried to suggest in the above discussion—as an implicit critique of Harlem and the Jazz club scene as restrictive communities of meaning, as a sign of Rufus's inability to fully interrogate his homosexual practices, and as an unbearable experience of placelessness and deprivation—then it seems important to account for the way the novel further stresses Rufus's racialized, queer impermanence. An important place to begin is in thinking more carefully about why chapter 1, where all of this angst and alienation is described, is entitled "Easy Rider," and why it is contextualized by an epigraph from the early blues musician W.C. Handy:

I told him, easy riders
Got to stay away,
So he had to vamp it,
But the hike ain't far.

Of its most recognized meanings in the African American cultural context, the term "easy rider" has been used as a *sexual reference* to a type of lover as well as a *musical reference* to a blues man's traveling guitar.[37] According to a 1949 description of the term as a sexual connotation, it can mean "a male lover who lives off a woman's earnings."[38] As a reference to a musician's guitar, the term "easy rider" is the chosen nomenclature because the guitar itself "could be slung across [the blues musician's] . . . back when he wished to travel."[39] These two meanings, given W.C. Handy's imperative that easy riders "got to stay away," come to suggest that, for the purposes of the novel, being an "easy rider" is as much a *migratory sexual identity* (always pressured to not be "here") as it is a *transient way of subsisting* (always, like a blues musician, ready to move on to the next "gig"). Understood in this way—as identity and method—the term "easy rider" is not simply a reference to Rufus as a womanizer and musician,[40] but is more fully accounted for as a symbolic figure for the predicament in which Rufus finds himself—attempting to negotiate a social landscape where the geographic and social history of queer subjects of color has been erased.[41] One may want to resist this reading—opting to literalize the meaning of "easy rider"—but this can happen only at the expense of denying the complexity of Rufus's identity beyond his career choices and treatment of women (or, relatedly, suggesting that his misogynist practices have nothing to do with his queer sexuality).[42] When the reader first encounters Rufus in the introduction to the novel, Rufus is an unemployed, homeless, and disillusioned hustler negotiating his frustrations and fears through anonymous sexual encounters with other men. He is, literally, a black man without black friends and with very little connection to his family and Harlem community. Rufus is the "easy rider" in one of its most complex and unusual of senses—he inhabits an exiled sexual identity and engages in transient subsistence.

One of the interpretive consequences of framing the novel's first chapter through the racial and sexual chronotope of the "easy rider" is a heightened attention to the *simultaneity of factors* (i.e., race, gender, sexuality) influencing Rufus's migratory impulse.[43] Of course, it is not only that these factors are simultaneously present, but that, in the very way W.C. Handy's epigraph suggests, their coterminousness is given a distinctly spatial dimension. According to Handy, for example, the easy rider is under the compulsion to "vamp it"—to leave, to be anywhere but here—but as Handy concedes, "the hike ain't far." This last assertion inscribes an unusual dimension of proximity on the easy rider's exodus—paradoxically suggesting that the easy rider can be "banished" and simultaneously "near." Such a peculiar spatial configuration mirrors chapter 1's central sociogeographic dilemma: Rufus's interstitial proximity to, but distance from Harlem (his family) and the Jazz club scene (his friends) on the day he commits suicide.

If we are to take seriously the implication that Rufus's movement, particularly his nomadic/interstitial movement, matters a great deal in further understanding the novel's attention to questions of identity, knowledge, and responsibility in oppressive contexts, it is important to think about these peculiarly geographic practices as "queer migrations," as forming part of a long tradition of queer people negotiating hostility, desire, identity, and community belonging through movement.[44] *Another Country* indeed envisions various possibilities of "queer migration" for its male characters—enabling some, like Eric (Rufus's white friend and former lover), to enjoy all that is understood to be liberatory in its practice: *escape* from restrictive social norms and commitments, *exploration* of new sexual and social possibilities, and *transformation* both of consciousness and material circumstance. For Rufus, however, the promise of "queer migration" is brought into significant crisis (partly, of course, because Rufus himself does not fully acknowledge his movement, or at least part of it, as a quest for identity). Rufus finds himself negatively affected by the locations he ends up drifting between; he experiences his migratory attempts, not as fulfillment and transformation, but as fundamental impossibilities.

There are at least two significant reasons why this is the case. The first has to do with the differential effect race has on queer migration; the second has to do with whether Rufus "takes responsibility" for his identity given this particular circumstance. According to Bob Cant, the liberating prospects of queer migration have remained discontinuous in relation to lesbian and gay ethnic minorities due, in part, to the important function family collectives and family relationships play in societies where oppression by race and class is significant.[45] In communities where the family collective is seen as haven against poverty and racism, Cant argues, exodus necessarily comes at a (social, economic, and political) price. Rufus's movement away from Harlem, however, is never *explicitly* described in terms of sexuality, nor does Rufus ever seem to acknowledge his family life as being an economic or political haven. Such an explicit contradiction between Cant's account of migration for queer ethnic minorities and Rufus's own experience is instructive. Rufus's experience, for example, challenges Cant's presumption that the movement away from home, for queer ethnic minorities, is primarily conceptualized as a consciously "queer" decision (that is, as motivated solely by sexuality) and that the only reason for staying with family would be racial and/or economic. Such an opposition between sexuality and race/class does not begin to fully capture the ways that these are often imbricated for Rufus. Furthermore, Cant's explanation privileges race and class as the most pertinent issues affecting queer ethnic migration and, in this very way, fails to account for queer subjects whose motivations for migration are multiple (economic, racial, and sexual) and, often, simultaneous. One might even say that Cant relies too heavily on an idealized vision of the role of family in ethnic minority groups, for as Rufus's experience makes explicit, family is not always enjoyed as a refuge, but in fact is often experienced as a type of burden.[46]

We need not assume, in other words, that Rufus's decision to leave home in order to work (first for the navy and later as a musician) necessarily leaves out queerness at the expense of race and class, or vice versa. Queer migration, in the way practiced by Rufus, helps us to understand how certain acts of resistance are not consciously articulated, but still indicative of nonpropositional knowledge, of insight people have about the world that is not always expressible in immediate propositional truths (i.e., through words, concepts, theories, etc.). Understanding Rufus's movement as nonpropositional knowledge is crucial. As Susan Babbitt clarifies, we should be careful not to minimize the radical potential of nonpropositional knowledge for it is "perhaps the *only possible access* . . . [oppressed people may have] . . . to the kinds of epistemic standards that would permit effective radical criticism."[47] To the extent that queers of color are constituted negatively within several dominant paradigms, they often lack the epistemic community and standards that would add credibility (intelligibility and articulatability) to their experience and knowledge. To the extent that this is the case, their emotions, attitudes, and ways of behaving and moving in the social world are indeed some of the only ways they may have of expressing their insights. Regarding Rufus, it behooves us to acknowledge his movement as a form of nonpropositional knowledge that begs interpretive company and solidarity against the oppressive circumstances in which Rufus finds himself trapped, ideologically and spatially, as a (queer) black man.

Regardless of what his behavior points us to, Rufus does not seem to "take responsibility" for his identity in any straightforward way. In fact, Rufus cannot be described as exhibiting "integrity" about his identity, if by integrity we mean that Rufus is willing to risk behaving and identifying in ways not scripted by the racialized and homophobic status quo. As previously mentioned, Rufus has a sexual relationship with Eric (his white friend), but denies any queer identification through which he might revisit and reinterpret his sense of self. Likewise, he pursues a sexual relationship with Leona, a white woman from the South, but cannot separate his attraction for Leona from racialized revenge fantasies against the white race.[48]

We might do well to remember that Rufus's lack of responsibility for his identity haunts him, *costs him his life*, whereas other character's lack of responsibility for their identities constitutes something like a missed opportunity—one that will, no doubt, present itself again considering that time, resources, and at least some basic sense of belonging tends to be on their side. Eric, for example, may be said to take responsibility for his nonnormative sexual identity when he reveals his desire for Rufus and "stands behind" his identity as a man who desires other men. Attributing responsibility to Eric's actions, however, perhaps too quickly leaves unaccounted for the messiness of such responsibility—the possibility that Eric's declared love for Rufus may have more to do with white guilt and a fetishistic desire for black men, than with courageousness in the face of homophobic hostility. The novel intimates as much when Eric begins to consider his relationship with Rufus in light of his Southern upbringing and the racialized fantasies of his youth:

part of Rufus' great power over him had to do with the past which Eric had buried in some deep, dark place; was connected with himself, in Alabama, *when I was nothing but a child*; with the cold white people and the warm, black people. . . . They laughed differently from other people, so it had seemed to him, and moved with more beauty and violence, and they smelled like good things in the oven. But had he ever loved Rufus? Or had it simply been rage and nostalgia and guilt? And shame? Was it the body of Rufus to which he had clung, or the bodies of dark men, seen briefly, somewhere, in a garden or a clearing, long ago, sweat running down their chocolate chests and shoulders, their voices ringing out, the white of their jock-straps beautiful against their skin, one with his head tilted back before a dipper—and the water splashing, sparkling, singing down!—one with his arm raised, laying an axe to the base of a tree? . . . Perhaps Rufus had looked into his eyes and seen those dark men Eric saw, and hated him for it.[49]

Eric's "acceptance" of his desire for Rufus is tied to Eric's childhood idealization of the black working poor and to the sexualization of their bodies. His capacity to "stand behind" his desire for Rufus is facilitated by a combination of white guilt mapped onto a racialized erotic desire for black men. Likewise, it is Eric's economic and racial privileges that facilitate his queer migration to Europe, not to mention his ability to financially "keep" his young lover, Yves. In contrast to Rufus's constricted form of queer migration by means of enlisting in the navy and hustling, Eric has comparatively more options. Any responsibility we might attribute to Eric needs to take his racial and economic privileges into consideration.

That Eric is depicted in this complicated manner suggests that the novel does not seek facile distinctions between those characters *who are* and those *who are not* "taking responsibility" for their identities. The novel, in fact, clarifies that *none* of the characters take full responsibility for their identities. More importantly, it suggests that taking responsibility for one's identity is differentially constrained by networks of injustice that structures life opportunities and resources.[50]

UNCERTAINTY AND INCOHERENCE

If Baldwin's novel can be seen as promoting critical dialogue on the need to take responsibility for oneself and one's identity in contexts of systemic oppression, why is such a dialogue overburdened with failures and trauma, with pain and uncertainty? Indeed, one of the most disconcerting features of Baldwin's *Another Country* is that even as the novel posits the need for social change, it depicts a series of characters who rarely succeed in bringing about that change. In the light of such unsettling outcomes, it is no wonder that critics have been recently characterized as eager to read the novel as transcending sexual confusion and the failure of interracial harmony. According to Kevin Ohi, commentators as varied as Emmanuel Nelson, Michael Lynch, Terry Rowden, and William Cohen have misread the novel by stressing moments of resolution and self-awareness at the expense of understanding why confusion figures so prominently alongside moments of sought-after clarity. As Ohi notes, moments of sought-after transcendence and self-revelation unquestionably occur in the novel, but instead of representing states of achieved clarity these moments exist as nonrevelations, as experiences determined by confusion and self-doubt.

Ohi's point is well-taken. Unfortunately, his own answer to the question of why incoherence figures so prominently in the novel does not do enough justice to the novel's complex understanding of identity and knowledge. Whereas previous criticism may be faulted for evading the novel's peculiar engagement with incoherence, Ohi can be questioned for underreading its epistemological, ethical, and indeed referential significance. Ohi concludes that every instance of confusion in the novel plays a purely "structural" role and that—other than providing instantiations of the narrative difficulty of knowing—the novel has little to say that is in conversation with "a concept of political intervention modeled on representational politics."[51] With its theoretical overemphasis on the indeterminacy of meaning and its undervaluing caricature of "representational politics," Ohi's claim is unsupported by the text. Ohi particularly overstates the case when he claims that the "traumatic opacity" that prevails in *Another Country* is "as incommensurable as it is inconsolable and as incomprehensible as it is essential."[52] The opacity prevalent in the novel is "incommensurable" not as a point of fact but to the extent that characters in the novel prove themselves incapable of taking responsibility for how they understand themselves in the world, refusing to assimilate the possibility that their identities seriously hinder (and, at times, substantially help) them objectively understand the circumstances around them (i.e., the interracial and homosexual friendships they foster and the mechanisms of power that permeate them). In other words, moments of incoherence in *Another Country* might be most usefully theorized as social, rather than as purely narrative, phenomena. In this sense, one might come to see the novel's thematization of incoherence as referencing a paradigmatic feature of systemic oppression and as the epistemic and communicative crisis that Baldwin seeks to render intelligible.

Attending to Baldwin's own recollections of living in Greenwich Village in the 1940s, one can detect correlations between the confusing racial and sexual politics that Baldwin was experiencing personally and those he chose to write about in the novel. In fact, Baldwin began writing *Another Country* in Greenwich Village in 1948. Consider the similarity between the following two passages as just one example of how crucial Baldwin's observations are to an analysis of his novel. In "Here Be Dragons," Baldwin writes, "At bottom, what I had learned was that male desire for a male roams everywhere, avid, desperate, unimaginably lonely, culminating often in drugs, piety, madness or death. It was also dreadfully like watching myself at the end of a long, slow-moving line: Soon I would be next. All of this was very frightening. It was lonely and impersonal and demeaning."[53] Now, compare this to what Baldwin writes in *Another Country*:

He remembered the army of lonely men who had used him, who had wrestled with him. . . . They were husbands, they were fathers, gangsters, football players, rovers; and they were everywhere. . . . Days or weeks or months might pass—or even years—before, once again, furtively, in an empty locker room, on an empty stairway or a roof, in the shadow of a wall in the park, in a parked car, or in the furnished room of an absent friend, they surrendered to the hands, to the stroking and fondling and kissing of the despised and anonymous sex.[54]

I want to suggest not that the meaning of Baldwin's novel lies in reference to the author's biography, but rather that Baldwin's treatment of the thematic issues central to the novel (desire, confusion, and a suicidal attitude toward the self) is motivated by an understanding of society and is not fully explained in terms of textual indeterminacy. Baldwin was unequivocal during his lifetime about the necessary and even "inevitable" presence of incoherence in his writing because he understood the United States to be in a profound state of incoherence (regarding race relations in particular), and he saw it as his life's work to engage that incoherence in a purposeful manner.[55]

Ohi is correct to emphasize the impossibility of achieving transparent self-knowledge in the novel, but he is less convincing when he associates a lack of transparency with a lack of intelligibility in any and all cases. The following section examines crucial passages in the novel that further prove how incoherence, far from being a *purely* structural feature of the novel, is actually central to the novel's embedded thesis on the relations among identity, experience, and knowledge. Specifically, I address some pivotal moments in the lives of two characters (Eric and Vivaldo) that help to constitute the novel's conclusions about social fragmentation and the need for people to risk, at times, their sense of self in an effort to better understand it.

RISKING (DIS)ORDER

Toward the end of the novel, when Eric and Vivaldo are finally able to have some time alone—away from their lovers and mutual friends—a powerful conversation takes place that has implications for understanding the relations among identity, oppression, and incoherence. It is at this moment that Eric and Vivaldo finally broach the subject of their sexual desires for both men and women (Eric from the perspective of a self-identified homosexual man and Vivaldo from a primarily heterosexual perspective), sharing a deep sense of frustration and confusion about what their desires mean for their current and future relationships. This confusion is interesting not as an "incommensurable" and "inconsolable" fact but as an issue entirely dependent on the forms of oppression that both men are subject to and the risks they are willing to take to see themselves, and the world in which they live, differently.

Eric, for example, having recently made love with his close female friend Cass, begins to openly question his sense of himself as a homosexual man.[56] Vivaldo, without fully understanding the value of working through his confusion, advocates for circumventing altogether the issue of his sexual identity—referring to his own sexuality as an ambivalent one and arguing that he and Eric both need to accept the constitutive uncertainty of their bisexual predicament: "*I* can't be sure . . . that one fine day, I won't get all hung up on some boy—like that cat in *Death in Venice*. So *you* can't be sure that there isn't a woman waiting for you, just for you, somewhere up the road."[57] In a manner consistent with Vivaldo's privilege as a heterosexually identified man, Vivaldo takes for granted a correspondence between Eric's sexual uncertainty and his own and then passes off his own lack of responsibility for his identity (i.e., his easy assumption that his sexual practices and sexual desires have no purchase on his heterosexual identification) as an inevitable mode of operation. The reference to Thomas Mann's novel *Death in Venice* further shows that for Vivaldo love and relationships are not about how one identifies oneself but about impulse and desire in the abstract. Love and desire, for Vivaldo, are simply things that happen to one, not phenomena that are constrained by one's self-identifications and social location. Of course, Vivaldo could not be further from the truth on this issue. How one identifies oneself and how one is seen in the world indeed influence how one desires and how one practices that desire with others, and the novel goes to great lengths to demonstrate this.

Responding to Vivaldo, Eric accepts that he may never achieve certainty about his desires but does not allow this to excuse postponing processes of self-reflection and self-critique about his identity: "Indeed . . . , I can't be sure. And yet I must decide. . . . I mean, I think you've got to be truthful about the life you have. Otherwise, there's no possibility of achieving the life you want . . . or think you want."[58] Eric cannot be certain whom he will end up loving, a man or a woman, and yet he "must decide" on a way of life to see that particular possibility through. He must be "truthful" about the uncertainty that constitutes his sexual desire, but he must "stand behind" his nonheteronormative behavior to fully understand the consequences of that behavior. Eric seems to understand, in other words, that how he chooses to identify himself and, consequently, how he chooses to lead his life and to be seen in the world have ramifications for the types of experiences and knowledge he will acquire. Given this understanding of the value of self-identification for knowledge production, it seems clear why Eric would distrust Vivaldo's desire to leave the question of identity undecided, as if it had no implications for one's practice in, and perspective on, the world. Furthermore, Eric's response to Vivaldo does not do away with the uncertainty of his desires for both men and women (the uncertainty does not simply vanish because Eric makes choices about his identity) but acknowledges that his uncertainty about his sexuality and sexual identity is more than a matter of psychological interiority or individual sexual preference. His uncertainty is, in fact, shaped by social forces. Therefore, Eric's response implies an understanding that the indecision he feels about identifying himself as heterosexual or homosexual has to be evaluated in regard to the ways these two identities are not equally valued options, how they are decidedly unequal modes of identification and how one often functions at the great expense of the other.

Eric's response to Vivaldo holds an embedded epistemological thesis: in order to know even complicated things like desire, one needs to make decisions that, in one form or another, amount to sustained personal and social commitments—sustained lines of inquiry—that have a stronger purchase on one's life than one intends. By this I mean that, as Babbitt has pointed out, the situations in which we take total control over outcomes infrequently constitute the types of learning experiences needed to radically reinterpret our lives.[59] This is particularly true in contexts of systemic social oppression, for in these contexts one often exists, consciously and unconsciously, as a mode for its perpetuation. In other words, what one is able to comprehend as being good for oneself may in fact be good for the perpetuation of oppression and may not facilitate a more accurate account of how one often thinks and strategizes, desires and feels, in relation to oppressive regimes of power.

Take, as a brief example, Vivaldo's suggestion that he can have sexual relations with men as a favor to them, as an acknowledgment of their need for him, but not with any sense of being changed by the encounter. In Vivaldo's eyes, this benevolence toward homosexuals may be liberating but does not implicate him in the logic of homosexuality.[60] Eric, of course, opposes Vivaldo's characterization of himself in this way and responds by associating responsibility for one's identity with intellectual and emotional labor, with personal risk. He tells Vivaldo, "If you went to bed with a guy just because he wanted you to, *you* wouldn't have to take any responsibility for it; *you* wouldn't be doing any of the work. *He'd* do all the work. And the idea of being passive is very attractive to many men, maybe to most men."[61] Eric implies that what Vivaldo understands as good is primarily a way for Vivaldo to avoid questioning his sense of self. He exposes the true purpose Vivaldo's benevolence serves—it minimizes personal risk and maintains the heterosexual status quo. Eric further demystifies the notion that one's ability to objectively understand oppression, and one's relation to it, lies simply in intent. Likewise, he clarifies how understanding oppression often requires stamina and courage, a sustained awareness that comfort may signal stagnation and that fear and anxiety may signal potential growth and breakthrough.

Taking responsibility for one's self in the manner suggested by Eric—as a risky, against-the-grain, sustained line of inquiry—is the novel's thematic core. Yet, the novel does not represent the process through which one *successfully* takes responsibility for one's self. It addresses the ways in which one can lose track of that possibility. In fact, the novel concerns itself with characters that have not been able to understand how their social location impinges on, as much as it informs, their horizon of possibility. One of *Another Country*'s most interesting explorations of the relation between social location and knowledge makes this feature of the novel more explicit. This example shows that at the same time the novel emphasizes incoherence, its formative subtext stresses the process by which even utterly confused characters can gain more or less accurate understandings of their social predicament.

Close to the end of the novel, an unusual scenario unfolds. Vivaldo experiences an unexpected "revelation" vis-à-vis a particularly queer sexual attraction to an unknown woman at a bar:

He looked at the blonde again, wondering what she was like with no clothes on. . . . He wondered about her odor, juices, sounds; for a night, only for a night; then abruptly, with no warning, he found himself wondering how Rufus would have looked at this girl, and an odd thing happened; all desire left him, he turned absolutely cold, and then desire came roaring back, with legions. *Aha*, he heard Rufus snicker, *you don't be careful, motherfucker, you going to get a* black *hard on*. He heard again the laughter which had followed him down the block. And something in him was breaking; he was, briefly and horribly, in a region where there were no definitions of any kind, neither of color, nor of male and female. There was only the leap and the rending and the terror and the surrender. . . . What order could prevail against so grim a privacy? And yet, without order, of what value was the mystery?[62]

In the midst of an otherwise unremarkable contemplation of this woman's "odor, juices, [and] sounds" and momentary longings to be with her "for a night, only for a night," Vivaldo suddenly, and without warning, finds himself wondering how Rufus (if he were alive) might have reacted to this woman. To his surprise, Vivaldo's queries take the form of an out-of-body experience. Vivaldo briefly loses all desire (shocked at his unexpected recollection of Rufus), only to have it come "roaring back, with legions" when he suddenly finds himself *inside* Rufus's body. Shocked at the ambiguous source (and force) of his sexual arousal, Vivaldo imagines Rufus snickering: "*aha . . . , you don't be careful, motherfucker, you going to get a* black *hard on*." The remarkable awakening of desire that results from merging with Rufus's body positions Vivaldo "briefly and horribly, in a region where there [are] . . . no definitions of any kind, neither of color, nor of male and female. There [is] . . . only the leap and the rending and the terror and the surrender." This is a peculiarly evocative moment in the novel because the experience is understood simultaneously as a dreaded, intersubjective manifestation of (queer) racialized desire by Vivaldo and as a chaotic "region" where race and gender have little relevance. Because this region is described as stripped of the circumstances that led to Rufus's sense of isolation and death, Vivaldo's menacing revelation of the desire that overtakes him when he merges with Rufus, into Rufus, represents a distinctive moment of convergence for the novel. Indeed, the allusions to Rufus's suicide (through words like "leap," "rending," "terror," and "surrender") suggest that the trauma Vivaldo undergoes in this new location has implications for what readers are to believe the novel is saying about both Rufus's and Vivaldo's experiences of self-knowledge.

This is apparent when the novel shifts its attention from Vivaldo's shock at finding himself in a region with no definitions to the consequences of being there. In a profound culminating moment of free indirect interior monologue, the novel asks, "What order could prevail against so grim a privacy? And yet, without order, of what value was the mystery?" These questions seem to reflect the notion that when queer desire is taken seriously, no prior gendered or racial system of ordering the world can remain intact. More important, however, without some alternative way of reconceptualizing the world according to this formerly suppressed reality, there is no use in the revelation.

The implications of these two questions for Vivaldo's actions are crucial but require some unpacking. Vivaldo makes sense to himself through the logic of heteronormativity and moral individualism. These two ways of ordering the world are placed into crisis by the shocking revelation of his racialized desire through and for Rufus and through and for other men and women. While Vivaldo experiences confusion and fear, the true dilemma is that he does not risk adopting an alternative way of conceptualizing this new and uncomfortable reality. Because no new order is ventured to replace the previous one, Vivaldo understands the instability as chaotic rather than generative.

As the novel clarifies, this is a pattern of complacency with terrible consequences, for "when people no longer knew that a mystery could only be approached through form . . . , they perished."[63] Vivaldo experiences desire (through Rufus) as chaotic because the "order" through which Vivaldo is accustomed to seeing the world obscures the complexities of (queer) racialized desire. The novel's conviction that a "mystery" can only be approached through "form," then, emphasizes the importance of risking alternative ways of life, of risking the disorder necessary to sustain alternative social orders. Understanding one's relation to structures of oppression, as the novel suggests, involves unraveling forms of identification—indeed, it involves ending some forms of identification—but not in indiscriminate ways and certainly not by leaving a vacuum in their stead. Risking identities in this manner, far from implying that Baldwin rejects identity, suggests that identities can actually reference and illuminate (to varying degrees of accuracy and comfort) aspects of the social world. Seen in this way, feelings of incoherence and chaos are not examples of textual indeterminacy but are cognitive and affective registers that have liberatory potential.

IDENTITY, REFERENCE, AND THE "REAL"

This reading of Baldwin on identity raises vital questions for contemporary literary and social theory. Principally, it stresses the necessity of situating identities in nuanced and less alarmist relations to social constructivist theses. For example, the suicidal account of knowledge acquisition in Baldwin's novel grants complexity to the relation between identity and knowledge (going so far as to assert the necessity of "dying"—of ending certain forms of identification—in order to know) without claiming that all identities are thoroughly and always suspect forms of subjection. Some identities, like Vivaldo's, get in the way of solidarity and comprehension precisely because of the function that identities serve as means of making sense of the social world *in particular ways*. Identities are profoundly mediated (socially constructed) realities. Still, it is of no advantage to render all identities suspect simply on these grounds. Such an emphasis obscures not only the differences in mediated realities but also the prospect that some identities have greater epistemic and political value than others—and that they gain this value not in self-evident, transhistorical ways, but rather contextually and through the great effort and self-reflexivity of people and communities working toward a more just world.

Underlying this argument is a realist concern similarly articulated by the feminist political theorist Lois McNay, a concern regarding the still-fashion-able theorization of subjecthood solely from within "negative" paradigms of knowledge production, paradigms where violence is ascribed to any and all forms of normative claims and subjecthood is only and always a form of subjection.[64] A realist approach to the emphasis on subjecthood as subjection notes the rigidity of this equation, arguing that it erases difference by attributing to all forms of subjecthood a pernicious origin and hence necessitates its subversion. When one reduces all identities to forms of subjection that one must subvert, one cannot for example begin to ascertain why Vivaldo's decision to leave the question of his sexual identity open-ended might in fact be wrong, or why the taking up of a publicly nonheteronormative identity could in fact help him to understand features of the social that would otherwise remain unintelligible to him because of his privileged identity as a heterosexually identified white man. It may be that Vivaldo needs to end his sense of self. However, an indiscriminate imperative to subvert identity does not fully capture the difficult moral and emotional work, the decision making and moral risk taking, that people like Vivaldo (situated at the intersection of ideological, historical, and material circumstances) will undertake when deciding how best to subvert identities. Critics might say that Vivaldo subverts heterosexuality by keeping his sexual options as a heterosexual man open, but such a reading would have to erase the novel's emphasis on the ways that pernicious forms of masculinity remain intact, and are even fostered, when men have sex with men.

Related to this account of identity (and its reformulation of the subjecthood-as-subjection model) is another realist concern regarding projects that attribute a linguistic indeterminacy and contingency of meaning to all texts. While these projects may be thought provoking and often illuminating, they fail to some extent to theorize a complex account of reference. Ohi's approach, for example, makes apparent certain aspects of linguistic representation that go unnoticed in other conceptual frames—and for this reason projects like his are important as part of the repertoire for critical social inquiry. Yet such readings may not be sufficient for understanding what any particular indeterminacy, in any given context, might mean. Additionally, philosophical realists have argued that indiscriminate approaches to highlighting the indeterminacy of meaning in texts are often guilty of epistemological denial, of occluding their own epistemological foundations to make other approaches particular or ideological so theirs, in rhetorical contrast, come across as universal and true—all without having to substantiate why and on what grounds the truth value of their claims regarding the indeterminacy of meaning should be believed.[65] My argument bears repeating: insight garnered from, say, deconstructive reading strategies must be tempered with the understanding that these forms of reading may foreground aspects of a narrative that are overlooked by other approaches but will not sufficiently explain the function of indeterminacy in any given context. This is so because they remain unwilling to differentiate between kinds of indeterminacy and because they seem reluctant to theorize what Mohanty (drawing on the philosophers Charles Sanders Peirce and Richard Boyd) refers to as "degrees of epistemic access."[66]

The deconstructive practice of attending to the indeterminacy of meaning in texts reflects a more general disposition toward knowledge and the social that often shirks away from questions of reference. According to Mohanty, such questions are associated with the now outdated claims of epistemological foundationalism (i.e., "the view that knowledge and inquiry should ultimately be grounded in a privileged class of beliefs, or a method, which are themselves uniquely resistant to falsification through new evidence, to changes in knowledge").[67] Mohanty argues that the critique of epistemological foundationalism, while valuable, only partially succeeds as a springboard for contemporary social theory, because it erroneously attributes to theories of reference and objectivity a reductive politics—a "nostalgic desire to seek extratextual certainty and to avoid epistemic complexity."[68] But theorizations of reference and objectivity need not be associated with the illusion of error-free "certainty" for them to be meaningfully used in social analysis. For example, if Marxist projects do not, for any number of reasons, accurately describe our world or effectively promote the needs of the people they claim to represent, we need not evacuate from these social movements the "degrees of epistemic access" they offer us through their approaches, successes, and failures.

To situate a critique of epistemological foundationalism is, on the one hand, to acknowledge its importance and, on the other, to show where an extreme skepticism goes wrong. In this way, social inquiry can shift to address complex questions pertaining to political criticism and social change—How do texts, in fact, reflect reality? Who are our own people? How do we learn from experience?[69] The shift does not mean that these questions are now easily answered, but rather that the prospect of error is no longer seen as opposing the possibility of objectivity and reference. The emphasis is on degrees of access and on remaining self-reflective about the mediated quality of experiences and identities.

At stake here is the extent to which texts like Baldwin's can be said to reference the social world, offering degrees of epistemic access. Put differently, at issue is the degree to which we believe that discussions of reference simply rehearse a "nostalgic desire . . . to avoid epistemic complexity." What I have tried to show is that epistemic complexity is exactly what hangs in the balance when critics undertheorize the novel as a form of social analysis and when they exaggerate claims to the indeterminacy of meaning in Baldwin's text. Rehabilitating reference is not an attempt to avoid epistemic complexity. In fact, attending to reference opens up difficult questions regarding politics and objectivity.[70] For instance, consider Eldridge Cleaver's claim that *Another Country* risks being an irresponsible novel because the characters it portrays do not represent the "real" black experience of social resistance. While I do not share Cleaver's conclusion that Baldwin's novel is unrepresentative, I want to stress that developing a compelling counterresponse does not solely involve proving the representativeness of the text (by showing how it represents the ways "real" people act). One important answer to the question of *Another Country*'s unrepresentativeness lies outside a narrow definition of representation. In the pages that remain, I will make some concluding suggestions about the role unrepresentative narratives play in acquiring crucial knowledge about the world.

In a brief philosophical reading of Samuel Delany's autobiography, *The Motion of Light in Water*, Susan Babbitt makes a series of important observations regarding the relation between knowledge and narration. She writes:

> Delany notices that he was never able to remember some incidences of his life *until he began to tell a story of a certain sort, motivated by a commitment to a direction of thought and action.* He claims that he had to develop a certain orientation, in theory and practice, in order to understand some things about his life that were actually part of his conscious memories and experience. There were things that he remembered and knew that he had experienced, but to which he could not give appropriate significance.[71] (my emphasis)

Drawing, first, on Delany's assertion that his own capacity to know depended literally on the kinds of stories he was capable of telling—some of which cognitively excluded events and emotions because the stories could not give them "appropriate significance"—Babbitt goes on to emphasize Delany's even more radical understanding of the epistemic significance of storytelling. Delany places the epistemic value of storytelling in its germinative capacity and not, strictly, its representative one. Delany resists the naive understanding of narration as simply representing reality and dares to complicate knowledge acquisition by highlighting the always theory-laden (i.e., situated, partial) nature of what and how we know. Babbitt adds a crucial qualification to Delany's important claims: she distinguishes Delany's nonfoundationalist account of knowledge from its potential coherence with radical postmodern skepticism. She distinguishes, in other words, between the postmodern notion that discourses construct reality and the realist notion that discourses are always somehow impinging on and impinged upon by reality. The point, however, is not to make a too-strict separation between narration and "the real" but to acknowledge that the real is not simply what is thought about it and that some narratives, because they highlight certain features of the social as opposed to others, give us the necessarily *interested* possibility of understanding our lives—and all the ideologies and experiences that constitute them—in a particular way. This understanding of the relation between knowledge and narration, Babbitt reminds us, differs from philosophical perspectivism or radical postmodern skepticism because it recognizes that narrating reality in different ways does not, strictly speaking, change reality with each perspectival shift. The important realist claim, here, is that narratives will organize and influence the social but never completely determine it.

Building on the foregoing realist account of the relation between knowledge and narration, I would say that Cleaver's concerns about representativeness in Baldwin's novel can be challenged without making use of traditional understandings of representation. If the black characters in the novel are not recognized as representing real black experience, such a question of referential accuracy needs to be problematized with an acknowledgment that narratives need not be representative to be epistemically useful. This is not to say that all unrepresentative narratives are useful but to acknowledge the germinative, as opposed to the strictly representative, quality of narrative. Indeed, based on Babbitt's insights, this concluding account of *Another Country* might be ventured: perhaps what Baldwin wanted to say about the very real experiences of resisting racial and sexual oppression could not be fully accounted for until he was disposed to write something with a critical objective in mind and with a new and distinctive story to tell—a novel that staged the death of an African American protagonist early on, for example, and prompted white characters and a black character to think deeply about race and sexuality, together (in proximity to each other), but with great cognitive and experiential distances to overcome. Baldwin's novel might not be representative—in the sense of documenting what has already been—but his story might still be germinative in a way that helps elucidate what many of us, for better or worse, have been dying to know: that the possibility for human flourishing is both founded on and mired by the identities that we have made and that have been made of us; that the task in front of us, then, is not to avoid this fact but to engage it and to do so with the only resources we have, our capacity for self-reflection and our courage to change. The consequences of not doing so, Baldwin would add, are plainly for us to find out, for it is an all too present, all too tangible reality that "people pay for what they do, and, still more, for what they have allowed themselves to become. And they pay for it very simply: by the lives they lead."[72]

CHAPTER 3

QUEER LATINA/O MIGRANT LABOR

> Away, she went away.
> But every place she went
> they pushed her to the other side
> and that other side pushed her to the other side
> of the other side of the other side.
>
> Gloria Anzaldúa, "Del Otro Lado"

> Movements in and away from different contexts. La cachapera se mueve (she moves) to avoid passing; to avoid becoming a figment of the Anglo imagination consumed by and reduced to protesting ethnocentric racism; to avoid being silenced; to avoid being socially reduced to her construction in el mitote. . . . In what spaces and through which movements can the cachapera, jota, pata, marimacha find responses to her gestures and words that take pleasure in the abundance of her meaning?
>
> María Lugones, *Pilgrimages*

In this chapter, I return to the issue of "queer migration" raised briefly in Chapter 2 in order to resituate it within queer US Latina/o discourse of the 1980s and 1990s. In Chapter 2, it was important to read Rufus as a kind of queer migrant; his negotiations with racism and homophobia manifesting in his transient behavior, in the labor he expended moving through various liminal spaces, in and out of various communities. It is not clear, however, that Baldwin's novel as a whole sought to push our thinking in this respect. If it did, it raised more questions than it answered regarding nomadism as practice and symptom of queer social resistance and negotiation. The novel did foreground the failure of Rufus's migratory strategies and even offered the conceptual metaphor of the "easy rider" to register a more complicated sense of Rufus's compromised racial, sexual, and spatial transgressions, but it did so in a manner that was only suggestive of queer migration as spatial praxis for the queer ethnic subject.

The term queer migration has been used by scholars to reference the *international* movement of gays and lesbians, as well as to signal *intra-national* patterns of migration, most frequently referenced as rural to urban dislocations.[1] My use of "queer migrant labor" is related to these, but in a manner closer to what Andrew Gorman-Murray has theorized as "embodied queer identity quests," referencing queer mobility at a more local and hermeneutic scale.[2] This understanding of queer migration through the body and as a form of deep social inquiry does not presume the logic of migration-as-emancipation, the belief that when queers move (away) they become free. Instead, it finds the knowledge acquisition possibilities of spatial resistance worthy of further interrogation. I am interested in "queer migrant labor" as a reference to plural forms of spatial resistance and analysis. Queer migrant labor references strategies practiced at various geographic scales by people searching for ways to express themselves sexually and socially in forms not sanctioned by the communities in which they reside.

Two further qualifications are important here. My use of "queer migrant labor" in this chapter is distinguishable in emphasis and focus from what Anne Marie Fortier describes as the primary ways that race and sexuality have been discussed under the rubric of "queer diaspora." I do not foreground in this chapter, for example, the pernicious effects of the internationalization of US gay and lesbian politics, that is, the processes whereby particular historical constructions of identity politics (particular to the Western world) are taken to be universal and mapped onto other national and cultural contexts.[3] I do, however, explore what it has meant for queer US Latinas/os in the 1980s and 1990s to engage and often adopt a distinctly US form of gay and lesbian "coming out" politics—how they mobilized critiques of it as they practiced it, experiencing its limitations in their own lives, its undergirding spatial logic enticing queers of color to consider moving further and further away from communities of color. Similarly, this chapter is influenced by, but not uniformly concerned with the transnational emphasis in the second important usage of "queer diaspora"—

the queering of traditionally defined ethnic or national diasporas. Rather, this chapter interrogates migrations within the United States, with a focus on the distinctly spatialized labor of intelligibility, the labor of making sense of oneself and making sense to others in oppressive contexts.

Queer Latina/o migrant labor, broadly speaking, is a way of acknowledging various spatial practices of resistance and survival. These practices range in scale, purpose, and effect and include such overtly spatialized practices as "queer exodus" (i.e., the flight of queer people from presumably limiting communities of "origin" to presumably more liberating communities of "choice") and cruising for sex (i.e., the public negotiation of stigmatized desire in response to the explicit heteronormativity of the public domain).[4] Additionally, these practices include strategies of survival and negotiation that do not seem, at first glance, to have any significant relationship to spatiality. One might consider, as an example, the "psychological" negotiations of queer people of color in heteronormative environments. What writers like Gloria Anzaldúa help us to understand about such necessary processes of self-evaluation (in light of racist and heteronormative value systems that influence how queer people understand and feel about themselves) is that such processes actually involve queer subjects in transit and in place—they involve queer subjects responding to various spatialized ideologies. For Anzaldúa, coming to consciousness as a queer mestiza is not simply a matter of deciding to think differently about herself and her interests, but is preceded by practices of spatial retreat: retreat into semiprivate spaces like her room ("I locked the door, kept the world out")[5] and retreat from the daily intimacies and demands for "loyalty" that buttress heteronormativity and homophobic self-hatred ("She has to learn to push their eyes away. She has to still her eyes from looking at their feelings—feelings that can catch her in their gaze, bind her to them").[6] Anzaldúa reminds us that such spatial buffers, no matter the scale at which they are practiced, also have spacio-cognitive consequences. The process of retreat (and meditation) that Anzaldúa refers to as the "Coatlicue state" is also a foundation for future movement and insight (what she calls "a prelude to a crossing"), a stage of retreat/assessment that one must inhabit before establishing a politicized consciousness/movement.[7]

Rather than catalogue multiple spatial practices of queer Latina/o resistance, this chapter is concerned with making a conceptual distinction between two types: practices that explicitly address spatiality, like queer exodus, and practices more often conceived purely as identity practices that have an undertheorized and/or underacknowledged spatialization. The goal in both of these cases is to foreground the epistemic consequences and challenges of such practices, understanding how an examination of the spatiality of such strategies highlights the knowledge acquisition process for queers of color in contexts of multiple oppressions. "Queer exodus" is conceptually significant to queer Latina/o thought of the 1980s and 1990s. One can think here of Anzaldúa's framing of homophobia as the "fear of coming home," or her mantra, "Not me who sold out my people but they me," developed as a reminder that her marginalization was not of her choosing. For this reason, the bulk of this chapter explores how queer migrant labor—away from, and toward, the family/ethnic collective—helps us to theorize the spatialization of knowledge in oppressive contexts. Marivel Danielson has already noted the centrality of home to queer Chicana/Latina cultural production, theorizing these cultural workers as "homecoming queers . . . , subjects in the process of coming home through creative expression and critical consciousness."[8] By "homecoming," Danielson means a profound reconceptualization of home, not simply a nostalgic return. This brings her closer to Catriona Rueda Esquivel's framing of "Chicana lesbian fictions" as confrontations with networks of patriarchy and colonialism that have rendered Chicana lesbian bodies, knowledge, and subjectivity opaque if not entirely erased in the Chicano historical imaginary.[9]

My contribution to this body of work is to further interrogate queer Latina/o representations of knowledge acquisition and the spatializations upon which they often rest, spatializations that map distances away from and toward family/community and that range in emphasis, from the politics of imposed exile and consequences of "chosen" estrangement, to the fear of being left behind or the danger of being rendered newly vulnerable in foreign political/social geographies). Critics have been rightfully leery of developmental progress narratives that position migration away from home and nation as the idealized route to sexual freedom and that ossify communities of origin as backward, as sites of impenetrable homophobia.[10] This chapter builds on this critique, but it frames the issue slightly differently. Queer Latina/o writers and theorists in the 1980s and 1990s found themselves in contexts (often violent) where the logic of "migration-as-emancipation" came into crisis but still had purchase for them as queer racialized subjects, not as an idealized route toward "freedom," but as a counterhegemonic acknowledgment that they were negotiating new subjectivities and knowledge through the very act of surviving collectivities through movement. This migratory sensibility, a product of queer racialized labor, infuses a broad range of queer Latina/o cultural production with what I call a *prepositional* repertoire of desired relationality, making sure to be "near," "within," "from," "beside," and "among" communities of color whenever possible. In this way, the rubric of queer migrant labor shares similarities with Gayatri Gopinath's South Asian "queer diasporic imaginary."[11] Both repudiate the historical erasure of queers from the communal/familial imaginary and both challenge the fear-inducing (border-policing) idea that queers of color pose a paradigmatic threat to family, community, nation, and liberation.[12]

The concluding section of this chapter—"Identity *as* Spatial Praxis"—shifts from spatialized practices of resistance that are clearly demarcated and addressed as such, to those practices of resistance traditionally understood aspatially, under the purview of psychology, cognition, and identification. I reconsider José Esteban Muñoz's discussion of queer people of color and their "disidentificatory" actions and expand on the attentiveness to space to which such a concept refers. In this way, I emphasize how identities are not arbitrary social constructions, even as they are malleable and changing. An assertion on which my argument in this chapter rests is that queer Latina/o identities and subjectivities are harnessed in direct engagement with the *spatialization* of knowledge and power in the social realm. All identities and subjectivities, to be sure, are situated and informed in this way. However, some are passively informed by this understanding, and others are formed in direct acknowledgment. The queer migrant labor discussed in this chapter is not accidental labor; far from being simply a random thematic of queer Latina/o cultural production, it actually indexes, to greater and lesser degrees of accuracy, the way communities are structured spatially to control knowledge production and behavior.[13]

"SPINNING OUTSIDE THE ORBIT OF THAT FAMILIAL EMBRACE"

In the introduction to *Loving in the War Years*, Cherríe Moraga famously writes of the need to distance herself from the Chicano community in order to more adequately understand the social networks of power at work there.[14]

"I . . . fought to free myself from my culture's claim on me. It seemed I had to step outside of my *familia* to see what we as a people were doing."[15] With this framing, Moraga certainly echoes other Latina lesbian writers in understanding queer exodus as a practice and path of consciousness raising.[16] However, her framing comes under critique for coming dangerously close to rehearsing a dominant logic that authorizes intellectuals through rhetorics of estrangement and displays of detachment. Lora Romero argues, for instance, that Moraga idealizes her position outside of mainstream Chicano politics, implying that community members who never "leave" *la familia Chicana* are inherently unable to assess the community's failings.[17] Such a disavowal of "organic intellectuals," writes Romero, allows self-proclaimed exiled critics, like Moraga, to "represent themselves as the consciousness of the people and to fortify the institutional practices that deny participants in popular movements the right to represent themselves."[18]

While Romero may be correct to imply that Moraga's *Loving* shares a tense relationship to practices that reinforce "the fantasy of a population that is 'nonintellectual,'" such an emphasis risks misunderstanding the value Moraga places on her queer and racialized displacements.[19] Moraga privileges both her distance and her estrangement from the Chicano community as important mechanisms through which her politicized insights are acquired. However, she manages to communicate this via images of social conflict and repressive violence that give a particular resonance to her claims. These references situate Moraga in a series of conflictive negotiations, often of constrictedness in many communities, and offers the reader rich emotional and material contexts through which the practice of distancing oneself from oppressive circumstances can be understood as praxical—as movement that is itself analysis and reflection, movement that is not simply first-order thoughts and reactions, but is an assessment (in a spatialized manner) of one's values and the values of one's communities.

Moraga recalls, for example, how as a young adult she had perfectly assimilated the homophobic and sexist values prevalent in her everyday relationships, so much so that intimate aspects of her life, like her own sexuality, were closed off from certain possibilities: "The sheer prospect of being a lesbian was too great to bear, as I fully believed that giving in to such desires would find me shot-up with bullets or drugs in a gutter somewhere."[20] As she points out, it is not simply that certain options were closed off—in the sense of not even being charted—but that the prospect of lesbianism was, in fact, already imagined, charted out in a violent manner. And it is precisely this violence that Moraga continuously reflects upon. The images of distress that Moraga invokes, for instance, range from dreams of forced incarceration in prison camps to descriptions of violent bodily dismemberments.[21] Although they are not references particular to Chicano communities, they represent in a cumulative way the extent to which fear of violence and hatred looms over the queer Latina/o political imaginary of the 1980s and 1990s and how it heightens the desire in queer Latinas/os to search for alternative locations where they might nurture insight and challenge set values without fear.

Moraga's anxiety over her own safety and struggle for political connection and personal fulfillment is a major thread running throughout *Loving*. In a rather circuitous manner, however, this anxiety is exemplified in her heightened sensitivity to the struggles faced by others. We might read, for instance, Moraga's first visit to Mexico City's basílica as an example of such enhanced empathy. Upon first visiting the popular basílica and its display of Mexico's iconic symbol of national belonging (La Virgen de Guadalupe), Moraga becomes particularly attentive to the problems caused by the electronic walkway installed in the basílica to funnel visitors past the image as quickly as possible. When witnessing the distress and determination of the most impoverished Mexican women to remain on the electronic walkway, in order to appropriately venerate La Virgen, Moraga leaves the church profoundly disturbed.[22] She writes of "knowing how for so many years [she] had closed [her] heart to the passionate pull of such a faith that promised no end to the pain."[23] We might interpret the emotional response to the experience of struggle she witnesses as resonating with her experience of feeling marginalized and estranged from the Chicana/o community she longs to be a part of; it could even be said that this scene dramatizes Moraga's inability to act publicly and accept a Catholic (Chicana/o) spiritual vision that acts against her acceptance of her own racialized sexuality. Similar to the women struggling to remain on the moving walkway, Moraga writes throughout *Loving* of struggling to establish a sense of place and belonging within "*la familia Chicana*," despite circumventing practices (such as suspicion of mixed-raced Chicanas/os and the normalization of heterosexist and patriarchal values) implemented by the Chicana/o community.[24] This ability to identify with others in the process of struggle is a common motif in

Moraga's early writing.[25] Consequently, images such as the one detailed above carry heightened meaning. Filtered through Moraga's experience of alienation from the Chicana/o community, the moving walkway that she describes the Mexican women struggling against works to metaphorically represent the factors (e.g., ethnic nationalism, heterosexism, and patriarchal hegemony) that together create the "system" of oppressive social relations within Latina/o communities, the "moving sidewalks" that allow queer Latinas/os public participation in the cultural collective only in a standardized, fleeting, and strictly tributary manner.

The angst that permeates Moraga's writing, and that manifests itself in her empathy for others, is a belief in shared fate and an assertion of political solidarity. Not only does Moraga assert, in her work, a visceral awareness of the violent circumstances lesbians of color encounter in the United States (as is evident in the title of one of her poems, "We Have Read a Lot and Know We Are Not Safe"), but also Moraga refuses to leave such an attentiveness unconnected to other struggles around the world ("But it is not safe / Ni for Me. / Ni for El Salvador."[26] Romero's claim that Moraga idealizes her position outside of the Chicano community needs to be contextualized, then. While we should take seriously Romero's caution not to quickly assume that communities of origin inherently inhibit political consciousness, we should also be careful not to polarize the issue and assume discourses of distance and/or retreat unproductive.

Moraga is not the only Latina lesbian of the 1980s and 1990s to consider the epistemic and political consequences of queer exodus and queer migration. As a feminist philosopher and popular educator, María Lugones has taken very seriously the enticements and entrapments of queer exodus—ultimately rejecting the logic of needing to move away from communities of "origin" to communities of "choice" in order "know." Still, Lugones offers useful and moving analysis of how queer Latinas are often defined into incomprehensibility within Latino communities, the unfathomability of women loving women making it seem like the only two options are to conform to social standards or to abandon the prospect of social intelligibility and relationality within community. Lugones theorizes the liberatory potential usually attributed to movement away from barrios and toward spaces of lesbian socializing and organizing. While restraining herself from "advocating," in any simplistic sense, a separation from barrio communities, Lugones nevertheless gives a base-line credence to the self-preserving migratory instinct of queer Latinas in contexts of homophobic duress.[27] Making note of the "tortillera's" circumscribed presence within Latina/o communities, and observing, in particular, the pernicious circuits of gossip through which the tortillera is never addressed as such in the social, but is consequently ascribed a ghostly presence through gossip, Lugones questions the effectiveness of any acting and speaking on the tortillera's own behalf:[28]

> La tortillera exists en la comunidad only as a pervert. Perversion constitutes her and marks her as outside of countenanced relationality. Her sociality is alive and constructed en el mitote (*in gossip*), in her absence. . . . How could she make sense except in her silence, without uncovering her mark? How could she speak a sense that does not betray her, that does not turn against her? . . . La cachapera is silent, her meaning is made by others. El mitote imagines her as most vividly social and anomalous, but the anomaly is tamed through lack of direct address, through a denial of dialogue.[29]

As Lugones suggests, the means of defining a positive tortillera subjectivity and sociality are often severely limited. This failure to access some form of positive intelligibility within the Latina/o community leads to very narrow avenues of empowerment for the queer Latina in proximity to family and community. When heterosexism is violently naturalized through practices, institutions, and ideologies that depend on their appearance of neutrality, queer experience is deemed inconceivable. And so, the logic follows, to the extent that she is not imagined in some minimally positive sense within the Latina/o community, the queer Latina remains "absent." And to the extent that she remains absent, she is incapable of making sense to that cultural collective. She lacks a sanctioned self through which she can negotiate a sociality. As Lugones rhetorically suggests, borrowing from lesbian philosopher Sara Hoagland, "That which does not exist cannot relate to anything or anyone else."[30]

Moraga, like Lugones, is aware of the disempowering relationality queer Latinas/os encounter within the ethnic collective, and she explores the topic of this cultural unintelligibility in both her autobiographical and fictional work. In the introduction to *The Last Generation*, where she ultimately addresses her adult relationships with family and relatives, Moraga cleverly combines images of childhood inadequacies with feelings of powerlessness to represent her lack of sociality and presence in her home environment as a childless woman. Understanding her *lack* in a context where women *naturally* "make babies," Moraga describes herself as inconsequentially present, "the space occupying the middle of the sofa."[31] In her play "The Hungry Woman: A Mexican Medea," Moraga's protagonist is a queer Latina caught between her desire for women and her desire for Chicano nationalist cultural belonging. Describing herself as "a dying breed of female," as "the last one to make this journey," Medea arguably represents a woman socialized to understand herself in relation to Chicano nationalism, patriarchy, and heteronormativity.[32] In a significant way, she is the ultimate transgressor because her love for women is—quite literally—a painful annihilation of her sense of self.

What Lugones's and Moraga's work suggests is that if the queer Latina seeks the social sanctioning of her community, she is often forced to compromise her sociality by being assumed into the cultural collective's standard image of its constituency. Consequently, the queer Latina learns to acquire a public guise through which she maintains cultural intelligibility and relative safety. According to Lugones, "Heterosexual is the status that she may actually seek through her manner of presentation, including her speech, her compliance and alliance to heterosexual norms, including explicit displays of homophobia."[33] Acquiring a heterosexual persona through her silence, the tortillera participates in her own invisibility, a mirror displacing the self (into the privacy and anonymity of night clubs) and reflecting the other.[34]

This "heterosexual rehearsal," which Lugones implies as succeeding only in collaboration with other Latina/o community members who participate in her "production," is an arduous and violent daily process of communal self-denial. The erasure, silencing, and self-hatred that the queer Latina undergoes in trying to negotiate social norms is more than enough reason to value what seems to be (under certain circumstances) her only alternative: to flee. In search of a voice, of a place where her words may have meaning and her actions may have beneficial consequences, the queer Latina makes steps toward fleeing—what Lugones terms "movement towards movement"—to locations and communities where she may begin to create meaning for herself.

Lugones's "movement towards movement" is at base a recognition of the epistemic value of actions that bring about alternative social relations.[35] Alternative social relations can make queer Latinas/os happier and more comfortable, certainly. More importantly, they can place queer Latinas/os in epistemically privileged positions. Susan Babbitt, for instance, argues that it is often only when oppressed individuals are distanced from the accustomed social and political ways of relating to others that they can actually acquire more adequate personal and political understandings of their social situation. This argument—regarding the relationship between distance and knowledge—is different than what Romero glosses as problematic in Moraga's writing. Certainly, queer Latinas/os who distance themselves from family and community networks do not automatically have a cognitive advantage on every matter pertaining to the community. Still, they may have initiated a process (both spatial and cognitive) that is not inconsequential to their formations and self-understandings as Latina/o and queer. Babbitt terms this process "transformational experience," and she theorizes such a process by engaging with the controversial philosophical tradition of distinguishing between rational choice and objective interests. Babbitt proves most provocative in proposing a theory of rational deliberation that more fully accounts for "false consciousness," a fundamental misapprehension of one's own situation resulting from deep-seated ideological oppression. As I want to show in the following few pages, drawing on Babbitt's analysis opens up possibilities to more adequately account for the epistemic value of migratory movement in resistance to oppressive circumstances.

One of Babbitt's central concerns in her essay, "Feminism and Objective Interests: The Role of Transformational Experiences in Rational Deliberation," is to openly address the liberal approach to rational deliberation in order to critique instances where it proves inadequate in representing ideological oppression. The major failure of the liberal approach, Babbitt argues, is that it defines rational choice in terms of what someone would choose under various types of *idealized* cognitive conditions and that it suggests an *unchanging* subject in the process of achieving different stages of consciousness.[36] Babbitt's major interest in this essay is to critique the liberal view's obsession with the unchanging subject and to problematize the definition of what qualifies as useful/liberatory cognitive capacities. Ultimately, Babbitt's argument is a realist account of the causal relation between transformational experiences and rational deliberation.

One reason the liberal view fails according to Babbitt's framework is that it does not link and interrogate the social situatedness of the ideologically oppressed in relation to their ability to reason.[37] Because of this, the liberal view cannot attribute importance to transformational experiences in producing the very situations that can teach people more objective truths about the world. Using the example of Thomas Hill's Deferential Wife (a woman described as deriving her core sense of self from deferring to her husband), Babbitt examines the condition under which a liberal view fails to be adequate. The uniqueness of this example, Babbitt reminds us, is that the Deferential Wife does not defer to her husband only in certain circumstances, or only in return for her husband's deference in other occasions. The Deferential Wife defines herself (her sense of pride, success, and failure) in terms of her subordination.[38] The liberal view would argue that the Deferential Wife's liberation is predicated on her ability to stay true to her (current) values and interests while deliberating (under idealized conditions) over her deferential status.[39] But this view, Babbitt argues, fails to acknowledge the importance of transformational conditions that necessarily precede the desired change:

If [the Deferential Wife] is to choose what is best for *her*—even if she has access to full and complete information about what would be good for her under different conditions—she has no reason to choose a full sense of autonomy. She has not the kind of self to which such a sense of autonomy could be applied. . . . In order for it to be rational for her to desire autonomy in the sense that rules out her habitual servility, her actual sense of self would have to be transformed so that habitual servility is not what defines it.[40]

What Babbitt clarifies in her critique of the liberal approach, and what ultimately makes her analysis a realist accounting of identity, is that objective knowledge in fact relies on theory-mediated practices. Furthermore, these practices are not simply ones that we can willfully enact without ourselves moving to different "locations" and without changing in the process. Babbitt is able to conceptualize the possibilities of achieving more objective knowledge about oppression without retaining reductive notions of the subject as unchanging. She can argue, in a provocative manner, that the Deferential Wife needs to practice a different sense of self in order to make decisions that are in her self-interest. Babbitt's argument is further enhanced by an emphasis on the relationship between space and knowledge production, which in the case of the Deferential Wife means that she may need to leave certain situations (i.e., her restricted sociality in sole proximity to her husband and his values) and enter new ones (perhaps a women's consciousness-raising group) in order to better understand her circumstances.

Babbitt's theory of transformational experience helps us account for the epistemic consequences queer Latinas/os often attribute to queer exodus. I draw now from an image Babbitt uses in her discussion of the Deferential Wife to emphasize the concrete implications her ideas may have on queer Latina/o exodus:

> Vividly imagining oneself in some position does not usually involve transformations. This is why vivid imaginings are usually different from something like a mind-altering drug experience or a hallucination. When we vividly imagine ourselves in some situation, we are usually in control of the interpretation of the event. In a drug experience or a hallucination, the control is not there, so that often a person experiences herself in a state of emotion, desire, commitment, or relationship that she does not choose. Not only does that person experience herself in that situation, but she also acts and engages according to what she *is* in this other state, experiencing the consequences and so on.[41]

What I want to suggest, based on Babbitt's account of transformational experiences, is that while queer Latinas/os can vividly imagine alternatives and utopias, this exercise in visions, as Babbitt proposes, is less likely to involve transformations than those situations where one's capacity to imagine social change is not limited and constrained by existing (oppressive) social relations. With this understanding of transformational experiences we might understand the practice of, and desire for, distance as an initiation into a (potentially) mind-altering process, where the "deferential" queer Latina/o of the 1980s and 1990s acquires new meaning and alternative perspectives on his/her life from new locations.

THE "CRISIS" IN QUEER LATINA/O EXODUS

The motif of queer exodus is crucial to understanding certain impulses in queer Latina/o cultural production of the 1980s and 1990s. Yet, to acknowledge queer exodus as a significant social phenomenon, and to suggest that this type of queer distancing allows for *certain* insight and politicization, does not imply that queer exodus functions only in a progressive manner and only toward liberating ends. In fact, I want to provide some examples that suggest, in the words of Lugones herself, "why to think of choosing to leave communities of place is to think of the wrong activity in resistance to domination."[42]

One could reasonably argue, for instance, that queer exodus is one of the keys to contextualizing Richard Rodriguez's conservativism about ethnic identity in his autobiography *Hunger of Memory*. His infamously "liberal" distinction between the public and private domain arises, one might reasonably argue, from his inability to foresee a queer identity successfully flourish in proximity to, and in relationship with, his ethnic home and community. While *Hunger of Memory* does not overtly reference queer subjectivity, to argue that it might actually function on an implicit model of queer exodus would locate the book in a very interesting way: as illustrative of the impoverished outcomes of relying on a theory of sexual liberation premised on deracination, an uprooting that makes it quite difficult to reconcile a more coalitional and holistic politics of place. To understand *Hunger of Memory* in this way, as one extreme on a very broad spectrum of attempts at queer Latina/o empowerment, is to suggest that this often ostracized text, despite debates to the contrary, exists on an ever-evolving continuum of queer Latina/o relationships with exodus. Furthermore, understanding *Hunger of Memory* in this manner reveals that beyond examining *why* exodus is readily advocated/practiced or *how* it ends up working as trope in certain texts, critics should also be in the habit of documenting when queer exodus seems to backfire and to what extent.

Any cursory overview of queer Latina/o cultural production, beyond *Loving in the War Years* and *Hunger of Memory*—from the earlier writings of John Rechy, Arturo Islas, Gil Cuadros, and Terri de la Peña to later writings by Achy Obejas, tatiana de la tierra, Rigoberto Gonzalez, and Felicia Luna Lemus—will reveal a substantial questioning and deep suspicion of queer exodus as empowerment. In recent years, an increased attention to gay and lesbian ethnic minorities and their experiences with exodus has fostered in some the need to reconsider this tendency toward flight relative to its social, emotional, and political gain. Bob Cant argues that the liberating prospects of exodus for gays and lesbians have maintained a discontinuous relationship with lesbian and gay ethnic minorities due to the important function families and ethnic communities play in societies where oppression by race and class is considerable. As he suggests, queer ethnic minorities who migrate away often find themselves confined in restrictive roles within queer communities that accept their sexuality, but often marginalize and objectify their ethnicity.

Cant, as I have argued in the previous chapter (through my discussion of Rufus Scott), may in fact be exaggerating the importance of "the family" to queer ethnic minorities. The late sociologist Lionel Cantú has made an important critique of the trope of family, and its relationship to the study of Latino cultures and queer Latino men in particular, arguing that a conservative, anthropological ethno-centrism is evidenced when familism is ascribed an enhanced explanatory value for minorities and Third World people. The insinuation, Cantú rightly observes, is that even though everybody presumably grows up in some sort of family scenario and has the possibility of creating meaningful family relationships, the explanatory value of "the family" is only ascribed to certain cultural "others." However questionable Cant's reinscription of "familism" onto ethnic minorities may be, to argue as he does that distance from communities of origin often comes at a social and political price raises important concerns, for as much as exodus is practiced as recourse by the ethnic subject, its liberating prospects have proven to be quite complex, if not elusive.[43]

The challenges and traumas of negotiating ethnocentric racism and homonormativity in white gay and lesbian communities is one, recurrent and unique route in queer Latina/o cultural production of the 1990s for reassessing communities of origin as sites of queer possibility. Frances Negrón-Muntaner, in her film *Brincando el Charco: A Portrait of a Puerto Rican*, brings attention to this issue by fictionalizing it through a telephone conversation between her protagonist, Claudia (a Puerto Rican lesbian photographer) and the head of a gay publishing company. We learn through the ensuing conversation that Claudia's interests are in exploring Puerto Rican cultural identity through those who exist on its margins. Having been disowned by her family on the Island, Claudia finds herself inspired to explore Puerto Rican cultural politics as a route toward her lesbian identity.[44] Yet, as we learn through her struggle to get published, Claudia's work is deemed unmarketable for a "queer" (white) audience. As soon as the publisher begins to defend the reasons why Claudia's work will not be published, we are reminded of the tenuous and restricted sociality of queer Latinas/os in that space.

The publisher reassures Claudia, over the phone, of his genuine commitment to developing the visibility of gays and lesbians of color. The moment he expresses interest in her work (stating, "I truly like some of your stuff") his gaze lowers and focuses on the body of a young black male employee walking out of his office. Through this scene, we come to understand that the publisher's self-proclaimed commitment to the "visibility of gays and lesbians of color" is a commitment to a self-referential visibility—visibility for the queer person of color only in ways that please and do not threaten the privileged white patron. Citing Jackie Goldsby's essay, "What it Means To Be Colored Me,"

Tracy Morgan has made a similar observation that addresses the implications of this systemic acknowledgment/erasure: "The low level of concern about racism among many . . . [white] queers is derived, at least in part, from the 'tight reins held by gay print media that have resisted and restricted the free flow of ideas on the subject of racism in the gay male community, proving once again that ignorance isn't innocent; it's organized.'"[45] Negrón-Muntaner's scene dramatizes the limited ways in which queer people of color become accepted in queer (white) spaces: as either culturally assimilated queer "white" prototypes (as the eventual rejection of Claudia's "ethnically themed" work proves) or as ethnic objects of desire—eroticized bodies forced to fit into white fantasies.[46]

Queer Latina/o migration (from ethnic space to white queer space) is driven not necessarily by a desire to dissolve ethnic heritage and ties to communities, but rather a desire to express queer desire and sociability. Through the same telephone conversation with her publisher, Claudia is made aware, for example, that her reflections on lesbian identity are not deemed significant contributions because of their insistent ethnic references. Remarking on her work in scenes aesthetically juxtaposed as opposites—images of Claudia on the phone in a dark office with images of the publisher in an office with natural light entering through drapeless widows and reflecting off of white walls—he states, "If you're genuinely interested in marketing yourself as a Latina lesbian artist, you are just going to have to let go of certain issues. For example, I can tell you my readers are not concerned about colonialism—unless, of course, they are interested in the political implications of S & M relationships." The publisher reconciles queer ethnic concerns by decontextualizing and critiquing them through a narrow conception of who and what "the gay community" values. Here we see that queerness (in its universalized, presumably de-raced, de-classed form) not only becomes the privileged medium through which "the gay community" assumes a benign selection of "worthy" topics for discussion and circulation, but also the privileged manner in which "the gay community" systematically silences and objectifies people of color. Borrowing an observation from María Lugones in her critique of the lesbian feminist political movement, one could say that this scene depicts a queer movement that "lacks a taste for conversations inside locales and ways that risk its complicity with colonization, with our cultural and material erasure."[47] That the publisher smirks when he alludes to the "political implications of S&M relationships" further reveals not only a lack of interest in exploring those issues that could potentially implicate white queers in objectionable and coercive practices, but also a Lugonesian "arrogant" perception, which may pose the formative cognitive obstacle in addressing and dismantling oppressive practices.[48]

Far from being a marginal theme in queer Latina/o cultural production, the experience of needing to stifle one's values and political perspectives in order to negotiate alliances with white communities is often approached through the "case study" of interracial relationships. Writers like Gil Cuadros, Achy Obejas, Manuel Muñoz, and Juanita Sánchez, among others, have depicted the unhealthy compromises made by Latinas/os in return for relationships with white men and women. For example, Gil Cuadros writes, in *City of God*, of a young Chicano who learns to accommodate his white lover's racism by suppressing discussions of history and politics. "For our sake," the protagonist states, "I kept Sleepy Lagoon, Indian Massacres, and insecticides taboo subjects to avoid arguments and misunderstandings."[49] The protagonist internalizes his white lover's standard for deeming conversation topics "important and relevant," making their interactions, not only unbalanced, but superficial. We see this exemplified in the protagonist's concluding remarks, where he admits that despite his attempts to assimilate into white gay male privilege, he still remains objectified as an outsider: "They all treated me as . . . this little Mexican boy. . . . They said stuff like, 'Hot, Latin, brown-skinned, warm, exotic, dark, dark, dark.'"[50]

Due to experiences like these, queer Latinas/os come to share a heightened preoccupation with reevaluating their migratory strategies of negotiating oppression—in particular, rethinking their relationship to the family/ethnic community that has been, for many reasons and to different degrees, "left behind." Of course, the idea that queer Latinas/os "leave behind" the ethnic/family unit in order to negotiate desire and subjectivity always needs to be contextualized. Raúl Villa's astute critical reading of Cuadros within a larger Chicana/o literary-political tradition of "place-consciousness," reminds us that queer Latina/o migrations are never simply autonomous "decisions" to move away in order to actualize alternative forms of sexual desire and subjectivity, but are always complexly motivated and related to realities of urban displacement. Villa reminds us that the possibility of a "safe" home for queer Chicanas/os in Los Angeles is not only being eviscerated by homophobic practices in Chicana/o communities, but also that the possibility of any kind of Chicana/o home-place, "safe" or not, is simultaneously being undermined by actual destruction of Chicano communities by urban planners.[51] Queer migrations, therefore, respond to a variety of elements and sociohistoric specificities. Villa makes this explicit by reminding us of one of Cuadros's stories, "My Aztlán: White Place," and how even as the protagonist of this story is "speeding toward East Los Angeles, in flight from the white gay club scene on the Westside," he still finds himself escaping, but without a safe home to return to: "I was born below this freeway, in a house with a picket fence now plowed under. It was the same street my uncle and Tía lived on. . . . I've been here before, time after time, told my mother where our old house would be buried, near the call box, under the fast lane."[52]

While negative experiences in white communities have been useful tropes in queer Latina/o cultural production (significant in their ability to de-idealize the logic of queer exodus as "transformational"), valuing the Latina/o community as a sight of complex empowerment is also evident in less overt ways. In order to understand these more clearly, I want to provide a reading of a passage in Gloria Anzaldúa's *Borderlands* through the lens of "nonpropositional knowledge," which will help frame a discussion of how to understand queer Latina/o *fear of leaving home* as possibly reflecting latent political meaning. The point I want to make here, and that bears repeating, is that queer Latina/o cultural production challenges the logic of migration-as-emancipation, not always directly, but frequently with detailed attention to what it feels like to be negotiating hostilities in place and space.

The Epistemic Possibilities of Fear

Nonpropositional knowledge, Babbitt reminds us, refers to insights people have about the world that are not always expressible in immediate propositional truths. The examination of nonpropositional knowledge, therefore, is an attempt at understanding how emotions and behaviors are ways in which oppressed individuals make sense of their social world, a world that often robs them of concepts, histories, and communities to help give meaning to their lives. We need to examine queer Latina/o cultural production for the nonpropositional insights they have documented in relation to home communities. While some queer Latinas/os may lack the community resources of validation to address the systemic oppression in their lives, they may, nevertheless, *feel* and intuit in ways that reference objective features of their social world.

Emotions are knowledge-saturated indexes of the social world and our values.[53] They are epistemically significant and theory-laden, even when what they point to and make known cannot be fully articulated. We might think of Cherríe Moraga here when, in describing the difficulties she experienced being the only Chicana in her college, she reflects upon the importance of emotions that usually precede propositional understanding. "All along I had felt the difference," writes Moraga, "but not until I could put the words 'class' and 'race' to the experience, did my feelings make any sense."[54] What Moraga might be meaning here, on one level, is that sometimes we sense things intuitively that imply the need for analysis, but we do not (for several important reasons) come to any conclusions about it. The ability to eventually place meaning onto these feelings is fundamental, Moraga reminds us, to how well we evaluate and challenge oppressive situations and practices. However, "feeling like a nut," as Moraga describes her initial feelings of alienation, gestures toward important realities in the world (important *knowledge* about the world), that, if ignored, eliminates the very evidence on which theories of oppression and agency are founded.

I am retaining in this account a connection between personal experience and accurate knowledge. This is not to discount critiques that experienced-based knowledge has been overidealized, but to account for composite features of experienced-based knowledge—nonpropositional elements that have played a role historically, and can play a role in the future, for marginalized groups who lack the institutional and community validation to make sense of impressions, instinctual responses, and guesses. While we have learned greatly from understandings of experience as discursively mediated, we must also recognize the peculiar limitations of this formulation when taken to extremes. As Linda Alcoff has suggested, we should reject the "Lacanian-inspired claim that, in *all cases*, 'experience is a linguistic event,'" for if experience only gains meaning through discourse, then certain experiences, like the rape of an infant, are rendered meaningless.[55] Children who have been raped often do not have the concept of "rape" as a conceptual tool to negotiate and understand what has happened to them. However, their emotions and behaviors reflect, often with startling consistency, nonpropositional insights about the experience they have had. These behaviors, as registers of the world in which we live, need to be understood as epistemically useful. As psychologists have noted, the children who are sexually assaulted and who begin to exhibit indicators of emotional distress may not be able to articulate what is happening, but may be, nonetheless, communicating something about the world and their experience through their behavior and attitude. These symptoms of emotional distress, in fact, make us take notice and express concern. Traumatic symptoms are also fundamental indicators of why we understand sexual abuse to be wrong, why we understand it as a violation of an individual's autonomy. Should the case be that those sexually abused/assaulted no longer exhibited emotional distress, it would be much harder to argue as a society why this kind of sexual experience constituted an "assault," why it was wrong. Taking this example seriously, we should be more open to accounting for feelings, intuitions, and behaviors as manifestations of knowledge. Regarding queer Latina's/o's reflections on home, we should be open to understanding how some emotional responses, like fear of distancing oneself from Latina/o communities, may constitute nonpropositional insight about their political and social futures, rather than premature nostalgia for home.

There is a section in Anzaldúa's *Borderlands/La Frontera* where having an understanding of nonpropositional knowledge helps us understand some of the inferences being made regarding to the epistemic value of staying connected to and rooted in communities of origin. In "La Herencia Coatlicue," Anzaldúa speaks of her initial decolonial grapplings with her racialized sexuality, "el secreto terrible," and dramatically raises the problem of privileging distance and its cognitive consequences over the benefits of proximity and intimacy with the cultural collective. Urging attention to "cultural tyranny" in Chicana/o communities, Anzaldúa first intimates the need for distance by describing the unhealthy relationship with her culture and family as the source of her growing self-hatred. She tells us that her first awareness of herself as different from her family came well before her own sexual exploration; that, in fact, it is the "worried look" in her parents' eyes that communicates to her, as early as the age of two or three, that there is something fundamentally wrong with her.

Anzaldúa's growing tension with her family/community culminates in what one might typically understand as a stagnating idleness and depression, leading to a dual fear of looking within (confronting her racialized sexuality) and of becoming, in the process, lost, spiraling away from what she has known. Avoiding contact with family members, Anzaldúa undergoes a temporary withdrawal where she has no other recourse but to isolate herself, "lock . . . the door, keep the world out," in order to make some sense of herself in relation to her community.⁵⁶ In this manner, Anzaldúa explains her circumscribed experience within the coloniality of the Chicano/Mexicano border community—an experience of self-hatred and confusion imposed on her by a collective (and colonial legacy) ready to punish her difference in order to tame or erase it.

Given this experience of alienation and hostility, one would expect to hear, as is common with Anzaldúa, of a need to leave behind oppressive circumstances, to carry one's culture on one's back and search for those alternative social relations necessary for empowerment and change.⁵⁷ While this is one of Anzaldúa's migratory assertions, she makes a very interesting detour in this section. Instead of immediately speaking of fleeing *in order to be* and *in order to know*, Anzaldúa offers an alternative framing: a meditation, in the isolation of her room, on who she might be now and in the future, and who she might have been in the past, a deep decolonial digging.⁵⁸ Notably, this digging (which, in practice, feels like a demolishing) leads her to panic and fear that the journey she has initiated necessitates the elimination of her body for the sake of consciousness. Here is Anzaldúa's insightful description of the fear that accompanies the decolonization of one's mind—a decolonization, as Anzaldúa makes evident, which is both a painful journey *and* a metamorphosis:

she has this fear   that she has no names   that she
has many names   that she doesn't know her names   She has
this fear . . .   that if she takes off her clothes   shoves her brain
aside   peels off her skin . . .   strips the flesh from the bone   flushes out
the marrow   She has this fear that if she digs
into herself   she won't find anyone   that when she gets
"there"   she won't find her notches on the trees   the
birds will have eaten all the crumbs   She has this fear
that she won't find her way back.⁵⁹

Multiple ironies and spatializations are at play here. When one might justifiably expect Anzaldúa to rationalize distance, on account of having experienced violence, we see her giving voice to a fear that searching for another way to be (which in practice could mean searching in an other location) backfires, becoming an annihilation of self. The very route, however, to representing this fear—the coatlicue state—is a theorization accomplished through stasis, not movement, and is rooted in a reinterpretation of indigenous cosmologies and indigenous women's history of resistance.[60] The very route toward seeking new knowledge and critiquing Chicana/o "cultural tyranny," in other words, is not a distancing, but a decolonial anchoring and return—a decolonization of Chicana/o history by foregrounding indigenous women's subjugated knowledges and forms of resistance.

Rather than interpret Anzaldúa's association of introspection as destruction with ideological oppression, it is important to offer a complimentary spatialized explanation. The queer mestiza "fears" looking within, not only because she lacks conceptual tools, historical perspectives, and frameworks from which to make sense of her experiences, but also because the person she envisions becoming in the process of self-exploration is not sufficiently emplaced, situated relationally to others and to things. Her fear is not of "self-acceptance," of learning to be a more "authentic" self, but in fact a fear that her liberation depends on radical transformations, a fear that she *needs* to change (in ways that have not yet been previously mapped) and that such a change precedes certain insights. Anzaldúa's fear of introspection may have less to do with not finding "anyone" at the end of her journey, and more to do with being perplexed and concerned about who she thinks she will find "there," and what she thinks of that "place" in relation to where she has already been. My argument here recalls Babbitt's discussion of transformational experiences, urging complexity with regard to the practice of knowledge acquisition as implying and in many cases necessitating certain spatialized engagements.

We may want to think about Moraga here, and a section of *Loving* where she attends to questions of migration-as-emancipation, describing the process of accepting her sexuality as being inextricably linked to (and preceded by) a temporary moving away from her community. In "accepting" one's sexuality, Moraga seems to argue, one naturally seeks others who might be in a similar situation. Yet, while Moraga most clearly finds a community (the women's movement) that seems attuned to her needs and desires, she comes to slowly understand how inadequate they are for the decolonial lesbian politics she most desperately needs. Moraga argues that the women's movement failed to answer, or even show a concern for, the questions she had as a Chicana lesbian.[61] Not interested in cultural analysis based on monolithic understandings of "gender" and "sexuality," Moraga reassesses her situation. "What I need to explore," concludes Moraga, "will not be found in the feminist lesbian bedroom, but more likely in the mostly heterosexual bedrooms of South Texas, L.A., or even Sonora, Mexico."[62] This radically spatialized assertion of where knowledge resides, suggests that even if the route through which many queer Latinas/os gain initial insights about their sexuality is through distance and distancing, a richer, decolonial consciousness awaits in proximity to family, home, and community. Drawing on Moraga, I want to suggest that Anzaldúa's "fear" (so dramatically represented in her work by the description of bodily dismemberment and by associating introspection with chaos and not finding a "way back home") carries with it nonpropositional knowledge—that is, Anzaldúa's fear reflects (or, has the potential to reflect) a deeply felt and complex understanding of oppression as layered, an understanding that sees distancing from family and community not only as a strategic response to oppression, but also as a disturbing symptom of it.

My reading practice, here, perhaps belabors a point and makes too much of Anzaldúa's reflections on decolonial consciousness and space. Anzaldúa, however, is particularly unapologetic about her investment in the logic of "migration-as-emancipation." For example, *self-initiated* social and physical dislocation for Anzaldúa have no negative cultural ramifications: "Lo Mexicano is in my system," she asserts. "I am a turtle, wherever I go I carry 'home' on my back."[63] While this is an important political possibility to lay claim to—an open disavowal of being "out of touch" with the community or of "selling out"—Anzaldúa's claims can be pressed for failing, in this isolatable instance, to account for "contact zones," the real challenges and unavoidable mutations that many encounters with difference and power entail. Anzaldúa's assertion that culture and identity remain unchanged despite geographic and social distance is, surely, a rhetorical strategy confronting discourses of authenticity, Chicano nationalist critiques of feminism as nonorganic and foreign imposition. Nonetheless, such a claim seems to risk leaving unaccounted the relationship between social situatedness and knowledge, that is, the very real difference it makes to be situated, as a queer person of color, away from community and family.

Despite Anzaldúa's unapologetic engagement with the benefits of queer exodus, she also invokes a cosmology of inevitable "return."[64] This seeming contradiction can be best explained through nonlinear notions of time, echoed through the I Ching aphorism with which Anzaldúa begins the section of her book entitled *El Retorno*: "All movements are accomplished in six stages, and the seventh brings return."[65] "The return" Anzaldúa advocates is a traceable return, an accumulation of knowledge and a recognition of where the queer mestiza has been. It is a "return" that remembers—refusing to erase the pain and labor involved in the path taken ("I have come back. *Tanto me costó el alejamiento*").[66] It is also an analytic "return" that labors to make sense of the journey—to take inventory and differentiate "between the inherited, the acquired, and the imposed."[67] Finally, this "return" fulfills a kind of prophecy and political imperative, helping her readers link queer mestiza migratory labor as an *extension* of Chicano/Mexicano/Indigena decolonial politics. She reminds us that deracination does not have to mean depoliticization, and that as a queer mestiza she knows—through the way her body has *had* to move through the social world—not only that we can survive profound forms of oppression and violence, but that the queer mestiza's survival is the fulfillment of a profound decolonial promise: "The land was Mexican once / was Indian always / and is. / And will be again."[68]

As suggested by Anzaldúa's own conclusion, there seems to exist for the queer mestiza a decolonial investment in community that challenges the practice and perceived benefits of distancing oneself from community due to oppressive circumstances. This decolonial insight is often expressed in terms of a fear of detachment as well as fear of repeated abuse. There is a strong desire to stay (connected), and if not to stay, to *return*—to "leave bread crumbs" along the way so as to find the way back. The fear of being disconnected is tangible in queer Latina/o cultural production of the 1980s and 1990s, but the decolonizing practice of "homecoming" supercedes actual displacement, reminding us that the queer Latina/o body commits to never forgetting what it must occasionally "sever" and leave hind. "Even after the cut," Moraga cleverly reminds us, "they say the toes still itch / the body remembers the knee / gracefully bending."[69]

We Fight Back with Our Families?

The suggestion that Latina/o communities may in fact be crucial *and* viable locations for a queer politics, and the seemingly contradictory reality that queer Latinas/os often move away in order to express themselves in forms not sanctioned by Latino communities, is not a tension that requires resolution in the form of favoring one practice over the other. Rather, it seems that the practice of migration often influences new perspective on the possibilities of ethnic communities for a radical politics. Yet, it is important to heed the words of María Lugones when, in acknowledging such a tension between communities of "origin" and communities of "choice," and acknowledging the political possibilities of each, she does not leave the issue of queer exodus unpoliticized and undertheorized. Although Lugones wants for herself and other queer Latinas a culturally specific way of being that *does not close down multiplicity* ("a voice as a jota, a wide repertoire in daily things among people"), she also requires of this way of being a particular political vision, her "own sense of walking in some direction rather than wandering aimlessly and without sense in terrains prepared to swallow [her] whole or in parts."[70] In this way, Lugones maintains a critical disposition toward queer exodus, even as she acknowledges (as I have already shown earlier in this chapter) its benefits.

In fact, Lugones makes a series of critiques in response to queer exodus that deserve further consideration. Lugones suggests to us, for example, that strategies like queer exodus may indeed be resistant activity—necessary at times and full of useful epistemic consequences—but they certainly need not be associated interchangeably with *social* change. That is, we can acknowledge the epistemic value of alternative social locations (for the queer Latina/o in conflict with the ethnic collective), while still remaining accountable for the political and social possibilities that such acts of migration potentially *undermine*. I am speaking here of the fact that movement away from communities of origin often leaves those communities and their practices intact, unchallenged. One example that Lugones offers in order to further buttress this claim is that of closeted Latinas "migrating" on weekends to the lesbian bar. There these Latinas are able to "be" in a manner that they can never manage in the larger social space of heteronormative family and cultural relations. However, these same women may be unable to mobilize such experiences of lesbian sociality, experiences with latent political importance, in a manner that may change or influence their lives every other day of the week (i.e., at home, among family, or even at work). Certainly, Lugones acknowledges that the experiences of lesbian sociality at the bar cannot be left behind (simply willed away), and that these experiences often do influence and even organize some experiences outside of the bar. However, Lugones asks us to consider how the "taintedness" with which closeted Latinas experience their daily lives—"*With traces of the bar in the movements of the hips, the pursing of the lips to point to things, the taste of love and style directed strictly inward, toward a point inside that is locked beyond meaning*"—may never be a "taintedness" that is purposefully resistant or committed to enacting *social* change. Reflecting on the dilemma of lesbian bar culture potentially fueling complacency, Lugones writes:

Y mañana al jale. Con traces de la barra *in the movements of the hips, the pursing of the lips to point to things, the taste for love and style directed strictly inward, toward a point inside that is locked beyond meaning.* Como si fuéramos simplemente mujeres. *Not even bothered by the "conversations" ordered by heterosexual domesticity.* Que va, si a una ni se le ocurre pensar en ninguna lengua, ni con ningún conjunto de cicatrices y palabras, algo como *"ordered by hetersexual domesticity."* Oh, a veces se lo piensa, como algo abstracto, *taking a step back, like taking a picture for posterity.* ¿Y si mi mamá es tortillera? ¿Dónde? ¿Aquí entre las casadas y por casar, que saben tanto de showers para mujeres y beibis? No tiene sentido . . . ¡Ay que asco que se besen en la boca! ¡Ay virgencita, ni me lo cuentes!

[And tomorrow to work. With traces of the bar in the movements of the hips, the pursing of the lips to point to things, the taste of love and style directed strictly inward, toward a point inside that is locked beyond meaning. As if we were simply women. Not even bothered by the "conversations" ordered by heterosexual domesticity. It doesn't even occur to one to think in any language, nor with any set of scars and words, something like "ordered by heterosexual domesticity." Oh, sometimes one things about it, like something abstract, taking a step back, like taking a picture for posterity. And if my mother is a *tortillera*? Where? Here, among the wedded and to be wed, who know so much about showers for brides and babies. No, it doesn't make any sense. . . . How revolting that they kiss each other on the mouth! Holy mother of God, don't even tell me about it!][71]

The lesbian bar, in short, offers a space for momentary release, but not in a way that fosters politicization outside of the bar. The reality of this disconnection, Lugones suggests, is so great that closeted Latinas often cannot even entertain certain thoughts—like wondering if one's own mother is a tortillera and doing so long enough to consider changing one's behavior in light of that possible fact. Here, we might want to consider that once we reconceptualize Latina/o life as heterogeneous, as constituted by queers, it becomes less imperative to perpetuate heteronormativity out of a fear that we are an anomaly, that we are not of this place. Unfortunately, as the ending two sentences of Lugones's account suggest, closeted Latinas may even work against such prospects, acting against their own objective interests by ventriloquizing homophobic rhetoric in the presence of other women ("How revolting that they kiss each other on the mouth! Holy mother of God, don't even tell me about it!"). It is worth repeating here that all of this behavior is compatible with experiences in lesbian bar culture, precisely because the experiences at the lesbian bar are compartmentalized, and done so in a depoliticized vein.

Not all instances of queer migration should be understood as politically problematic. In fact, many instances of queer exodus, as Lugones herself notes, do indeed have ramifications of great political importance.[72] Such practices of exodus, while resistant and politically important, often perpetuate an understanding of communities of origin as stagnant, as places that constitute their members passively. They do this often implicitly and by inference, suggesting through the very act of exodus not simply the inadequacies of communities of origin for a radical politics, but the seeming impossibility of ever making them change. This is the tendency that Lugones identifies as problematic in the work of Marilyn Freedman and in her strict conceptual distinction between communities of "origin" and communities of "choice." Lugones writes, "Friedman sees passivity in communities of place: ossified hierarchies and roles. She misses the ingenuity and constant creativity in relationships among neighbors, people in families, and in relations that cannot be easily placed in the understanding of communities of place."[73] As an alternative to Freedman, Lugones asks us to reconceptualize communities of place as complex and heterogeneous. Lugones asks, "Why not think that as contradictory identities are formed within communities of place, these communities are revealed as not univocal, passing on and embodying an undisturbed common sense, but as complex and tense sites of identity formation?"[74] Here, Lugones promotes an account of communities of origin that opens them up for practices of social resistance that do not require uprootings.

Similarly, Moraga has made an observation, citing Mirtha Quintanales, regarding the need to reconceptualize Latina/o communities as places within which to dwell and grow, and why this reconceptualization might constitute a cognitive advantage for queer Latinas/os:

The critical issue for me regarding the politics of sexuality is that as a Latina Lesbian living in the U.S., I do not really have much of an opportunity to examine what constitutes sexual conformity and sexual defiance in my own culture, in my own ethnic community and how that may affect my own values, attitudes, sexual life and politics. There is virtually no dialogue on the subject anywhere and I . . . am quite in the dark about what we're up against.[75]

Implied in Quintanales's avowal of her needs as a Latina lesbian is an understanding that the familial/ethnic community is a location where conversations have a history—developed by struggles and (mis)understandings based on proximity—that have been formative for queer Latinas/os. As such, it would be a profound mistake and liability if they remained unexamined. As Moraga herself concludes, "We have not been allowed to express ourselves in specifically female and Latina ways or even to explore what those ways are. As long as that is held in check, so much of the rest of our potential power is as well."[76] Of course, this reevaluation of Latina/o communities does not imply that queer Latinas/os have always participated *equally* in these "Latino conversations." But it does account for a common frame of reference, and in a fundamental way, a desire to see Latina/o communities in all of their heterogeneity.

Understanding the ethnic community as a viable "site" for coalition and resistance is perhaps one of the most important consequences of queer Latina/o migrant labor. If we believe Moraga when she states that what she needs to explore "will not be found in the feminist lesbian bedroom, but most likely in the mostly heterosexual bedrooms of South Texas, L.A., or even Sonora, Mexico," we need to remind ourselves that such a conclusion was the result of queer migrant labor, or routes, detours, and deliberations that if erased produce confusion about the spatialization of knowledge and power in our society.[77] Without these routes, Moraga's claim to anchor queer Latina/o politics in conversation with Latina/o communities could sound like idealism and uninformed glorification. Queer Latina cultural critics are aware of the problematic nature of *longing to belong* and the danger involved in desiring sociality within an ethnic home(land) that often works against them. Lugones, for example, embraces the complexity of this political necessity for a politics of place and a politics of coalition, wanting to engage in the practice of understanding social categories like "women," "Latino," and "familia," not as strictly defined, but as emphatically open-ended, "as if you held a multitude of interrelated subjects in your attention and you thought, felt, understood yourself as among them in your own specificity and in the problematic character of that specificity, as enmeshed in both shifting and historically threaded but also ossified relations of solidarity and exploitation."[78] Similarly, Mary Pat Brady helps us to understand why, for example, queer Chicana engagements with traditionally heteronormative practices of Chicano nationalist resistance are not simplistic affirmations of such practices, but are, in fact, critiques and redeployments, often of some of their most basic and foundational assumptions.[79]

IDENTITY AS SPATIAL PRAXIS

The focus of this chapter has been the centrality of "queer exodus" to queer Latina/o discourse. By addressing one of its logics (i.e., the logic of migration-as-emancipation), I have foregrounded various responses to this tradition, calling attention to the actual phenomenon as a form of queer spatial praxis—as movement that calls attention to the situatedness of knowledges by attending to the perspectives fostered by the migrating queer subject in various locations.

By way of conclusion, I now want to transition away from negotiations that have explicit spatial dimensions toward the less overtly spatialized practices of identity and identification. In particular, I am thinking of those peculiar types of identity and identification that José Esteban Muñoz has termed "disidentifications." In *Disidentifications: Queers of Color and the Performance of Politics*, Muñoz advances a theory of "disidentification" and a theory of the "world-making" possibilities of performance art in order to contribute to a better understanding of the ways queers of color (specifically, queer artists of color) negotiate relationships of survival and empowerment with dominant cultures. Dominant cultures often sustain themselves by perpetuating ideologies that work against queer people of color and their attempts at sociopolitical self-realization and representation. Muñoz positions his work as an examination not only of the ways queer people of color navigate hostility in mainstream environments through disidentificatory methods, but how they teach others similarly situated to do so as well. "Disidentification," Muñoz argues, is a model of dealing with dominant ideology that neither seeks to assimilate within structures of dominance nor strictly opposes them. It stands in contrast with two models that seek to explain ways in which the Althusserian subject negotiates the interpellative pressures of dominant ideology.[80] The first model (identification/assimilation model) describes the actions of the "Good Subject" who assimilates without introspection or contestation and chooses the path of identification with discursive and ideological forms. The second (the counteridentification/utopian model) describes the "Bad Subject" who resists and attempts to reject the images and identificatory sites offered by dominant ideology and proceeds to rebel against the symbolic system. What is seen as a danger in both of these stock models (dangerous in the second because of the counterdetermination that such a system is said to install and anticipate) is seen to be reconciled in a third mode of analyses, that of "disidentification."

Part of the destructive relationship majoritarian groups insist on having with minoritarian groups is a debilitating social contract that performance art (especially the art noted by Muñoz by artists like Jack Smith and Carmelita Tropicana) self-consciously strives to disrupt. By allowing audiences to reimagine not only their codified relationships to genres of entertainment (and expectations of passive spectatorship), but also their compartmentalized relationship to politics and social oppression, performance artists often reaffirm the "world-making" potential of radical artistic creativity. Working with this notion of the possibility of social change through art, Muñoz moves beyond the isolated disidentificatory act (and its importance to individuals as survival strategy) to the *performance* of the disidentificatory act and its increasing importance in developing critical communities of social change. In this manner, Muñoz finds the concept of disidentification and the particular significance of *performing* disidentifications useful in unpacking the often misunderstood and neglected cultural and political significance of radical artistic work by queer people of color.

Practices of disidentification call attention, in very interesting and unexpected ways, to the spatiality of knowledge and power. Muñoz makes this particularly evident in his discussion of the transgendered documentary subject "Sara/Ricardo" in Susanne Aiken and Carlos Aparicio's two films *The Salt Mines* (1990) and *Transformation* (1996). In the 1990 film, Sara is one of the homeless transvestites and transsexuals of color being documented by Aiken and Aparicio in New York City. In the 1996 film, Sara has moved to Texas, shifted out of her identification as a woman, and goes by the name Ricardo (the name given to her at birth). Unpacking the issues at stake, Muñoz writes:

Ricardo . . . has taken on a heterosexual identification and a conversion to fundamentalist Christianity. Ricardo has even gone so far as to marry a woman from his church group. Even though Sara had breasts and had undergone years of guerrilla hormone therapy, he is trying to masculinize himself to fit into his new community. This masculinization includes having his implants removed, cutting his hair, and renouncing his homosexual desire.[81]

Sara's radical transformation to being identified, once again, as an anatomically born male (that is, as "Ricardo"), is read by Muñoz as an explicit re-formation of identity for the purpose of gaining access and mobility in another geography, the geography of heteronormative privilege. This new space is acquired through religious conversion and a marriage (to a woman). The space afforded by heterosexual identification makes possible the health care that Sara so desperately needs as a person living with AIDS. As Muñoz points out, Sara's *disidentification* with heterosexuality (by having her breast implants removed, by stopping hormone injections, and by marrying a woman) is not a liberatory disidentification on many counts. Nonetheless, the practice of disidentifying with heterosexual privilege is Sara's opportunity to gain access to health care as she confronts her deteriorating health. Importantly, this "access" is one that has an overt spatialization: Sara becomes "Ricardo" in order to be granted resources that she, as a homeless transsexual, cannot acquire on her own and from within that homeless transsexual (spatial) reality.

A significant mistake one might make in conceptualizing disidentifications as spatialized processes would be to associate only certain disidentifications, like that of Sara/Ricardo's radical transformation, with spatiality, while leaving other disidentificatory processes underacknowledged as instances of spatial praxis. For example, a short documentary film by Augie Robles, entitled *Cholo/Joto*, is exemplary for Muñoz's theorization of disidentification, in that the film's last images enact a moment of disidentification with the homophobic logic of Chicano nationalism. The disidentification occurs when the documentary subject, Valentín (played by Robles, himself), asserts a cognitive and emotional connection with barrio communities without having to displace his queer sensibilities, nor ignore instances of rampant homophobia. In fact, Valentín grounds his alignment with barrio communities and politics by attributing queer possibilities at the very core of Chicano nationalist rhetoric and iconography. Reconceptualizing his relationship to a famous mural of Ché Guevara in San Diego's Chicano Park, Valentín disidentifies with the sentiment behind Guevara's famous pronouncement, "A true revolutionary is guided by deep feelings of love." Rather than respond to what Muñoz refers to as the "entrenched misogyny and homophobia of masculinist liberation ideologies" that Guevara's image often represents, Valentín responds to the icon in a manner that conceptualizes a place for himself in coalitional struggle with his community.

Driven also by love, Valentín performatively states, "I'm not going to fight out of anger but because I love myself and I love my community."[82] In this way, Valentín is able to disidentify with liberationist iconography, inserting himself within a cultural history of resistance that did not have him, as a queer subject, in mind in the first place—a history that must now come to terms with queerness because queer Latinas/os have claimed, for themselves, a space in the barrio and its resistant politics. Importantly, the film contextualizes such a disidentification within the context of migration-as-emancipation. By alluding to the experience of racism in gay ghettos and homophobia in Chicano neighborhoods, the film foregrounds the act of disidentifying with Ché, not simply as a cognitive exercise enacted for mental sanity, but truly as a spatial remapping of political possibilities within Chicano communities and politics. The act of disidentification, in other words, remaps the barrio as a place to engage in desire *and* politics. Ché, for the Chicano joto in San Diego, can now be a revolutionary precedent without having to be idealized, or sanitized in the queer resistant imagination.

If Robles's film *Cholo/Joto* is suggestive of the implicit geographical negotiations at stake in disidentificatory practices, Horacio Roque-Ramírez's 1996 short story, "Cholo/Salvatrucho," can be read as making a similar assertion and much more explicitly.[83] In fact, Roque-Ramírez's short story is an important companion to the film *Cholo/Joto* precisely in its ability to show how practices of disidentification have variable consequences depending on *where* these disidentifications take place. "Cholo/Salvatrucho" is written from the perspective of a queer Salvadoreño living in the Mission District in San Francisco and describes in great embodied detail the geographical consequences of adopting a cholo aesthetic without cholo sociality. The "look" our narrator achieves is always understood as an achievement to be very proud of, but also one that is never truly "real":

Tu camisa Pendleton *de mentiritas*, de segunda, te cuelga muy bien. . . . el resplandor de tu cabeza recién rasurada, un estilo de *cholo falso* . . . tu propio estilo, *medio falso pero bien hecho*.[84]

[Your fake Pendleton shirt, from a second-hand store, hangs on your body very well . . . the shine of your recently shaven head, the style of a cholo wannabe, your own style, a little fake, but well done.] (my translation)

As cholo *replica*, however, this performance has disidentificatory viability only within the confines of queer space. This becomes most evident when, on the day the narrator decides to walk from his home to a gay club, he is assaulted by young Latino men hanging out on the street. The assault, interestingly enough, is preceded by the narrator's hyper-attentiveness to his cholo aesthetic in public space. Enthusiastic about meeting his date later that night, the narrator works to restrict such anticipation, describing it as emotion that does not have a proper place in male body comportment and especially in public: "La emoción que cargás es algo obvia hoy, más de lo normal que se permite en público, o que permite la seguiridad" [The emotion that you carry with you is more obvious today, more than what is permitted in public, or that security will permit].[85] Attentive to how his (cholo) body signifies in the barrio, the narrator reminds himself not to rush, that he must pace himself in order to blend in: "continúas caminando, sabiendo muy bien que no debés acelerar en absoluto. Solo un paso bien medido es el que menos atención te puede dar en estas partes de tu barrio" [you continue walking, knowing very well that you should not increase your pace by any means. Only a carefully measured pace is what will least draw attention in this section of your barrio].[86] Unfortunately, none of the narrator's initial efforts help him avoid a confrontation with some young men on the street, a confrontation which forces him into a profound self-reflexivity and attentiveness to his body comportment:

Sabés que ya es demasiado tarde para no llamar la atención al darte vuelta para una de las otras calles y que no hay manera de evitar que te vean. . . . Con cautela, tomás mejor control de tu ritmo, ni muy creído ni tan sonriente. Independiente, pensás. Ahora si les prohibís a tus aretes que se muevan tanto, que no digan nada, que no te dilaten de lo que sos, y a lo que vas con tantas ganas. Tratás de no tomar ninguna posición exagerada, aunque tampoco dejás de querer sentirte un poco mas máchito que antes, lo suficiente para indicarles que no sos De La Hoya per que tampoco sos maricón profesional. De repente te das cuenta que esta vez no hay salida y que sólo tu buen semblante de niño-vato bien portado y un poquito amanerado te puede salvar.[87]

[You realize that it is too late to not call attention to yourself by turning around and heading down one of the other streets; there is no real way of avoiding being seen. . . . With a great deal of caution, you take better control of your rhythm, not too conceited nor too friendly. "Independent," you think to yourself. Now you prohibit your earrings from moving so much, so that they don't reveal anything, so that they don't communicate what you are and where you are going with such anticipation. You try not to make any exaggerated gestures, although you don't resist the temptation to think of yourself a little more macho than before, the sufficient amount to indicate that even if you are not from La Hoya, it doesn't mean by default that you are a professional fag. All of a sudden you realize that this time there is no escape and that only your resemblance of a well-behaved and slightly effeminate baby-vato can save you.]

Every aspect of his body and movement—from his pace to the way he restricts his earrings from moving—seems for the narrator to have crucial communicative functions. By controlling these, or imagining that he can, the narrator hopes to project an "independent," bipartisan persona, nothing exaggerated, nothing too macho, someone who just needs to walk by, someone who will not disturb and does not seek to be disturbed. The narrator ultimately fails in projecting such a sensibility and attributes such a failure to a stubborn naiveté on his part regarding the prospect of disidentifying with the cholo "look" without attending to the constraints and consequences of such a disidentification:

Otra vez te acordás que los disfraces en la discoteca son una cosa, y los de la calle otra. Pero vos seguís de necio confundiendo los dos en todas partes.[88]

[Again you realize that the costumes at the club are one thing, and the one's on the street are another. But you continue, stubbornly, confusing the two everywhere you go.]

In other words, although one would be wrong to say that the narrator *asks* to be assaulted on the street, it is precisely the narrator's choice of a cholo aesthetic that brings him into a symbolic economy of meaning on the street. And it is by acknowledging this symbolic economy of meaning—by acknowledging that he need not give up his disidentification with the cholo aesthetic, but that he also need not assume such disidentifications have no geographical limits and consequences—that the narrator helps us to understand the spatial concerns and constraints of enacting "successful" disidentifications.

This is not, by any means, all that there is to say about this short story, nor about the work of Horacio Roque-Ramírez as a historian and creative writer.[89] However, my reading of "Cholo/Salvatrucho" does emphasize this story's importance in helping us understand practices of disidentification as forms of spatial praxis—as instances of social resistance and agency that address (as much as they become impinged upon by) the spatialization of knowledge and power. Broadly speaking, this chapter has been concerned with spatial analysis in queer Latina/o discourse of the 1980s and 1990s. In it, I have sought to understand some of the *migratory* ways that queer Latinas/os have negotiated social and epistemic well-being in oppressive contexts. Particularly, I have wanted to emphasize the embodied theory-making that can be gleaned by attending to the experience-based writing and cultural production of queer Latinas/os, especially with regard to those uniquely "migrant" forms of labor necessary for acquiring and producing knowledge in oppressive contexts.

CHAPTER 4

SHIFTING THE SITE OF QUEER ENUNCIATION

> The urgency for lesbianas Latinas to speak is undeniable. From Carla Trujillo's challenge to Chicana lesbians to "fight for our own voices as women" to Emma Pérez's declaration that "marginalized groups must have separate spaces to inaugurate their own discourses, nuestra lengua en nuestro sitio," the call to create our language, to name ourselves, becomes a critical task of survival.
>
> Yolanda Chávez Leyva, "Listening to the Silences"

> I have come to believe over and over again that what is most important to me must be spoken, made verbal and shared, even at the risk of it being bruised or misunderstood. [I have come to believe] that the speaking profits me, beyond any other effect.
>
> Audre Lorde, "The Transformation of Silence"

To familiarize oneself with the literary production of queer writers of color is, arguably, to witness the importance of crafting a subjective, politicized voice for the abject desiring body. One need only peruse the work of writers as diverse as Audre Lorde and Gloria Anzaldúa, Ricardo Bracho and Essex Hemphill, among others, to see firsthand how resistance and enfranchisement have often been nurtured through narratives where identity and politics are written about *from* the perspective of queers of color. While the importance of this history and practice cannot be overstated, critics of queer ethnic literary production would be remiss if they did not attend to divergences from this tradition, divergences that might not only yield social insights complementary to those produced by first-person narratives, but would also highlight how such insights come to be generated so astutely and provocatively, not only through narrative content, but through narrative form. When and how do queer writers of color differ from this first-person tradition of narration, and what conceptual and critical consequences arise from such departures?[1] If, as the historian Yolanda Chávez Leyva has noted, the urgency to speak is "undeniable," why has such speaking and its "profits" (to borrow language from Audre Lorde) been revisited in some queer ethnic literary production?[2]

I offer some preliminary answers to these questions by turning to the work of the queer Chicano writer Manuel Muñoz and the queer African American writer Randall Kenan, arguing that their work develops a provocative, multifocal narrative approach to queer experience and identity. This approach, which I describe as *shifting the site of queer enunciation,* astutely decenters queer speaking subjects, doing so in a manner that not only equitably distributes narrative responsibility for queer experience and identity, but that also enables a deeper understanding of the intersubjective and social contexts in which queer subjects come into being. By shifting the anticipated "location" and articulation of queerness—moving it from the queer subject proper to the queer subject's siblings, friends, parents, and neighbors—Muñoz and Kenan transfer some of the burden of queer representation. More importantly, they expose the web of relationships and discourses that constitute queer experience and queer identity in any given context. Such a narrative approach, precisely because it provides what the philosopher María Lugones would term a "peopled sense" of queer experience, produces a fundamental break with logics of domination that refuse marginalized subjects their "social girth," that is, their relationship to various people, places, histories, and socialities.

Shifting the site of queer enunciation, as a narrative practice, provides an opportunity to foreground the following set of observations: (1) that queer experiences are actually *coproduced and shared* by larger collectives, even though these larger collectives often deny their own implicatedness in queer sociality; (2) that in fact it takes studied work to deny such implication, and that such a denial leads to a kind of existential distance that is thoroughly produced rather than natural; (3) that some nonqueer people actually work to resist the logic of social fragmentation mandated by homophobic societies, and that they do so, at times, by bearing "faithful witness" to acts of queer social resistance—even when it is dangerous to do so and even when such acts place them in opposition to homophobic "common sense"; and (4) that queer people define themselves in relation to some of the same webs of cultural meaning that heterosexuals around them draw from, and that, in this sense, queers are engaged participants in the dialogic production of cultural meanings and therefore fundamentally part of the collective experience and imaginary.

Before discussing Muñoz's and Kenan's writing, it is important to briefly acknowledge that narrating queer stories from perspectives other than those of queer subjects can have profound sociopolitical implications. This is particularly so given a political climate in which subaltern resistance is continuously misrepresented through the lens of "individual," "rational" modern agency.[3] María Lugones argues that such a conception of agency is, in reality, a fiction that tends to impede rather than to enable oppressed peoples. She reminds us that the notion of effective individual agency actively hides the institutional setting and backing of commonly understood "individual" potency. It entices people with the apparent power and efficacy of their own individual deliberations and decisions, even as the oppressed have the everyday experiences to understand that their acts of resistance cannot successfully intervene socially unless they are backed up by others.[4] While Lugones acknowledges that it often feels as though agency arises from us alone, she argues that such a feeling actively thwarts a more complex understanding of how one's own intentions arise in social contexts and among people, and that our intentions respond to a nexus of "intentionalities" that are given "up-take" or are diverted and morphed by other constellations of intentions and the institutional backings that support them. With this complex vision of intentionality Lugones argues that the oppressed actualize an "active subjectivity," a mode of responding to oppression that is not the modern conception of agency at all. This is so primarily because "active subjectivity" is a practice that is lacking not only institutional backup but also such institutional backup in a self-aware manner. "Active subjectivity," according to Lugones, is a type of subjectivity that replaces the illusion of individual agency with a horizontal attentiveness to how intentions travel from person to person. "Active subjectivity" in this sense remains attentive and invested in the possibility of actualizing social change, even as it reveals the deeply contextual and attenuated nature of social action and meaning making.[5] From such a complex understanding of active subjectivity and intentionality, the writings of Muñoz and Kenan gain importance for their innovative narrative approach. By providing rich descriptions of what it feels like to bear witness to queerness in a complex social context—explicitly elaborating on queer experience as taking shape in contexts of great interaction, ideological influence, and competing intentionality—Muñoz and Kenan make explicit and further expand on the notion of queerness as social, coproduced, and shared.

MANUEL MUÑOZ'S HETERODIEGETIC INTERVENTIONS

Manuel Muñoz's collection of short stories, *Zigzagger*, is impressive with regard to the scope and emotional integrity with which it depicts formative experiences in the sociality of queerness. Muñoz's attentiveness to small-town community life—and the social consequences of that life for how sexuality and intimacy will be played out by those who constitute the community—holds a special place in Chicano letters. Like its literary predecessors (from Rolando Hinojosa's *Estampas del Valle* and Tomas Rivera's *Y no se lo tragó la tierra* to Arturo Islas's *The Rain God* and Ito Romo's *The Bridge*), *Zigzagger* addresses intimate relationships, communal history, and vernacular knowledge. However, quite unlike most of its predecessors, Muñoz's stories are some of the first to make queer experience a tangible, albeit attenuated, presence in the midst of small-town Chicano community life.

I examine three short stories from this collection, stories that convey a sense of queer experience as social and shared precisely because they narrate it from a perspective other than that of the queer subject proper. In the short story "Good as Yesterday," for example, a sister's perspective provides an intimate account of living and learning alongside a queer younger brother. In "The Unimportant Lila Parr" a rural Mexican American community reflects on the murder of a young gay man in their town. In the title story, "Zigzagger," a young man's sexual awakening is narrated in its complex sociality through his parents, who witness its aftermath, and through the son himself, who is fundamentally changed by the experience.

Among the claims I make in this chapter, I emphasize that there is an important *heterodiegetic* approach that undergirds these three stories. Crucial information is conveyed about the sociality of queerness when queer experience is narrated, not directly from a character within the story's action (a *homodiegetic* approach), but from a narrative voice outside of the experienced events.[6] Through an omniscient style of narration, for example, these heterodiegetic narratives provide readers a sense of the diversity of people experiencing queerness, giving us access to the many ways queerness is being conceptualized by people situated differently in relation to it.[7] Muñoz's narratives, however, do not, strictly speaking, convey a plurality of perspectives in any given story, and in fact, they often rely on a specific focaliser to consider queerness from a particular perspective (solely from a sister's or solely from a mother's point of view, for example). Still, by writing in a heterodiegetic mode—from a narrative voice outside of the experienced events—Muñoz conveys a subtle but crucial insight about the often *muted sociality* of queerness. His narrative approach, in other words, makes visible the shared quality of queer experience, even if those people sharing in it are not cognizant of it or are not compelled to narrate a story about it. Though focalization helps narratives like those of Muñoz convey an intimate sense of the interiority of characters (e.g., of what they are thinking and feeling), such an interiority is still not at the self-consciously discursive level implied by homodiegetic narratives, where characters have something to say in an explicit way about what they are experiencing.[8]

The three narratives I examine all work within this heterodiegetic logic; however, each is further distinguished by the degree of narrative proximity it employs toward queer ethnic subjects and the insights on muted agency and queer experience that such proximity can convey. In the short story "Good as Yesterday," Vero's intimate perspective on her relationship with her queer younger brother conveys an up-close and embodied understanding of queerness, particularly as it unfolds within the psychological and geographic context of a small Mexican American town in central California. Focalized explicitly through Vero's perspective, the story describes with great detail the emotions and tensions that arise for her in bearing witness to Nicky's struggles as a young gay man. For example, when Nicky is brutally assaulted by neighborhood boys his own age on his sixteenth birthday, Vero is irrevocably affected by it; the incident forms in her mind the moment at which she is compelled (however imperfectly and ambivalently) to love and support Nicky in his complicated sociality:

She has always wanted to tell him that she loves him because of how he came home on his sixteenth birthday. He had come home running. He had come home bleeding.

In one of the alleys in their neighborhood, six boys had dragged and beaten him. All six of them had taken turns, boys he went to school with, boys from another neighborhood, boys he grew up with, boys he had secretly fooled with on back porches. Gaudio, Peter, Alex, Fidel, Israel, and Andy.[9]

Vero's desire to communicate to Nicky that he is loved, as we see in this passage, is a desire to mitigate the emotional, physical, and symbolic damage caused by the violence he is subjected to on his birthday. As we later come to understand, this assault forever changes Nicky; this is so precisely because such an incident represents more than an isolated confrontation. The assault affects Nicky so profoundly because it is carried out communally, by people with whom he has shared intimacies, and because the violence functions for these other boys as their own right of passage, as a symbolic affirmation of their nonabject place within the collective heteronormative order.

Unfortunately Vero's intention to communicate with Nicky that he is loved (in light of such communal and intimate violence) is severely constrained by a peculiar form of speechlessness. That Vero has always "wanted to tell him" that she loves him but never actually has is a significant feature of the type of social stigma they are both facing, *together*, due to Nicky's gender-nonconforming behavior. Although Vero finds it difficult to verbalize what is happening to them—precisely because what is happening (to Nicky and Vero) is something that homophobic communities work hard at erasing from the social—such a difficulty communicating verbally does not trump the cognitive and emotional alignment being established by Vero in regard to her brother. She may not be able to communicate with him all that she knows of his victimization on his birthday, but she has assimilated enough information about the insidiousness of such violence to see herself in the capacity of bearing faithful witness for him.

One dimension of Nicky's victimization that perhaps does not get fully assimilated by Vero is the *sexualized* nature of the violence. There is in fact an undeniable sexual history to Nicky's victimization, being that some of the boys that assault him are also boys he had "fooled with on back porches"—a sexual dimension that once taken into account helps readers to recontextualize the *kind* of physical violence that arises in response to illicit sexual desire. For example, the sentence structure employed in describing such violence makes evident the repetitive abuse to which Nicky is subjected. The two abrupt sentences close to the beginning of the passage—declarative sentences ending in gerunds and contained between longer sentences—narratively produce a contrast (both visual and audible) suggestive of the intimate spatiality and activity of the physical assault. Revisiting such a sentence structure with the knowledge that at least some of the violence is motivated by wanting to *disavow* homosexuality in themselves and *avow* it in Nicky brings forth a sexualized dimension to what might be meant by "all six of them had taken turns."

To read this violence as *sexualized* violence is not to argue that the assault on Nicky is in fact a rape, but more accurately to resist the tendency to desexualize homophobic violence. With this in mind it is important to understand Vero as someone who is assimilating many more things than she is able to fully process or articulate. Although Vero's growing understanding that Nicky needs to be protected (i.e., that what is happening to him must be resisted as opposed to perpetuated) cannot be communicated verbally or directly, it remains a compelling accomplishment given that homophobic violence between men is frequently erased and desexualized as a cultural phenomenon, or, if not erased and desexualized, it is often justified as a necessary right of passage.

Tied to Vero's complex alignment with Nicky is an understanding of the added hostility to which he is subjected precisely because of the lack of publicity he can bring to the specific form of violence he experiences. Closeted with his family about his homosexuality, Nicky is constrained in his ability to make his family respond to his *actual* lived experience. They can respond to the violence inflicted on his body, but they are unable to understand the full import of the homophobic violence to which he has been subjected. Instead they can respond only given their superimposed understandings of who they assume him to be and what relationship they assume he has with other men, with women, and with the world as they know it. This added burden of isolation, which Nicky must deal with on a very personal, emotional level, does not escape Vero's attention. In fact Vero is particularly aware of their mother's absence in this respect. Because the mother cannot attribute queerness to her son, she is unable to understand the violence in its specificity. The failure to read queer identity and experience results in the mother's circumscribed effectiveness in responding to the actual situation in front of her. Given this understanding, Vero's response to Nicky takes on a maternal approach, an approach that reflects not only her own growing sense that she is *responsible for* Nicky as a sister, but that she is responsible for him in the absence of their mother's help:

And when their mother had tried to calm him down, saying, "Who did this to you? Why did they do this to you? Why?" Vero had known that their mother did not know anything about Nicky and how the cuts and deep bruises spelled out who he really was. . . . Vero had tried to clean him up. She had wanted to tell him that it was okay and that she loved him, but he had his head bent down and cried the way the mothers and grandmothers did at funerals. He had his head down and she had felt like their mother, looking at his beautiful black hair, the cuts on his ears, the scratches on his neck. She wondered why on earth he believed he could act like this with the boys at the high school and not expect this outcome. . . . "Nicky," she had said, but that was all she said.[10]

Their mother's inability to *read* how the cuts and bruises "spelled out who he really was" further emphasizes Vero's attentiveness as a complex (albeit imperfect) act of critical social literacy. She is learning to "read"—in an embodied, culturally specific way—the circumstances affecting Nicky, not only as they pertain to him and his gender-nonconforming behavior, but also as they pertain to the network of cultural expectations to which they are both subject. Vero is in the process of acquiring this skill of reading deeply into the social, but that process is constrained by the very embodied and culturally specific forms of knowing to which she has access. In other words, Vero tries to support her younger brother—assessing correctly that her mother is not sufficiently informed or prepared to provide him with support—and finds recourse in adopting a maternal stance. Unfortunately this maternal stance does not solve, in any easy way, Vero's own doubts about Nicky's behavior, her own doubts that, in some way or another, Nicky is at fault for the violence that is visited upon him.

Vero's attentiveness to her brother is an imperfect attentiveness, perhaps most obviously because, as a member of a community permeated by homophobia, she can receive no social support for the particular disposition she is exhibiting toward her brother. In fact there is no ready-made community of meaning prepared to support her exploration and understanding of what, in all of its complexity, she and her brother are experiencing, separately and together. I say *separately and together* to emphasize that there is a difference in being the person whose body is visited upon by social failure, with psychological and physical violence, and being the one who shares in that experience through, for example, empathy. This difference, however, does not have to be in opposition to the idea of such an experience being shared. Vero comes to understand, at least in part, Nicky's experiences of isolation. She does not know these experiences in their totality, but she knows enough to feel implicated in that produced isolation and knows enough to work against that communal production, even if she finds his effeminate behavior objectionable, and even if she finds herself at a loss for words with which to tell him that he is loved.

The imperfect quality of Vero's attempts at bearing witness to Nicky's pain is crucial to what I am arguing about the effectiveness, not only of this story's thematic focus, but also of its narrative approach. By focalizing the narrative from the perspective of Vero, we are able to see the real difficulty of bearing "faithful witness" to queerness *as* social.[11] It is clear, for example, that Vero and Nicky are constantly being reminded by others that in a homophobic society queerness should not have a social and shared presence; it must always remain demeaned and isolated, stripped of its relational possibilities. Vero's friends, for instance, warn her often of her little brother's gender nonconformity: "*Tell your little brother to stop acting like that. Tell him to stop looking at the guys like that. They don't think it's funny.*"[12] This warning coheres with the logic of social fragmentation that needs to police the boundaries of gender difference in order to continue the "purity" and "naturalness" of the gender dichotomy. By suggesting that Nicky stop acting "like that," Vero's friends are enforcing an understanding of queerness as not having a proper social space, as not even having a proper discursive presence because they won't even speak its name. Of course by having to address "it" as an issue, they are implicitly admitting to "its" existence, but by their tenacity in reminding Vero over and over again that she needs to "mind her brother," these women reaffirm their status as cultural carriers responsible for the status quo; queerness will have no sociality precisely because they will it so and precisely because their will is backed up by a larger ideological and structural framework. The physical assault Nicky is subject to, then, is merely another actualization of this logic of gender purity. Likewise the logic behind the verbal warnings and the physical attack are further buttressed, albeit unintentionally, by the mother's own ignorance of her son's queerness; the mother's silence in this respect produces yet another assurance that queerness cannot have a sociality, for surely, if your own people cannot give you social backup, who can?

Even though Vero is aware of the obstacles that her brother faces, and even though she sometimes succumbs to their professed logic,[13] she consistently *tries* to back him up. The important part of Vero's complicity with Nicky, the importance of her collaboration with his queerness, is that she often refrains from conveying her culturally ingrained reactions to his overt femininity. And it is through this process of ignoring her misgivings (about his gender nonconformity, about his choice in men, about his choice in friends) that Vero aligns herself with him and his difficult coming-of-age decisions, a tenuous alignment demanding a great deal of intersubjectivity, of worked-at connectedness.

To a certain extent Vero's actions seem selfless in the traditional sense of the word: more preoccupied with the other, willing to sacrifice her needs for others. I resist using the term here, however, for its inaccuracy in reflecting the real sense of self that Vero maintains as she aligns herself with her brother. The narrative in fact suggests that she can collaborate with Nicky only to the extent that she remains present with her sense of self as she extends and aligns herself with her brother. To be sure, the narrative encourages us to understand Vero as always having been the type of person to look after her brother. However, the narrative also highlights the emotional and intellectual labor involved in being a faithful witness. In other words, the narrative goes to great lengths to suggest that this is both a predisposition of Vero's and that such a witnessing is a great deal of work.

One of the most concrete examples of Vero's worked-at commitment to Nicky has to do with the fact that Nicky actually falls in love with a young man with whom Vero was once sexually intimate, and that these two young men begin a sexual relationship. This unanticipated relationship becomes a source of pain and discomfort for Vero.[14] To say that she overcomes emotions of betrayal and anger is not completely true, for it is clear that she must repeatedly talk herself out of her feelings of jealousy, talk herself out of emotional responses that would leave Nicky further isolated, responses that would not take into account how differently situated they are in relation to the organization of their community.[15] When Nicky's lover, Julián, is jailed for unpaid speeding tickets, Vero is the one who, unbeknownst to her parents, secretly drives Nicky for visitation on weekends. There she is often upset by Nicky's overt effeminacies, but she is also restrained in how and when she brings this to his attention. Her awareness of his lack of options forces her to remind him only in the most pressured of circumstances. One of these circumstances occurs when they are waiting in line to enter the detention center with the other female visitors:

Vero walks forward. The voices of her friends keep chiding her. *You do too much for that brother of yours, Vero. Let him be his own.* She stands and waits with him. Her feet hurt. She has a job at the auto parts store in downtown, a family-owned business losing out to the new strip mall, a job where she stands all day at a counter. She is twenty and unmarried in a place where most have either left or married by that age and she knows so many of the men in town from the store. . . . They buy spark plugs and fan belts, handing them over to her with hands just as smooth and young as hers, the wedding bands glimmering. She could have it worse, she knows. She could lose the job if the strip mall takes away too much business. She would have to move to another town for work, she knows, and then what? How long can the Impala run without her father fixing it as he used to? What would happen to her little brother if she were not around?[16]

The experience of waiting in line to enter the detention center serves Vero as a physical and emotional reminder of her own needs, desires, and anxieties. Standing in line with Nicky, *for* Nicky, she is reminded of working all day on her feet. This causes her anxiety, not solely because she is physically tired, but also because she is reminded of her situation as a single woman working in an auto-parts store, in contact with married men whom she is often attracted to. This is an important moment in the story because it shows that the moment of reaching out to her brother is also a moment of thinking more critically about her own life. Their lives are surely very distinct, and in fact much of the ideology around gender in the town seems to suggest that they should understand their experiences as utterly different. Yet, as the story suggests, in the resistant act of aligning herself with her brother against the grain of what her family and community is telling her, she explores connections and possible similarities between her brother and herself.

Vero understands, in a profound way, that Nicky needs her in a manner that she does not need him. This becomes apparent in a seemingly inconsequential moment as they proceed in the line to enter the detention facility and must be searched before entering. Since Nicky has brought a series of sealed letters for his boyfriend, sealed and wrapped with orange ribbon, the presiding officer informs him that nothing sealed can be brought into the detention center. This causes Nicky a great deal of frustration that Vero quickly responds to: "Nicky looked pained and when he turns to Vero to begin protest, she gives him a look that says, *Do it*. It is not the way he wanted it to be: these cards are for Julián Orosco, the man he thinks he loves."[17] Because Nicky cannot bring himself to ruin the cards by opening them, and because Vero "can hear the shifting of someone impatient with both the old man's adherence to the rules and Nicky's foolishness in bringing the cards in the first place," she takes the cards away from him and begins unsealing them herself: "She is careful not to rip the envelopes completely and it pains her that she is doing this for her little brother. There are fifteen cards in all and she does the math in her head, the money he has spent for the visit: the cards and the chicken, the cookies and the magazines. She has given him spending money. She has made too much of this possible." That she has perhaps "made too much of this possible" shows that Vero is not unaffected by the homophobic logics of her community, logics that acknowledge the reality of homosexuality precisely in the elaborate forms with which they seek to keep it from manifesting. Muñoz's narrative, however, is interested in the struggle with these logics. The narrative goes on to communicate both the embarrassment and the restraint Vero experiences at seeing her brother so effeminized by his "womanly" devotion to the details of the gifts he brings to his lover: "Vero cannot look at Nicky as he struggles to put the ribbon back in place. Behind them is the rustle of irritation. Nicky cannot get the ribbon to fit again, *but she waits patiently for him to finish because she knows that when he sees Julián, he wants everything to be in order.*"[18] It is precisely in the lovingly, conflicted, but always *corroborating* ways Vero speaks of and acts alongside her brother that we get a sense of queerness as belonging to more people than simply the queer subject proper. I would like to emphasize that it is through the sister's intimate perspective that we also get a deeper sense of the work it actually takes to be a "faithful witness" to queerness as social—to understand, for example, one's deep implicatedness in how queerness will be lived out precisely because one forms part of the sociality in which queerness comes into being as muted or flagrant, as boastful or persecuted. This story, then, gives a rich account of queerness as being intersubjective: as taken in, assessed, and manipulated, by those closest to the queer subject. This is conveyed precisely by the way the narrative is focalized through the sister and not Nicky. By "shifting the site of queer enunciation" in this manner, Muñoz renders Nicky's experiences permeable in the sense that they are exposed as constituted relationally. Furthermore the fact that this narrative is heterodiegetic adds an extra sensibility to the muteness of this intersubjectivity. If Vero had narrated the events herself, in the first person, the sociality conveyed from that perspective would have been of an entirely different order, one that perhaps erroneously implied an *articulate* self-consciousness, erasing through mere narrative structure the experience of intersubjectivity as it was actually lived.

It is from this strategy of narrative proximity that Muñoz moves on to employ a radical distance from queer experience in the short story "The Unimportant Lila Parr." In this story the queer subject is dead, strangled, his body left naked in a roadside motel at the edge of the small town in which he was raised. What this story lacks in leaving unexplored the particulars of his queer subjectivity (or for that matter the intersubjectivity he shared with others) it gains in providing access to the mentality of those *existentially furthest* from him and his experiences. This includes, among other people, his own father (simply referred to in the narrative as "the man"), who epitomizes existential remoteness through his inability to acknowledge his son's homosexuality. The idea of being *existentially* distant, as opposed to literally or physically so, is important to emphasize here, given that the story takes place in a small town characterized by intimacy and closeness. In fact such a contrast raises a question: How does one become estranged from those one is physically and to some extent emotionally closest to? This is an important question to ask, particularly given the hostility queer people encounter primarily from family members who resist being witnesses to their complex experiences. Muñoz's narrative goes a long way to answering this question by suggesting that estrangement, especially estrangement from queer experience, is an unnatural production, a social manifestation that requires labor. This is so because existential distance, particularly as it develops in direct contrast to the town's close social networks, must be worked at in order for it to exist at all. In fact all psychological and emotional separations in the story are conveyed not simply as created separations, but as laborious constructions that, once created, must be self-consciously sustained.

For instance, well before the young man's murder an extreme existential distance is created and sustained by his mother (referred to in the narrative simply as "the wife") in relation to the other townspeople.[19] This existential distance arises in part in the context of an unprecedented inheritance; after an accidental collapse of a barn, which causes the death of their employer, Mr. Parr, the man and his wife inherit from the mourning Mrs. Parr all of their valuable possessions (their home, their car, their farming land and orchards). With this inheritance comes a great deal of attention and a change of lifestyle for the man and his wife. The substantive difference, however, does not arise from the change in economic status, but from the wife's desire to mark the change, both in her daily activities and in the way the town perceives her. This means, for example, that she likes to go into town and "spend more time than she needed to"—a deliberate performance of leisure in order to clearly demarcate her financial status. In particular she enjoys purchasing items that the townspeople will notice. Although she is careful not to spend beyond her means, she deliberately purchases items that do not need to be wrapped or put into paper bags: "About once a month, she walked out of the flower shop with a large basket of daisies. Or she purchased homemade soaps that smell[ed] like oatmeal-honey and lavender, with triple-looped lace as a handle." It is important to note that this behavior arises in response to the type of town in which she lives, a town small enough for residents to monitor behavior and close enough for them to share perceptions and circulate information. It is in response to this social framework that she comes to feel and act with the rigidity and pretentiousness that she does:

The man's wife drives a fairly new car and she knows that she's been in this town long enough for people to remember how she came into her prosperity. She knows they recognize her car as the Parrs' second-best. She sits rigid against her car seat when she drives, both hands on the steering wheel. Staring ahead, she pretends not to notice people, only bothering to wave at those who greet her first when they step into the crosswalk. She recognizes the change in herself—she doesn't look at people in the eye anymore, only their hands, what they take, and what they give back.[20]

Through her ways of behaving when she is in town—her rigid body comportment, her arrogant self-awareness, her hyperawareness of the townspeople and what they know about her and her hand-me-down prosperity—we come to understand how an existential distance in such an intimate and communal place is always artificial, how it is a separation that once created must be sustained if it is to have longevity.

Where, with whom, and to what effect existential distances of this magnitude are created and maintained in a small town is of particular importance to the queer subplot of this story. One must note in this regard that queer people are often central to the production of certain types of existential distancing. That is, to the extent that queer people need avenues of privacy through which queer sociality and sexuality can be explored without hostility, they often make use of the existential distance (and often require it) for certain types of homosexual sociality. Queer people cultivate practices of cruising, for example, ways of behaving sexually in public spaces that negotiate and resist the public demand for heteronormativity. In this sense it is important to understand existential distance as a produced "achievement" with complex valences. In other words extreme benefits are reaped from having heterosexuals unaware of homosexuality and its modes of being in the world. Muñoz's short story, however, does not have in mind the most queer-positive valences of this existential distance, or if it does, it wants to remind us through the death of the young gay man that existential distance from homosexuality—from its subjectivity and intersubjectivity—is produced with the logic of fragmentation in mind, with the logic of gender purity and with the logic of homophobia and homohatred. One of this story's greatest achievements is to remind us that queer experience does not take place in some no-place, but in fact negotiates the same geography that other people (with their own illicit practices) negotiate.

It is within this theme of existential distance and its artificiality that the man's estranged relationship to his son's murder and his son's illicit behavior gains significance. From the moment he first hears of his son's murder to the instant when he must identify his son's body at the coroner's office, the father cannot bring himself to acknowledge what the police and coroner's reports suggest, given the evidence: that he was found naked in a motel room, that two needles were found on the nightstand, that a young man his son's age was detained in the next town and was being charged with his son's murder. From the father's narrative perspective none of this information can be assimilated into his conception of himself. He experiences the murder with a great deal of shock, and as the narrative goes on to reveal, it is precisely the insinuation of sexual indiscretions that seems to weigh most heavily on his peace of mind. "He begins to wish," the omniscient narrator tells us, "that it had not been a roadside motel room, but a car accident, a negligent diesel truck, something that would remove the responsibility on his son's part."[21] By focalizing the narrative through the father's perspective the story conveys the cognitive and emotional dissonance with which queer experience has the semblance of being "recognized" but is always inevitably deferred. From the father's perspective this is all we can know about queer experience: that it leads to dangerous situations and that it causes a great deal of pain for families. From this partial perspective we see only a father's confusion and his mode of coping through denial—a behavior that is further buttressed by the tightly knit community that seems to rally behind his confusion and mode of coping. The people who work for him in the orchards, for example, do not approach him to talk, but work faster and harder in order to leave less work for him to worry about and more time to grieve, alone. Within such a tightly knit context—where neighbors purchase groceries for him and workers demonstrate affection through acts of personal sacrifice—the intimation of homosexuality stands out as an anomaly. Queer sexual experience comes to stand as irrevocably disrupting family and community life.

Yet it is precisely this disposition to understand queer experience as isolatable, as a social phenomenon that one can feel justified in feeling a great deal of estrangement from, that Muñoz's narrative approach helps to circumscribe. It is through the braiding of various perspectives—perspectives that include but are not limited to the father's on the days following the murder—that we get a fuller sense for how estrangement is constituted in this town and how queerness in particular comes to form a part of, as opposed to existing apart from, this shared context. I have already made some comments about the mother producing her own estrangement from others in the town. However, it is precisely the confirmation of this behavior through the focalized perspective of the townspeople that gives us a more accurate understanding of her distance from them as produced. They witness and comment on how she clutches her purse in symbolic performance; they notice that she wants to be seen. This forms an important parallel backdrop for understanding the father's estrangement from his son's queer experience.

By finally focalizing the narrative through someone other than the father, in particular through the motel owner's perspective—the one person in town who knows who frequents his establishment and the many reasons that bring them there—we come to know that the father himself has withheld a very important secret from everyone (perhaps even from himself). As the narrative explains, the father has been having a long-standing affair with his white neighbor, Lila Parr, and the affair has always taken place at the roadside motel where his own son was murdered. This affair is not revealed to us until the very end, when the narrative is focalized through the motel owner's perspective. Looking back on the narrative from the perspective of the motel owner we understand that any lack of acknowledgment on the father's part, any asserted confusion and repulsion regarding his son's sexual indiscretions belie the concrete ways that the father and son have objectively shared similar spaces (the motel) for similar reasons (illicit sex). Queer experience is part of the larger pattern of social secrecy that constitutes the small town's community life. Queer experience exists in time and space and in relationship to the same people, institutions, and ideologies of secrecy that the rest of the town responds to. The motel, in short, enacts a heterotopic quality, in that a heterotopia has the ability to juxtapose in a single real place several emplacements that are incompatible in themselves.[22] The father's and son's sexual indiscretions are inextricably linked in space and time, not simply literally to the motel, but also to the range of social circumstances that make the motel a location of purpose for social subjects in need of covert locations. It is with such information in mind—information that would not be available to us without multiple people accounting for the story—that the father's existential distance regarding his son's homosexuality in particular is understood as having an utterly produced quality. The father can continue to see his son with a great deal of fear so long as he continues to sublimate the reality of his own affair.

One of the major theoretical achievements of Muñoz's writing is its ability to communicate—through form and content—the very real ways that queer experience is a social and shared experience, even as oppressive ideologies work at making it seem less real and shared, and even if the queer subject often seems isolated in the process. As I have tried to point out, queer people come into being and come into a sociality in relationship to others. That queer people often feel isolated is in fact a kind of relationship to the people who surround them. The examples of "Good as Yesterday" and "The Unimportant Lila Parr" prove that estrangement from and proximity to queer experience happens as people with different forms of ideological or institutional backup make them happen. The isolation and violence that queer people are subject to are not by any means natural; they are produced in the very real ways that everyday people live out their lives. When Nicky, for example, starts to adopt a more effeminate and outlandish style (starting to socialize with other flamboyant and effeminate boys in his town), his behavior is not natural per se, but resistant behavior: it is a response to oppressive gender norms and constitutes a resistant sociality. Likewise when the father in "The Unimportant Lila Parr" does not allow his own experiences of sexual indiscretion to inform his relationship to his son's indiscretions, he is *working* at severing a connection that is undeniably real. The father and son share, if nothing else, a similarly spatialized mode of enacting desire through the heterotopic site of the motel. Together they form part of the town's nexus of relationships that require secrecy and that, whether acknowledged or not, are linked in a shared sociality.

Because I want to emphasize this understanding of queerness as social and shared as one of the consequences of Muñoz's narrative approach, I want to end my discussion by briefly addressing the title story, "Zigzagger." Unlike the other two stories, "Zigzagger" uses focalized perspectives from both the queer subject *and* his family and community, shifting narrative perspectives throughout the story. Centering on a young Chicano man's sexual awakening, this story refuses (through content and form) to isolate his agency or his subjectivity as something independent of other people. Muñoz does this precisely through the omniscient narrative style and alternating narrative perspectives with which he provides a collective account of what it means to be a part of, as opposed to *apart from*, the values, experiences, and concerns of a small Mexican and Mexican American community. This is conveyed most explicitly in the undeniable ways subjects in this community are inscribed psychologically and experientially with shared ways of thinking.

The young man's first cathartic homosexual experience stands out in the narrative as mired in religious dogma. Recalling the emotionally charged and titillating experience, he transitions from describing his sexual encounter in realistic terms ("He allowed the man's hands to grab his waist . . . he felt the hot press of the man's belly, the rough texture of hair") to describing the encounter as an incident with a satanic demon:

The man, his back broad, grunted heavily. . . . The man's sound made him grow, pushing the boy higher and higher, to where the boy could see himself in the arms of the man who glowed in the darkness of the canopy of branches, his skin a dull red, the pants and boots gone. And though he felt he was in air, he saw a flash of the man's feet entrenched fast in the ground—long, hard hooves digging into the soil, the height of horses when they charge—it was then that the boy remembers seeing and feeling at the same time—the hooves, then a piercing in the depth of his belly that made his eyes flash a whole battalion of stars, shooting and brilliant, more and more of them, until he had no choice but to scream out.[23]

Such a fantastic account in a fundamentally realist narrative can provide a perplexing experience for some readers. However, given the manner in which the young man's extraordinary experience is situated within the context of his mother's own religiosity and within the town's circumscribed religiosity, his seemingly implausible recounting gains a great deal of significance as a perceptual consequence of living among others in a shared and complex tradition of negotiating religious doctrines.[24] The young man's mother, as the story makes a point to foreground, understands sexuality through religious dogma in a manner altogether consistent with the way that her son comes to experience his first homosexual encounter. Attempting to cope with what she knows to be her son's sexual indiscretions the morning after he returns home drunk from a night of dancing at the town's local dance hall, the mother speculates:

She wonders if her husband knows now, if he can tell how the side-to-side swivel of the dancers at the hall and the zigzag of their steps have invited an ancient trouble, if her husband knows the countless stories of midnight goings-on, of women with broken blood vessels streaming underneath their skin from the touch of every man. . . . She wonders now if her husband has ever awakened at night, dreaming of dances where bags of church-blessed rattlesnakes have been opened in the darkness of the place, the mad slithering between feet and the screams, the rightness of that punishment, the snakes that spoke in human voices, the rushed side-to-side movement of the snakes before they coiled underneath tables to strike ankles.[25]

As the example of the mother shows, the son is not the only one whose experience is fundamentally influenced by religious indoctrination. Mother and son in fact share an understanding of sexuality as a problem, one that if not suppressed requires some form of punishment. Indeed the impulse to judge others and oneself by the religious standards of fear and retribution set by church ideology is embodied in the everyday thoughts and actions of the people in the town. This emphasis comes across most poignantly in the way the narrative emphasizes the religious dogma and fears that the entire town is up against as they prepare for the Saturday night dance-hall party. In a series of rich details the town is described as entirely focused on this dance, but up against the disapproving eye of the "churchgoers."

> Saturdays in this town are for dancing. The churchgoers think it is a vile day, and when they drive by the fields on their way to morning service, they sometimes claim to see workers swaying their hips as they pick tomatoes or grapes. They say that nothing gets done on Saturday afternoons because the workers go home too early in order to prepare for a long night of dancing. It is not just evenings, but the stretch of day—a whole cycle of temptation.

The churchgoers do not exact their moralizing gaze without critique. Among the community leadership are war veterans who serve as administrators for the use of the Veterans Hall. These veterans are described as resisting the moralizing tendencies of the majority of churchgoers, some even strategically narrating sexually explicit stories of debauchery during war time, of "Korean girls spreading their legs for soldiers and the relief it brought," in order to scandalize the churchgoers into silence.[26]

By braiding these perspectives into one narrative, Muñoz renders the young man's "fantastic" first sexual experience "of" the community in a substantial way. Even though his homosexual experience can never be directly acknowledged as such, it is through the heterodiegetic narrative approach implemented by Muñoz that the young man's experience can be given a sociality and a rootedness which the rest of the community seems unable or willing to admit to, if only because they have not even conceived of homosexuality so intimately. Through such a narrative approach this young man's cultural education is given proper social reference. By narrating the story from various perspectives Muñoz reminds us of shared and overlapping horizons of possibility.[27]

RANDALL KENAN RESOCIALIZING QUEERNESS

Shifting the site of queer enunciation, as I have been arguing, is a literary practice that intervenes politically at the level of social literacy, at the level of reading deeply into the social. Such a narrative practice reformulates how queerness is traditionally understood—as belonging, in some shameful and isolatable way, to the queer subject proper—by foregrounding the manner in which (and the people through which) queerness gains consistency or is denied a presence in the social. To suggest, as I have, that some of the most compelling narratives in Manuel Muñoz's collection of short stories exhibit a strong commitment to this *resocializing* of queerness is not to imply that Muñoz is the only writer who engages in this critical politics of narration. A broader narrative tradition exists, one where we might venture that James Baldwin in 1962 and Manuel Muñoz in 2003 serve as indispensable benchmarks.[28] As bookends of a sort, they frame the experimental work that developed in the second half of the twentieth century. Puerto Rican writer Luis Rafael Sanchez's 1966 short story "¡Jum!" chronicles the violence experienced by an effeminate, Puerto Rican black man, not through his perspective, but through the voices and experiences of what literary critic Larry La Fontaine-Stokes describes as the "murderous, intolerant mob composed of his formerly affable neighbors."[29] Cuban American writer Miguel Elías Muñoz's 1985 novel *The Greatest Performance* is narrated by two childhood friends who bear witness to each other's common history of resistance and gender nonconformity. Because its characters share a horizontal attentiveness (a mutual bearing witness) to each other's predicaments, the novel shares the burden of queer representation in a way that also gestures toward critical reflection on gender, race, and nation. The pioneering work of Mariana Romo-Carmona should also be understood within this trajectory. In her first-of-its-kind 2001 Spanish-language anthology, *Conversaciones: Relatos por padres y madres de hijas lesbianas e hijos gay*, Latino parents are asked to speak about their lives and relationships with their gay and lesbian children. The work of that anthology abides by the logic of shifting the burden of queer representation away from queer subjects. Among the many interesting consequences of such an approach, however, is that at least one of the parents requested to contribute an account comes out in the process, leaving us to ponder the question of where exactly queerness can be said to reside.[30]

Perhaps the most obvious example of a writer who fits within the tradition but who has morphed the practice into a trademark writing style is the acclaimed contemporary African American writer Randall Kenan. His first novel, *A Visitation of Spirits*, has received attention by critics who see the novel in conversation with Baldwin's writings, particularly the aspect of Baldwin's writings that cast queers as both deeply in conflict with and deeply enmeshed in communities of place. These critics do not all agree on which writings best foreground the literary continuities between Baldwin and Kenan, but they all seem to share an admiration for Kenan's ability to situate queerness within complex historical moments and concrete relationships, and to make such situatedness a moment of reflection about the community at large.

Sheila Smith McKoy, for example, argues that the novel's genius is in resituating black homosexuality into the "lifescapes" from which it arises. She writes, "Kenan's portrait of the brilliant and tortured Horace Cross is as much about the politics of coming out as a black man as it is a coming out narrative about the rural south."[31] This is so, precisely because "each of the characters who populate the novel confesses to some kind of sexual misconduct," even though these characters are never able to use such experiences as foundations from which to understand Horace's own cultural and sexual "transgressions."[32] Ironically, then, Horace remains cognitively and emotionally isolated from others through one of the very cultural practices (i.e., silence around sexuality) that constitutes that community and it's socioreligious heritage. In other words, Horace paradoxically "belongs" to his community by participating in culturally learned behavior that keeps him isolated from others. Sharon Holland is mindful of this irony, and its debilitating consequences for the queer black subject, when she comments, "It is quite apparent that Horace has inherited . . . [a rich] black imaginative landscape, but he is denied access to it nonetheless [through one particular feature of that landscape]."[33] Holland's account functions as a sobering reminder that enhanced understandings of the queer subject *in sociality* do not change homophobic realities per se, but in fact often make the "hard-edgedness" of these realities clearer to us. Which means that the *kind* of social literacy gained by such a practice of shifting the site of queer enunciation is the ability to read queerness as belonging to more people than simply the queer subject proper. Queerness, like that of Horace, belongs to a rich history of sexual repression in his community, his ultimate suicide a mirror for the community to see deeply into themselves.

Kenan does not shy away from the pernicious social realities within which queers of color must learn to negotiate and nurture solidarity. However, it is by momentarily postponing the queer subject's thoughts and feelings, and strategically writing from the perspective of those subjects who share sociocultural and psychological space with queers of color, that Kenan accomplishes some of his most powerful insights. For example, in his touching short story "The

Foundations of the Earth," a seventy-year-old African American woman—Mrs. Maggie MacGowan Williams—must deal not only with the unexpected news of her estranged grandson's accidental death in a car crash but also with the much less anticipated news of his homosexuality. Raised Baptist, in a rural community, to understand homosexuality as nothing other than "an unholy abomination," Mrs. Williams is faced with a particular moral dilemma at her grandson's funeral. It is on this occasion that she encounters, for the first time, her grandson's grieving white lover, Gabriel.

When Gabriel tries to approach Mrs. Williams at the funeral home to express his condolences, the narrative allows us access to Mrs. Williams's reactionary thoughts: "How dare he? This pathetic, stumbling, poor trashy white boy, to throw his sinful lust for her grandbaby in her face, as if to bury a grandchild weren't bad enough. Now this abomination had to be flaunted.—Sorry, indeed! The nerve! Who the hell did he think he was to parade their shame about?"[34] There is nothing particularly liberatory about hearing this homophobic rant; however, the importance lies in the sustained ethical effort, on Kenan's part (and on the part of queers of color more generally) to hear Ms. Maggie Williams beyond the homophobia, to bear witness to her and her process. When all of the immediate family gathers at Mrs. Williams house after the funeral, we get a very different response from her.

Gabriel approached. As he stood before her—raven-haired, pink-skinned, abject, eyes bloodshot—she experienced a bevy of conflicting emotions: disgust, grief, anger, tenderness, fear, weariness, pity. Nevertheless she *had* to be civil, *had* to make a leap of faith and of understanding. Somehow she felt it had been asked of her. And though there were still so many questions, so much to sort out, for now she would mime patience.... Time would unravel the rest.... She reached out, taking both his hands into her own, and said, the way she would to an old friend: "How have you been?"[35]

The moral dilemma arises for Mrs. Williams as she attempts to negotiate the disjuncture between her religious disposition to dislike Gabriel (because of his "sinful" relationship to her grandson) and her self-reflective disposition to hold herself accountable for the "bevy of conflicting emotions" that she is experiencing. Although Mrs. Williams, on the day of the funeral, is inclined to disapprove of Gabriel's presence, it is clear from the moment she first sets eyes on him that she is capable of bearing witness to his suffering in a way that trumps any homophobic impulse to require of him some shameful, repentant confirmation of his "sinful" life: "Gabriel had come with the body, like an interpreter for the dead. . . . He came, head bowed, rheumy-eyed, exhausted. He gave her no explanation; nor had she asked him for any, for he displayed the truth in his vacant and humble glare and had nothing to offer but the penurious tribute of his trembling hands. Which was more than she wanted."[36]

The "truth" that Gabriel displays in his "vacant and humble glare" and through the "penurious tribute of his trembling hands" is that he is grieving, grieving in a disarmingly familiar way, the way *anyone* who has lost a lover might grieve. His is an all-too-common embodiment, and it is to Mrs. Williams's credit that she does not violate this vulnerable state by asking of him what his body already confirms: that he is, whether she accepts it or not, her dead grandbaby's lover.

The hallmark ethic in this short story is foregrounded in Mrs. Williams's struggle to negotiate some of her most deeply held values. Throughout the story, she repeatedly forces herself to inhabit a space of insecurity and contemplation, a disposition that reflects an integrity about those things she cannot, or does not yet, fully understand. Mrs. Williams, for example, enjoys evenings on her back porch contemplating the curve of the earth. She reminds herself that what she perceives with the naked eye as flat land is, objectively, curved. Mrs. Williams is drawn to the idea, humbled by the idea, that what she perceives to be true is not. The ethic of this story, then, grounds itself in Mrs. Williams's disposition to reconsider some of her most deeply held beliefs in light of new information. This includes reconsidering her homophobia in light of her grandson's sexuality. Mrs. Williams, in fact, manages to reconfigure her relationship to queerness by coming to acknowledge that what pains her most is not attributable entirely to the news of her grandson's homosexuality, but to her sense of having lost an opportunity for connection with him in light of homophobia. Mrs. Williams holds herself accountable for being unaware and for, perhaps, having driven her own beloved grandson away. The cognitive and emotional reconfiguration here—which I am stressing as a reconfigurement of her relationship with queerness—is one where queerness is acknowledged in the social as a feature for which one is responsible. This is conveyed most clearly in Mrs. Williams's attempt to get her mind around her grandson's relationship with another man, to "realign her thinking" in regard to all relationships that are sexually intimate: "Maggie thought of her grandson being attracted to this tall white man. She tried to see them together and couldn't. At that moment she understood that she was being called on to realign her thinking about men and women, and men and men, and even women and women. Together . . . the way Adam and Eve were meant to be together."[37]

Mrs. Williams—because she positions herself in the social in a way that is self-reflective—is able to engage with queer life in a manner that has implications for her sense of the world. Queerness is no longer a feature of the world that she can approach with all of the values that she had previously acquired at a distance; queerness is now a reality to which she must remain accountable. Mrs. Williams's acknowledgment is an achievement, a labored-toward outcome, perhaps left indiscernible without the commitment of writers like Kenan to shift in narrative perspective (to momentarily postpone the queer subject's point of view) in order to bear witness to queerness as social and shared.

IN THE MOUTHS OF THE PEOPLE ONE LOVES

Muñoz and Kenan contribute immeasurably to this tradition of "shifting the site of queer enunciation," especially by stressing the tangible but often muted implicatedness of various people in the sociality of queerness. Their narratives are powerful interventions, not because they *replace* the urgency of the queer speaking subject, but because they momentarily postpone and reorient that urgency, strategically redeploying what Emma Pérez has called the necessity of *nuestra lengua en nuestro sitio*. The "critical task of survival" becomes modified in this process—not so much the need to find separate spaces in order to inaugurate our own discourses, not so much the need "to create our language, to name ourselves," but the need to find ourselves enmeshed in and constitutive of our communities, to find ourselves implicated in everyday community life (in messy, ambiguous ways, in loving and violent ways, in articulate and never-been-said ways). The critical task of survival becomes, not so much the need for voice, not so much the need to speak one's name, but the need to remind oneself that one has a name in the streets—that someone, somewhere, knows our name—and that there is abundant pleasure and "profit" in finding one's tongue, so to speak, in the mouths of the people one loves.

CHAPTER 5

CHO'S FAGGOT PAGEANTRY

Of course I'm a faggot, darling. I'm a flaming faggot, darling. I am fanning the flames of my faggotry.
Margaret Cho, *I'm the One that I Want*

You know, I walk down the hallway, they be calling me names: they call me faggot, they call me sissy. I said, "Oh yeah? You forgot. I'm also a model and an actress, so FUCK YOU TOO!"
Margaret Cho, *Notorious C.H.O.*

As implied in the previous chapter, finding people who might bear faithful witness to queerness, and who might take responsibility for the role they themselves play in how queerness gets to be enacted and understood in the social domain, is a surprisingly difficult undertaking, replete with the anticipation of belonging and social back-up (on behalf of queer people) and the sobering reality of community indifference and betrayal. In response, writers like Manuel Muñoz and Randall Kenan have worked to fill a void, narrating stories and perspectives from those (parents, siblings, and community members) who might otherwise rob us of our relation to them. This ethical act of imagination is, in one sense, a pedagogical intervention: teaching others that we belong to, and are responsible for, each other. In another sense, it is a powerful reminder that bearing faithful witness to queerness is actually more common than we think, but that it happens in such hostile contexts of heteronormative duress that it remains sporadic, subtle, and frequently unintelligible. The need, then, for queers to see ourselves acknowledged and valued by family and community is perhaps best described as a desire to see those subtle acts of witnessing *amplified*—made large and strong, made relevant—as a commitment to make lasting change in the communities we inhabit together.

The need to experience solidarity in amplified forms, loudly and publicly, is nowhere more provocatively met than in the stand-up comedy of the self-described "fag hag" and "backbone of the gay community," Korean American comedian and actor Margaret Cho.[1] Her highly acclaimed performances of unabashed solidarity and identification with gay male subculture, what we might otherwise call her shameless "faggot pageantry," are unique instantiations of bearing faithful witness to queerness, not because she claims to represent gay men accurately or in their full complexity and diversity, but because she highlights the fractured (compromised) locus from within which gay men negotiate active subjectivities, and from which she herself negotiates survival as a racialized, queer woman.[2] This fractured locus is not "shared" in any conventional sense of being experienced or understood similarly, but it is collectively discerned through defiant acts of witnessing and coimplication, of valuing and creating connection to what would otherwise be marginalized and shamed.

Cho performs solidarity with gay men through the very medium of derisive humor often used to dismiss them as peripheral and marginal. The association of male effeminacy, homosocial intimacy, and gay male sex with ridicule or as comic relief are everywhere in popular culture.[3] Cho's performances reference this common understanding, but manipulate it toward other ends. Rather than avoid the stigma of faggotry, of gender and sexual "abnormality," Cho embraces it ("Of course, I'm a faggot, darling"). This performative embrace is not so much a liberal affirmation of gay men's humanity, as much as it is a radical honoring of gay male agency under duress. Cho's performances create the context whereby audience members must bear witness not so much to gay men's oppression, but to their irreverent resilience in contexts of potential humiliation and harm. When Cho recalls, for example, how her best friend in high school, a young black drag queen, experienced homophobic verbal assaults that sought to make his effeminacy an abnormality to be policed and marginalized, Cho bears witness, less to the pain involved in experiencing this homophobic violence, and more to her friend's unflinching and flamboyant resistance, particularly his impertinent association of male effeminacy with *amplification* rather than reduction, with status rather than disdain ("Oh, yeah? You forgot. I'm also a model and an actress, so FUCK YOU TOO!").

Cho's comedic centering of gay male subculture and resistance raises important questions regarding gay men and intelligibility, particularly with regard to how gay men have made sense of the world in which they live through humor, and how they come to make sense to others as humorous. What kinds of intelligibility are possible in contexts where gay men frequently figure as objects of ridicule or comic relief, and where the very form of resistance to that reductionary perception is humorous?

This chapter recalls the unique function humor has played as both stigma and social resistance in the lives of gay men, and it pays special attention to the specific place of "camp" humor in Margaret Cho's depiction of solidarity with gay men. Camp is a mode of performance and reception often associated with stylized gender expression, with theatricality and irony, and with the imbuing of new and often subversive meanings onto cultural products such as music, fashion, movie stars, genres, and stereotypes.[4] As noted by historian George Chauncey, camp can be traced to forms of cultural resistance established by homosexual men in the first half of the twentieth century. More than simply a development of cultural tastes in the face of homophobic hostility, Chauncey understands camp as a "critical perspective on the world—or, more accurately, a stance in relation to the world—that derived from gay men's own experience as deviants . . . [and that] helped gay men make sense of, respond to, and undermine the social categories of gender and sexuality that served to marginalize them."[5] Cho performs solidarity with gay men through a camp sensibility that favors, to borrow the language of literary critic David Bergman, "exaggeration" and "extremity," and that locates in gay male subculture a precedent not only for cultivating a "self-conscious eroticism that throws into question the naturalization of desire," but also a nonassimilationist irony and boldness in the face of oppression.[6]

Cultural critics Pamela Robertson and Jose Estéban Muñoz remind us that camp sensibilities, while traditionally associated with gay male subculture, have a rarely documented feminist and critical race tradition. For example, Robertson notes a feminist camp tradition that includes women (from Mae West to Madonna) employing a female form of aestheticism rooted in burlesque that runs parallel to gay men's deployment of femininity and female masquerade.[7] Robertson's feminist "tradition" of camp, however, begs reconsideration with respect to questions of race. It not only relies on the troubling exclusion of key women of color such as Carmen Miranda, Eartha Kitt, and Charo from this feminist tradition, but it also leaves underexamined (as Robertson herself notes) the ways in which camp's sex and gender politics have always been intertwined with discourses of race.[8] Rather than continue to portray camp as an implicitly *white* gay or *white* feminist sensibility, Muñoz refuses to exclude women of color and the politics of race, defining camp through the work of Latina lesbian performance artist Carmelita Tropicana as a crafted response "to the breakdown of representation that occurs when a queer, ethnically marked, or other subject encounters his or her inability to fit within the majoritarian representation regime."[9]

Understanding Cho's comedy within this feminist and critical race discourse on camp is important because her work unapologetically hinges on a camp understanding of gay male sexual frivolity, subversive humor, and gender nonconforming resistance at the same time that it arises from her own negative encounters with "majoritarian representational regimes." In several of her stand-up shows, Cho describes the detrimental impact of growing up as a young, Korean American woman without positive representations of Asians in the media. She describes this impact in terms of the gradual confinement and atrophying of her imagination, sense of self, and sense of future possibilities.[10] It is through gay men, and gay male forms of resistance, that Cho finds courage to face racism, sexism, and homophobia in her own life. Cho is unequivocal when she attributes her career stamina in the entertainment industry to the courage that she saw modeled by gay men.[11] Rather than yield to the systemic identity-denying pressures of dominant culture, Cho finds role models in the defiant young gay men of her youth (men who "believed in themselves when nobody else did"), teenage drag queens who were courageous, shameless, creative, and resilient in their response to oppression.

Cho's embrace of gay male lived-resistance to sexual norms and gender expectations, her acceptance of gender nonconforming gay men as hilarious and irreverent, might be said to run the risk of "ornamentalizing" gay men, according them space in the social imaginary but only as long as they remain peripheral and benign comic relief.[12] However, Cho's comedy arguably resists such ornamentalization in that she integrates gay men and gay male subculture into her own worldview and sense of agency. Cho's camp identification with gay men functions less a gesture of appropriation and more as an expression of affiliation, an anchoring of agency through a certain performative embrace of perversity. This is made explicit in Cho's work when she refuses to make such camp identifications with gay men palatable to heteronormative audiences. In a powerful move that combines stand-up comedy's long-standing engagement with shame alongside gay male and Asian American struggles against oppression (of which shame is constitutive), Cho works through sexual-racial shame on stage as an analytic, enacting what Celine Parreñas Shimizu has termed "productive perversity": a countering of the regulatory function of racial and sexual normalcy through the exploration of, among other things, hypersexuality.[13] Cho does not simply *identify with* gay male sexuality, but through a theatricalized, camp understanding of gay men and gay sex she proactively "disidentifies" with her own heterosexuality. Disidentification, according to Muñoz, is a powerful way to "transform a cultural logic from within."[14] It is a model of dealing with dominant ideology that neither seeks to assimilate within structures of dominance nor strictly opposes them. Cho's disidentification with heterosexuality works in two ways—as a mode of self enactment against the societal pressures that require women to express and experience desire in deference to the desires of straight men, and as a pedagogical technique, as a way of teaching other women (and men) how to disidentify with heterosexuality and, ultimately, how to change key heteronormative aspects of our social world.[15]

Cho celebrates gay men, not as an act of detached empathy or diffident longing, but as a way to recreate her own sense of agency in the face of racial, gender, and sexual oppression. Notably, an important and underdiscussed mechanism through which she performs this appreciation of gay men is through *racialized conduits*—particularly through performances that signify "black gay men/black drag queens" and through her caricature of her Korean immigrant mother. These racialized conduits, or what Kathryn Bond Stockton has recently theorized as "switchpoints," powerfully transmit the idea of the gay community as alluring (in their resistant and crafted perversity) and empowered (through a redeployment of their presumed marginality) by evoking the specific meanings and emotions usually attached to "black gay men/black drag queens" and Asian immigrant women.

Focusing on her first two recorded live comedy performances *I'm the One that I Want* and *Notorious C.H.O.*, this chapter attends to Cho's provocative faggot pageantry, arguing among other things that her camp identification with gay men and disidentification with heterosexuality rests both on the deployment of "black drag queen/black gay male" stereotypes as amplified representatives of "the" queer community's resilience in the face of hostility, as well as on Cho's hallmark performances of her Korean immigrant mother's familiarity with queer issues. Ultimately, Cho's acts of amplified solidarity are not simply acts of empathy for queer "others" but are actually assertions of interconnection anchored in the reformulation and embrace of perversity. These are performances of solidarity through shame that, in their very enactment, help claim a powerful, communal sense of sexual and racial agency, allowing Cho to point out and make sense of the fractured locus from within which she negotiates identity and survival.

SOLIDARITY BY DESIGN

In order to better understand the role gay men and gay male subculture play in Cho's comedy, I compare the organizational logic of *I'm the One* and *Notorious*, suggesting that a retroactive blueprint of her comedy's narrative architecture tells us something important about the provocative impact of her work. In comparing these two performances, one discerns the rough outlines of a parallel narrative structure: a three-part progressive narrative arc, with a fourth, nonlinear thematic dimension. Firstly, both performances begin with a gay "camp" aesthetic opening—reveling in seemingly apolitical frivolity and irony in contexts of serious ethical and political concern. Secondly, they follow up with a seemingly disparaging (skating on homophobic) reference to gay men or gay male culture. However, Cho utilizes this reference to gay men, and the potential harm or shame induced by it, as grounds for identification and solidarity with gay men. Rather than leave gay men "othered" she integrates and links gay shame to her own life experiences and active subjectivity. Thirdly, Cho's performances build on this identification with gay shame in order to disidentify with heterosexuality. In other words, her identification with gay shame becomes a strategy, not simply of critiquing heterosexuality, but dismantling it from the inside—by claiming queer space and queer desires as a woman who seeks sexual relationships with heterosexual men. The fourth feature of her comedy is not always sequentially located as the first three because it involves the clever use of race and racial "switchpoints" to highlight her solidarity with gay men. This is most evident in her use of "black gay male/black drag queen" vernacular as the default performative voice through which she represents universal sassiness and resilience in the face of homophobic and racial oppression. It is further buttressed through Cho's hallmark performances of her Korean immigrant mother, especially her mother's stereotype-defying familiarity with queer issues.

Cho's Gay Camp Beginnings

Both *I'm the One* and *Notorious* begin in a similar gay camp fashion, by irreverently gesturing toward serious ethical and political issues from a seemingly frivolous and ironic frame of reference. In *I'm the One*, for example, Cho defends her love of extravagant fashion designer Karl Lagerfeld ("with his white hair, and the big glasses, and a fuckin' fan. Like, like he's some kind of Spanish lady") within the context of PETA activists protesting Lagerfeld's fashion show due to the use of fur in his collection. This camp devotion to Lagerfeld in the context of protests is not a critique of PETA activists, since Cho reminds us that she shares PETA's political convictions by performing at their benefit concerts. Rather, the camp effect here is the playful establishment of purposeful incongruity and irony, the necessary platform upon which the pleasure of faggot pageantry can be experienced as generative rather than as derisive. Cho's response to protesters is to immediately parody their earnestness—not only by recalling one of their slogans ("Karl Lagerfeld *IS A MURDERER!* "Karl Lagerfeld *IS A MURDERER!*") and performing it in a humorous, raspy tone with her fist in the air for dramatic emphasis, but also by asking a performatively glib question: "Wouldn't it be fabulous if Karl Lagerfeld actually WAS a murderer?" Cho follows up by smiling at the audience and stating,

Like what if he fuckin' lost it one day, backstage at a show, in Milan. And bludgeoned Elsa Klensch to death with a platform shoe: [yelling and performing the attack] "I hate that blouse!" He would have to go to jail, and they would make him wear the orange jump suit. [Beat] I would call Amnesty International myself if that happened. [Beat] They would take away his fan. He would be on the pay phone to André Leon Talley: "André, could you send me a fan? Could you bake it in a cake, or stick it in your ass or something? I need a fan right away." He has to make one out of spoons [fanning herself with an imaginary fan, Cho walks back and forth on stage, pursing her lips, her head tilted back, suggesting an air of snobbishness and superiority].

Several layers of playful irreverence and irony are being explored here—all emanating from Cho's camp identification with gay men as presumed expert practitioners in irony, extremity, and extravagance. The "bludgeoning" of a famous fashion editor (and fashion-based murder-mystery writer!) with, of all things, a "platform shoe" by a renowned gay designer traumatized by a fashion faux pas ("I hate that blouse!"), followed by that designer's incarceration, and the "inhumanity" of stripping him of his trademark fan, not to mention the "torture" of forcing him to wear an orange (presumably ill-fitting) jump suit, contributes to an over the top comedic fantasy scenario, one where in true camp jail-house-movie fashion, contraband (like drugs or, in Lagerfeld's case, a fan) must be clandestinely acquired (smuggled in through body orifices and baked in cakes) or ingeniously created out of necessity (e.g., a fan made out of spoons). The play in gay male frivolity and irony is crucial to Cho's camp identification with gay men. In a homophobic world that at almost every turn demands acquiescence to binary gender expectations through tactics of coercive intimidation and punishment, a camp understanding of gay men explores the power of performing *indifference* to those expectations and consequences, showing us the seriousness and "politics" behind representations of gay men as *acontextually* extravagant and frivolous.

Whereas the camp aesthetic opening in *I'm the One* pivots explicitly on Lagerfeld as an extravagant, gender nonconforming arbiter of "taste," her opening routine in *Notorious* is less literally about gay male camp, reveling instead in exaggerated sexual frivolity and ironic playfulness. Cho begins her show by telling us, in a purposefully matter-of-fact way, that her response to the aftermath of the 9-11 terrorist attacks was not only to refuse being "terrorized by the terrorists," but more importantly to join the relief work at ground zero and, "day after day, giv[e] blow jobs to rescue workers." With an affect of comedic seriousness and tongue-in-cheek national duty, Cho reminds us that her "blowjobs" to rescue workers were acts of selfless volunteerism ("because we all have to do our part"). Echoing the tenor of media reports circulated in the aftermath of the 9-11 attacks regarding the heroic acts of regular Americans in a time of crisis, Cho feigns genuine contemplative insight, recalling the lessons she learned through days of diligent volunteer oral sex: "You find out a lot about yourself during times of crisis. And I found out that I lost my gag reflex. I call that 'a triumph of the human spirit.'" Notably, the camp effect here is not a devaluing of the lives lost through the attacks, nor is it a diminishing of the spirit of solidarity exhibited by everyday people in the face of crisis. The camp effect, rather, is a sophisticated questioning of the normativity upon which "national unity" is presumed and established. The camp effect here is achieved through the presumed impropriety of raising our erotic needs to the level of our national security needs. The performance of shameless sexual "service" in a time of national crisis is not simply an embrace of the improper for shock value, but the enactment of a camp sensibility, one that registers the historical devaluing of certain sexual practices and identities, one that invokes Comfort Women and a history of racialized sexual service in a time of increased militarization, and one that challenges presumptions of what American national unity might mean if Americans were understood in their full human capacity and erotic diversity.

HOMOPHOBIC INTERLUDES, GAY SHAME, AND IDENTIFICATION

The second feature of Cho's narrative arc is to move from camp openings that are playful and ironic to seemingly disparaging references to gay men. These are always brief moments in her work, but poignant nonetheless. They not only call attention to the underlying seriousness of Cho's performances (that is, that her comedy actively responds to a world that is hostile to gay men), but they also mark interesting turning points in Cho's enactment of solidarity with gay men. Through these moments, Cho reframes homophobic hostility (and gay shame) as the backdrop against which she enacts her own sense of personal and political agency.

In *I'm the One*, Cho moves from her performance of Karl Lagerfeld's effeminate extravagance to conclusively and unapologetically stating: "Karl Lagerfeld is such a faggot!" Cho follows-up immediately by imagining Lagerfeld's unfazed response to the presumption of insult. Tossing her head back to produce an air of snobbish indifference, pursing her lips, and frantically shaking her hand in front of her face as if holding a fan, Cho responds in an accent parodying Lagerfeld's German accent: "Of course I'm a faggot, darling. I'm a flaming faggot, darling. I am fanning the flames of my faggotry." Rather than contribute to the stigmatization of effeminate gay men through this stereotypical performance, Cho emphasizes Lagerfeld's *purposeful* extravagance and resilience under homophobic duress. She concludes by not only asserting a deep appreciation and respect for "faggots" as unapologetically perverse ("I love the word 'faggot' because it describes my kind of guy"), but also by claiming space in a lineage of faggotry, reminding her audience of her own "feral" cohabitation and co-implication with gay men at the margins of society ("some people were raised by wolves, I was raised by drag queens").

In addition to affirming the centrality of gay men to her "upbringing," Cho goes one step further and claims an identity as a type of woman ("I am a Fag Hag") who has been historically devalued and presumed a failure in large part because of her connection and commitment to gay men.[16] Cho reworks, through camp humor, the pejorative understanding of "fag hags" as failed heterosexual women on the periphery of gay male subculture. Far from being peripheral, Cho argues that "fag hags" are actually the gay community's underacknowledged "backbone." The evidence that Cho provides for this claim deserves attention on several levels, foremost because at this point in the performance she directly addresses the gay men in her audience. "Without us," Cho humorously scolds gay men, "you are nothing!" This feigned contempt is followed by Cho enumerating (with ironic asides and embellishments) the ways that "fag hags" have been central to gay male sociality:

We have been there all through history: guiding your sorry ass through the Underground Railroad. [Pursing her lips, crouching as she walks, looking back frequently over her shoulder, waving frantically in a "come here" gesture, and speaking in an exaggerated, "black-drag-queen" vernacular] "Come on girl, you need to hurry. Come on. Don't forget Kyle—you know he like to lag behind." [Straightening up, back in her own voice and with accusatory emphasis] We went to the *prom* with you. [Beat] We are still there by your side at the gay bars.

Cho's brief "fag hag" history lesson reminds gay men that their pursuit of sexual freedom has always involved, whether they like to admit it or not, the corroboration of a certain kind of woman—a woman willing (like the white abolitionists helping fugitive slaves) to break social mores and support quests for liberty. Because this "fag hag" solidarity has not been fully documented or deemed important enough to be memorialized, Cho borrows upon the legacy and impact of the Underground Railroad for dramatic effect. Elevating the status of "fag hags" to that of courageous abolitionists, Cho plays with the presumed absurdity of the comparison, pointing out in the process a shared history ranging from coming-of-age benchmarks (like attending prom night in high school) to everyday social gatherings at the local gay bar.

Cho's shift from the idea of the "Gay Underground Railroad" to referencing prom night causes laughter with her audience, in part because it moves from the absurdity of make-believe (that is, Cho performing in a "black-drag-queen" vernacular helping gays toward "freedom") to the absurdity of reality (where young high school students must find opposite gender "dates" in order to avoid feeling marginalized or inadequate). Prom night, as a heteronormative process of cultural regulation, is recalled as a shared historical benchmark, by the women who presumably fell in love with closeted gay men, and also by the marginalized women and marginalized men who consciously relied on each other, especially on prom night, in order to exercise rights of passage only deemed appropriate for idealized normative teenagers.

The critical narrative progression in *I'm the One*—from a gay camp beginning and a seemingly disparaging reference to gay men, to identifying and creating connection with gay men, gay shame, and gay male struggles as a platform for agency—is mirrored with intensity in Cho's *Notorious*. The camp discussion of volunteer oral sex at the beginning of *Notorious* is followed up, eventually, with a joke about a gay club in Scotland, a club whose name is so stereotypically "gay," according to Cho, that she tells her audience it might as well be named "Fuck Me in the Ass, Bar and Grill." The bar is named "CC Blooms," a direct reference to the name of the character that Bette Midler played in the movie *Beaches*. The joke is met with roaring laughter from the audience. However, it is important to note how close the humor in this joke comes to the homophobic denigration of gay men as pathologically sentimental (i.e., because they stereotypically adore media representations of female strength through adversity) and as perversely obsessed with "unnatural" sexual desires (e.g., anal sex). Cho uses this "fuck me in the ass" joke, not in a homophobic manner, but as a necessary platform and transition to her own abject life struggles as an Asian American woman. Rather than keep gay men "othered" by metonymically reducing them to the abject "irrationality" that anal sex signifies in the homophobic imagination, she immediately transitions to sharing that space of abjection and speaking of her own body, including her own anus ("There's been a lot of activity, in and around my ass lately") and menstrual cycle ("sometimes straight men freak out when I talk about my period, but I don't talk about my period that much, compared to HOW-OFTEN-IT-HAPPENS"). After an extended-comedic discussion of her own experience with "anal irrigation" and her conviction that straight men could never cope with the monthly reality of menstrual cycles, Cho transitions to speaking autobiographically about her challenges and personal shame as a struggling Asian American actor in a structurally racist entertainment industry. Notably, this is the trademark "serious" part of her shows where, as Rachel Lee notes, Cho transitions toward "talk," toward personal exposition and narration on questions explicitly having to do with her own experience with racial invisibility and racial stereotypes, with body-image issues, drug abuse, and a sense of failure and self-hatred.[17] In other words, Cho employs gay shame as a bridge and precedent, sharing the burden and space of abjection as a platform from which to examine her own life and struggles, and as a way to honor and learn from the tactics that gay men have employed in response to their own oppression. While Cho's autobiographical reflections and her celebration of gay men have become her hallmark signatures, rarely has the intimate narrative logic between the two—the foundation of one upon the other—been mapped. Cho embraces a camp understanding of gay men as a way to harness self-reflection and courage, as well as to practice new tactics of survival and resistance.

DISIDENTIFYING WITH HETEROSEXUALITY

A key feature of Cho's comedy is identifying with those aspects of gay male identity and culture that seem shameful within a heteronormative worldview. This identification with gay men and gay shame is not simply an opportunity to stand in solidarity with gay men, it is also a powerful way for Cho to assert her own "perverse" agency and disidentification with heterosexuality. Disidentification names a unique form of social resistance that challenges oppressive practices without claiming to be completely outside of oppressive logics. Cho disidentifies with heterosexuality in her shows, meaning that she critiques heterosexuality from within, dismantling heteronormative privilege for her audience as a woman who registers for them as ostensibly heterosexual.[18]

In *I'm the One*, Cho disidentifies with heterosexuality by irreverently celebrating gay men and gay male culture in contrast to, and at the expense of, heterosexual men. Referring to herself as unapologetically "heterophobic," Cho praises the presence of gay men in her life ("Thank god for gay men, THANK GOD for gay men"), asserting that were it not for gay men, she would have excised men entirely from her life. "I am scared of straight men," she admits. "They're so scary to me. They used to be not that scary because I used to drink a lot. And I was never sacred. I would just walk up to a guy in a bar, and be like 'Hey, STICK IT IN!' You can't really do that in sobriety." Cho confesses to an unhealthy heterosexual promiscuity while abusing drugs and alcohol, but she associates sobriety with clarity regarding why heterosexual women should rethink their attraction to heterosexual men. Cho repeatedly undermines the idea that heterosexual men and women are "natural" pairs. She does so by attributing to heterosexual men a pathological narcissism and false sense of security with regard to understanding women's sexuality. For example, Cho recalls fearing sexual experimentation with a woman because, as she tells us, she wouldn't be able to fake an orgasm "like usual." Here, Cho disidentifies with heterosexuality, not by asserting a lesbian or bisexual *identity*, but by admitting to a long history of unpleasurable heterosexual sex—all while remaining presumably heterosexual in her audience's eyes, and expressing, from that crucial and intimate positionality, disapproval and dissatisfaction with straight men. At one point in her show, Cho exaggerates the differences between gay and straight men in terms of appearance, arguing that straight men are failures when it comes to making themselves attractive and desirable. She communicates this best when describing the lure of male strip shows among straight women and referencing the Chippendale's dancers as the most ironic icons of heterosexual women's fantasies: "The Chippendales dancers are gay. They're gay. You know why? Because there is no such thing as a straight man with visible abdominal muscles. It doesn't exist. You need to suck cock to get that muscle definition." Cho illustrates this "abdominal muscle workout" by bending her head towards her crotch. She goes on to say that she likes telling that particular joke during her comedy routines because "all the straight guys poof out their bellies" upon hearing it. She performs these last lines, as Lee notes, "with cheeks puffed out and arms encircles in front of her as if around a protruding stomach," looking like "a huge blowfish . . . , [an] overblown depiction of panicked male heterosexuality."[19] Here, Cho is referencing the culture of negation cultivated among homophobic men in their quest to produce a seamless, untarnished, and ultimately "natural" gender and sexual identity. The idea that heterosexually identified men might admire their own bodies (as well as, perhaps, the bodies of other men) is the reason, Cho hypothesizes, why straight pornography includes "the most disgusting men you'll ever see in your life," because straight men go to great lengths to avoid the possibility of desiring men. Relentless in her disidentification with heterosexuality, Cho does not simply mourn the lack of good-looking straight men in straight porn, but she defiantly proclaims her preference *for* gay porn, performing speechlessness and disgust when describing what she finds offensive in straight porn: "I love gay porn, cause the guys in gay porn are hot. It's not like straight porn, ew, straight porn is so . . . ew, ew."

In "Notorious," we see a similar disidentification with heterosexuality through Cho's relentless performative identification with gay men and stereotypical gay male ways of being. "What I love most about gay men," Cho asserts, "is the way they are about sex":

There is a fun and frivolity that surrounds gay men and their sexuality that is not there for straight men and sex. I think if you are oppressed over who you want to sleep with, when you actually go and do it, you're gonna have a really good time. If you are hated for who you like to fuck, you are gonna kick up your heals and fuck. [Beat] And it is such an inspiration to watch.

Cho further performs appreciation of gay male sexual shamelessness by employing a camp caricature of the differences between gay men and straight men in personals ads:

A straight personals ad goes something like: [in a melancholic, almost sedated, voice] "Divorced, White Male, 41, seeks slender lady for long conversations, walks on the beach, and foreign films. Non-smoker, a plus." [Makes snoring sound] A gay personals add is like: [in a raspy, "Wild-West" cartoon-like male voice] "WANTED: ASS BANDIT. Hold up this caboose. Dick smoker, a plus." [Looking surprised and speaking in her own voice] I want to answer *that* ad.

For Cho, gay men are not just admirably carefree and expressive of their most intimate desires, they model courageous attitudes toward the body and sex that serve for Cho as welcomed opportunities to interrogate and understand her own life as a woman. Rather than understand gay men as simply quirky comic relief, she concludes by asserting how profoundly incorporated gay men are in her life and to her sense of self: "I learned everything I know about being a woman from gay men. I learned all about sex from gay men. I kinda have sex like a gay man. I act like a gay man most of the time, actually." The declaration of gay men as role models and mentors—as men whom women might benefit from emulating and learning from—intervenes not only in the homophobic logic that renders gay men peripheral (if tolerated), but also in feminist critiques of gay male misogyny, critiques of gay men as having little to do with women's objective life struggles.

THE RACIAL ROUTE TO FAGGOT PAGEANTRY

The effort in this chapter to better understand Cho's trademark celebration of gay men, and purposeful disidentification with heterosexuality, would be diminished without attending to the role certain racialized representations play in her comedy's logic. Cho's provocative "faggot pageantry" relies, rather curiously, on the deployment of specific *racialized* "switchpoints," racialized representations that powerfully (but with remarkable subtlety) transmit the idea of the gay community as desirable in response to a context that would rather understand them as dismissible. Bond Stockton uses the term switchpoints to reference "a point of connection between two signs (or two rather separate connotative fields) where something from one flows toward (is diverted in the direction of) the other, lending its connotative spread and signifying force to the other, illuminating it and intensifying it, but also sometimes shifting it or adulterating it."[20] This understanding of switchpoints is helpful for fully capturing Cho's comedic logic because it defers questions of cultural appropriation (and by extension questions of "authenticity") in order to better trace and understand the multiple ways in which meanings travel. The discourse of "switchpoints" is conversant with E. Patrick Johnson's assertion that cross-cultural appropriations are not always instances of "colonization and subjugation," that they also often "provide fertile ground on which to formulate new epistemologies of self and Other."[21]

In *I'm the One,* for example, Cho relies on a "black gay male/black drag queen" persona and vernacular as the default performative voice through which she represents universal gay male sassiness and resilience in the face of oppression. This association is created through intonation, embodiment, and use of African

American Vernacular English (AAVE) and slang. Importantly, this "black gay male/black drag queen" persona and vernacular parallels the media stereotype and controlling image of the "sassy black woman." This stereotype of black women erases structural racism and violence to produce caricatures—like "Bonquiqui" of *SNL* and "Shanaynay" of the *Martin Lawrence Show*—who are unjustifiably mean, pathologically narcissistic and hypersexual, and condescendingly cynical.[22] Cho's "black gay male/black drag queen" persona can be differentiated from the "sassy black woman" stereotype, however, in that oppression and social resistance are everywhere emphasized and linked to each other in Cho's show, contextualizing behavior as constructed, as produced in conjunction with the social world and its social agents, hence indexing important aspects of that world. This is not a justification for lending stereotypes validity and authenticity, but rather an acknowledgment that Cho engages stereotypes with a critical difference.

For example, Cho employs a "black gay male/black drag queen" persona in the Gay Underground Railroad skit mentioned earlier, where she invokes the history of "fag hags" assisting gays to "freedom" ("Come on girl, you need to hurry. Come on. Don't forget Kyle, you know he like to lag behind"). Through the use exaggerated effeminate embodiment, as well as slang terms rooted in African American vernacular (like "girl" to reference women) and shifts in pronoun and verb agreements ("you know he *like* to lag behind"), Cho enacts solidarity with gay men *through* "blackness." She uses this persona as well when describing her appreciation for the barefaced priority gay men stereotypically place on sexual encounters over their social commitments. Mimicking a gay man's "typical" way of addressing friends when it is "dick o'clock"[23]—that is, when "all the gay men in the club simultaneously start looking for dick"—Cho reminds women in the audience how gay men will "leave you so fast" if they have an opportunity to be sexually intimate with another man: "Girl, you can get a ride home, can't you? You can get a ride, you can take a bus, you can take the subway, you a big girl—you go girl! You go! No, I mean you *go*, BYE!" The use the ubiquitous "you go, girl" African American slang accompanied with vernacular shifts in pronoun and verb agreements ("you *a* big girl") contribute, finally, to a playful sense of sarcasm—a request to leave masked by a slang phrase of encouragement ("You go, girl. You go. No, I mean you *go*, BYE!").

Cho relies on this "black gay male/black drag queen" persona once again when she describes the importance of gay men in the lives of straight women, particularly as they impart expert advice on how to sexually please heterosexual men. In the same voice used previously to reference the gay male community, Cho gives an example of a gay man providing tutelage regarding "fast and efficient" head:

Girl, all you gotta do, when you down there, all you gotta do is you just have to stick yo' finger up his ass. That's all you gotta do. That's all you gotta do! Oh, please, do you want to go home? Do you want to go home? Okay, then, you can be home in five minutes watching Ally McBeal. Please girl, it is not nasty. It is not nasty! You can wash yo' hand at home. You can wash yo' hand at home! That's why I drive like dis. [Cho adds to the comedic effect here by pretending to drive, putting her hands in front of her, as if to be using a car steering wheel, while her index finger is pointing out.]

The comedic and critical effect of suggesting that a heterosexual man's pleasure can be enhanced through anal play, and that a heterosexual woman's dislike of sex with heterosexual men can be ameliorated by a gay man's advice on how to give "fast and efficient" head, is remarkably accompanied by representing gay men *as* "black gay men/black drag queens." Surely not all gay men speak like this, let alone black gay men. The stereotype of effeminate black men and their forms of speech and public resistance functions, however, as a short cut—universalizing the idea of gay-men-as-valuable (as inventive and alluring in their nonmainstream forms of publicity and resistance) by imbuing gay men with those qualities commonly associated with stereotypes of effeminate black gay men.

Cho's *Notorious* reaffirms the association of gay men with "black gay male/black drag queen" vernacular when she champions the publicity and righteous anger with which her drag queen friends in high school defended themselves against homophobic aggression. Pursing her lips, moving her neck and head side-to-side with the all-too-familiar performance of sassy black woman "attitude," and placing a hand on her hip, Cho channels her friends' compelling rebellion and righteous resistance:

I do not need anyone telling me who I am! I know who I am, I know who I am! Dis' a fucked up school. I hate dis school. I need to get my GED, that's what *I* need. Dis a fucked up school, I hate this school! You know I walk down the hallway, they be calling me names, they call me faggot, they call me sissy. I said, "Oh yeah. You forgot. I'm also a model and an actress, so FUCK YOU TOO!" [Cho snaps her fingers and walks away.]

This moment of precious rebellion in the face of devaluation is performed as an example of *universal* gay male resilience. However, this performance is indisputably racialized, and this racialization is crucial to how Cho communicates the transgressive nature of her identification with gay men and disidentification with heterosexuality. It bears repeating that at the core of this performance is the stereotype of the "black gay man/black drag queen," not to mention the stereotype of the "sassy black woman." Cho's performance might be said to avoid the danger of previous stereotypes and controlling images in that it attends to social context, channeling "sassiness" as ingenuity and resilience, rather than pathology—as an *appropriate* response to marginalization and oppression.

Cho's faggot pageantry cannot achieve its transgressive impact without blackness figuring prominently in the representation of gayness. This is not because racism has been eradicated and black gay men are now, miraculously, esteemed members of the larger gay community; rather, it is because black gay men, or more precisely the *idea* of "black gay men," signify extra-ordinary marginality and extra-ordinary resistance. Deploying "black gay male/black drag queen/sassy black woman" personas, Cho channels that signifying force. She does so, not in some derogatory attempt to simply and naively "act black," but more as a way of marking and making gay male and Asian American female resistance legible. Cho's appropriation of blackness is not unusual given the international symbolic importance of US black cultural resistance (from Black Power to hip-hop) for minoritized people and minority social movements. However, it is unique in that this appropriation of blackness is undertaken in the service of identifying *with* gay male shame and gay male resistance, as well as with the enactment of Asian American female agency in oppressive contexts.

An important counterexample to how black stereotypes are used in less progressive, actually offensive, and outright racist ways are the controversial, blackface drag performances of Charles Knipp.[24] He is a white gay man who performs as "Shirley Q. Liquor," an alter ego often described as a heavy-set, illiterate, single black mother of nineteen children, who collects welfare, names many of her children after fast-food restaurants, discount stores, and venereal diseases, and is considered by Knipp himself "the queen of ignunce." Black and gay groups alike have protested Knipp's performances, which are mostly held at white gay pride events and gay clubs (see banshirleyqliquor.typepad.com). Although defended by some prominent figures in the queer community (for example, gay black drag queen Ru Paul and lesbian comedian Julie Goldman), Knipp's performances of blackness are strikingly different than that of Cho's. The difference is not that Cho appropriates "blackness" in more "realistic" ways, but that she invokes the stereotype of "black gay men/black drag queen/sassy black women" in a manner that revels in perverse forms of resistance, in ways that highlight the power, beauty, and resilience of nonnormativity in the face of regulation and violence. Knipp's blackface performances seem shallow and unreflexive in comparison, making it very difficult to see them as upsetting (intentionally or not) the racial/gender status quo. Rather, as noted by E. Patrick Johnson in his discussion of Patricia William's scholarship, there seems to be a voyeuristic deployment of blackness in Knipp's performance, placing the illusion of "black culture" not only on display, but "at a condescending distance."[25]

Cho's camp engagement with blackness not only functions much differently than that of Knipp's blackface camp performances, but it also participates in a larger repertoire of racialized switchpoints. The most unusual, but important racialized feature of Cho's elaborate faggot pageantry is her caricature of her own mother—a depiction of a woman who despite stereotypical assumptions about Korean immigrant women is radically conversant with gay male subculture. Cho's performance of her mother is foundational to her elaboration of faggot pageantry—i.e., to her identification with gay men and disidentification with heterosexuality—because it is through this racialized depiction of Asian immigrantness that Cho references shame around Asian American stereotypes at the same time that she undermines such refracted shame by shifting the location where one would anticipate hearing positive things about gays. In this way, Cho is in dialogue with what Chandan Reddy has noted about the pernicious ways that immigrant communities in the United States are represented as pathological bastions of heteronormativity, proving their backwardness and unassimilability to Western modernity.[26] Cho breaks with this pathologizing of immigrant communities, enticing her audience to reimagine a more ample cultural geography in which queerness resides in good company.

In *I'm the One*, for example, Cho reminds us of the way her mother responded with concern when first learning of Cho's sexual experimentation with women. The concern Cho depicts, however, is not homophobic disappointment, but rather concern on the mother's behalf for the lack of communication and trust between her own child and herself. Manipulating her face and body to produce her signature caricature of her mother (i.e., scrunching her face, pushing her chin to her neck, squinting her eyes) Cho performs the phone message she remembers her mother leaving on her answering machine regarding her sexual experience:

Ah you Gay?! Ah you Gay?! Pick up the phone! Iffa you don't pick up the phone, that mean you gay. Only gay screena call. [Beat] You are gay. [Beat] Why don't you talk to mommy about it? You can talk to Mommy about every-ting. [Beat] You have a cool mommy. Mommy's uh-so cool. And Mommy know ALL about the Gay! I know ALL about the gay! They have-uh so many gay (*whaaaaa*!), so many gay all over, all over the worl'. So many gay all over the worl' [beat] but not Korea, not Korea! But everywhere else, so many gay.

Cho's use of broken English and facial exaggeration to convey her mother's "immigrantness" contrasts with the ostensibly pro-gay content of her mother's phone message. Although Cho humorously performs her mother's ambivalence regarding the existence of homosexuality in Korea, Cho further enacts her mother's unexpected support for and familiarity with gay issues when she performs her mother's recollection of Cho's early childhood:

You know I think you gay-uh when you born. Yeah, you born, I was a holding you. [Cradling her arms as if holding a baby, looking into her arms] She's a so beautiful, she's so beautiful, [suddenly acting surprised, presumably in response to something "baby Margaret" has done] uh, uh, uh . . . What a dyke! What a big dyke! [Acting happy] Yes you are! You are so dykey, ah?! Maybe one day you-uh grow up to be PE Teacher.

Here Cho inverts expectations: an immigrant parent having a conversation about her child's sexuality, an immigrant parent celebrating, of all things, female masculinity, or what Cho terms "dykeyness."

Rather than let her audience presume she is fictionalizing all of this, Cho reminds her audience in an encore performance that her parents owned a bookstore in San Francisco, and she describes her mom's familiarity with gay pornography in a manner that destabilizes the idea of immigrants as insular and parochial.

My mother was in charge of the gay porn. So every day she would unpack boxes of gay porn and try to talk to me about it. "Thees book, that's called "Ass Master." That's book for gay. Because-uh, gay [beat] they like ass. They like ass-uh soooo much they don't know what to do. I think they like ass TOO MUCH. I want to say you have to have ass-uh in-uh moderation. You cannot have ass all of the time. If you have-uh ass all the time, then it's not special. [Pause] I know gay, his name is Paul, and Paul is so nice-uh, but he only like two thing. Ass and Judy Garland, that's all. What kind of life is that! [Laughing and pausing] Ass Master. Mommy gonna look at Ass Master now. I have to look at it. I'm so-kurious. I'm so-kurious about Ass Master. Ass Master. [Pretends to open magazine] AHHHHH! AHHHHH![Laughs and looks away]. I wasn't ready for that! It was just ass right away. I wasn't ready for that. Ass right away. I wasn't ready for that. I thought there would be table of contents, then ass.

What does this representation of Cho's mother tell us? What does it communicate? Unlike the use of "black gay men/black drag queens/sassy black women" as switchpoints, as representatives of universal gay male resistance, Cho's camp performance of her mother functions to denaturalize the association of immigrant communities with homophobia. It works to destabilize where one might reasonably presume to hear nonhostile humor and insight on issues "pertaining to gays." Cho's performance of her mother's familiarity with gay issues functions, then, as a switchpoint in the other direction; rather than transferring the meanings and connotations usually associated with Asian American mothers to gays, Cho's work delinks immigrant communities from the homophobia that is usually and spectacularly attributed to their "culture." Referencing immigrant communities as familiar with, and constituted by, queer people and queer issues, Cho intervenes into the logic of domination which would keep these two groups not only ontologically separate, but incomprehensible to each other. More than conveying as sense of "tolerating" gays, Cho's mother conveys a profound queer sensibility, stating in her own opinion and broken English that the "worl'" is not constituted by heterosexuals on the one hand, and gays on the other, but that ultimately everybody "little bit gay." This framing of queerness as being present (to different degrees) in everybody, pushes back against the mother's previous statement that in Korea "there are no gay." Cho's mother, in fact, recalls (with a great deal of gossipy pleasure) "a gay story" about "daddy"—a story where intimacy between men and the possibility of deeply carrying for another man is thematized not as a Westernized notion associated with white gayness, but with Koreanness. The story we hear is about Cho's father as a young college student in Korea, and about the deep friendship he develops with a young man who one day, when they are both together on a picnic in the countryside, has the courage to declare his love for Cho's father. Cho's father responds with shock, we are told, because he also loves his friend deeply, but cannot communicate that love without fearing being ascribed a homosexual identity. Instead, Cho's father reacts homophobically and punches his friend in the face. This act of violence, we are told by Cho's mother, is deeply regretted by Cho's father throughout his life, as it is the last memory that he has of his good friend.

The strategic decision I have made above, to eliminate, in my summary descriptions of Cho's performance, commentary on her style as well minimize direct quotations of what she actually says, reflects my intention to momentarily postpone her comedic flare and make visible one of the thematic cores of Cho's performance: the seriousness of her subject matter. The conceptual-political importance of locating queerness as part of Korean everyday life (rather than associating queerness with the United States), and the strategic importance of acknowledging the father's life-long regret for remaining estranged from a male friend whom he once cared for so deeply, cannot be overstated. Cho is remarkable in her ability to *queer* the image of Korean immigrant families, to "shift the site of queer enunciation" in such a profound way that now Koreanness is the location from which we are able to hear—in a vernacular and seemingly autochthonous way—antihomophobic memories and ethical commitments. This is captured by Cho, effortlessly and as a matter of fact, when she performs her mother's paced reflection regarding her father's early homosexual panic and his later deep-felt regret: "So, moral of story: is if you gay friend says to you 'I love you,' DON'T PUNCH!"

BEYOND PUNCH LINES

Cho's stand-up comedy presents me with an opportunity to provide some closing commentary about queer race narratives and the process and prospects of intelligibility. There is nothing particularly funny, of course, about the violence that queers of color actually experience. But humor and the deployment of stereotypes are indeed tactics Cho makes masterful use of in order to cohabit with dominant logics and undo them from within. Cho enacts complex solidarities through her comedy, weaving irreverent racialized narratives that valorize faggotry. And audiences get it. Well, perhaps it is safer simply to say that they laugh. At what exactly, one can't always be sure. But I have my hunches. I am not confident that liberatory knowledge is all that is circulating in the auditoriums, among the people, when she performs. But this is a point that I have been meaning to get at. The value of queer race narratives does not hinge on some idealized notion that they impact everyone in the same way. Rather, the value of this work is that it pushes us to see and feel in ways that run up against dominant understandings. Certainly all forms of resistance can be co-opted or ignored, but again this is not the point. Queer race narratives deliberate about the social world in ways that have not yet been fully accounted for and that may offer social theorists new frameworks with which to contend. That is, queer race narratives offer us access to subjugated ways of seeing and feeling, to complex processes of resistance and agency. I advocate for more familiarity with these knowledges and subjectivities, not on the grounds that they explain everything about the social world, or that they explain the social world well in every instance, but on the grounds that they are attempts at epistemic decolonization, and that as such, they represent possibilities for new knowledge and social critique. We learn from the failures of these attempts, as well as from their success. Since they are accounts of a real social world, their failure to explain it at times can also yield better knowledge. What constitutes failure and success, error and accuracy, is certainly a complex question, one that will depend of course on how well communities of knowers take responsibility for the claims they make and for the kinds of literacy that they themselves have developed to make sense of the world.

NOTES

INTRODUCTION
1. Ayala, "Foreword," vii–viii.
2. Ibid., v–vi.
3. Ibid., vi.
4. Baldwin, "Notes for a Hypothetical Novel," 241.
5. For some representative examples of scholarship theorizing epistemic decolonization, see Alarcón, "Chicana Feminism"; Alexander, *Pedagogies*; Aldama and Quiñonez, *Decolonial Voices*; Anzaldúa, *Borderlands*; B. Christian, "Race for Theory"; Delgadillo, *Spiritual Mestisaje*; Hames-García, "Queer Theory, Revisited"; Johnson, "'Quare' Studies"; Lugones, *Pilgrimages*; Mignolo, "Delinking"; Mignolo, "Epistemic Disobedience"; E. Pérez, *Decolonial Imaginary*; H. Perez, "You Can Have"; L. Pérez, *Chicana Art*; Smith, *Decolonizing Methodologies*; Womack, *Red on Red*; Yarbro-Bejarano, *Wounded Heart*.
6. Moraga and Anzaldúa, *This Bridge*, 23.
7. See L. Pérez, *Chicana Art*, 4.
8. Crenshaw et al., *Critical Race Theory*, 314.
9. "Realism" in contemporary ethnic, feminist, and literary studies can best be understood as a philosophical corrective to the dominance of postmodern skepticism as an epistemological position in the academy (Mohanty, "Realist Theory," 97). Realists share with postmodernists a basic commitment to the idea of social construction but are less cynical about the attainability of nonpositivist object knowledge. Realists argue that objective knowledge is realizable not as definite certainty but through degrees and by taking background theories seriously. Since the mid-1990s, realists have expanded this view on knowledge and argued against a purely constructivist view of identity, noting among other things that what matters is not whether identities are constructed but "what difference different kinds of construction make" (Alcoff et al., *Identity Politics Reconsidered*, 6). For more on realism and

objective knowledge, see Hau, "On Representing Others," 156–60; Hames-García, *Fugitive Thought*, xx–xxvi; Mohanty, "Epistemic Status," 29–43; Mohanty, *Literary Theory*, 189–93; Moya, "Introduction," 12–14; Teuton, *Red Land*, 93–94, 178–79. On realism and the epistemic status of minority identities, see Alcoff, *Visible Identities*, 42–44, 125–28; Alcoff et al., *Identity Politics Reconsidered*, 4–5, 100–104; Hames-García, *Identity Complex*, 18–21; Macdonald and Sánchez-Casal, "Identity, Realist Pedagogy," 16–28; Mohanty, *Literary Theory*, 202–40; Moya, *Learning*, 37–45, 82, 86–87, 93; Moya and Hames-García, *Reclaiming Identity*, 33–64, 83–86, 312–15, 334–41; Siebers, *Disability in Theory*, 82–84, 126–27.

10. To argue, as I want to in this book, that understanding the social world in more "objective" ways depends on how well we engage with people resisting oppression, is not to argue that the oppressed *always* have keen insights about the world and about their own circumstances, nor is it to argue that "learning from" subaltern people is an easy task or even a task without fundamental ethical and political issues at stake. Within literary studies, for example, I am in agreement with Doris Sommer's claim that understanding the work of minority writers often necessitates "an unlikely program of training," particularly for readers expecting "to enter into collaborative language games . . . , as if asymmetrical relationships flattened out on the smooth surface of print culture" (*Proceed*, xi). Sommer advocates a reading strategy of "vulnerable comportment," over one of presumed accessibility and mastery, prompted by minority writers who, she writes, "astute about their own social circumstances . . . , set manageable limits around readers who mistake a privileged center for the universe, and who need obstacles to notice the circumstances of conversation" (iv). Sommer's thesis seems importantly supported by her analysis of Rigoberta Menchú. However, we may want to acknowledge Sommer's claim without agreeing entirely that all minority writers direct their attention toward teaching "Westerners" and other privileged people how to "read." Rigoberta Menchú's testimony and the Zapatistas' communiqués are important examples of minority writings that self-consciously gesture outward, toward "others," and whose vision of social change depends on such a relationship. However, these are not representative of all minority writing. In fact, Sommer's thesis does not account for literature written "horizontally," for other minorities; nor does it reflect the idea that privileged people often confuse minority indifference toward them with acknowledgment.

11. For more on skepticism, see Mohanty's discussion of Spivak, Culler, and Nicholson (*Literary Theory*, 11–16), as well as his discussion of de Man (25–46). Also see Alcoff, *Visible Identities*, 71–83, 169–76; Moya, *Learning*, 7, 10, 13–14, 89, 97–98; Teuton, *Red Power*, 23–24, 44–45, 123–24, 180–82, 203–4.

12. Mohanty, *Literary Theory*, 213; Moya and Hames-García, *Reclaiming Identity*, 12–13.

13. For an overview of the critique of identity, see Alcoff, *Visible Identities*, 11–132.

14. Alcoff et al., *Identity Politics Reconsidered*, 6. One key to arguing for the plausible accuracy of identity claims is to refuse collapsing political identities with transparent ethnographic descriptions. The terms "gay" or "queer" may not, for example, describe how every person in APLA's target audience thinks about themselves, but the terms point us to an analysis of society and oppression, and to forms of resistance. These may not fully hit their mark, and may need to be changed over time, but they nonetheless gesture toward possibilities and avenues for resistance and solidarity.

15. Alcoff et al., *Identity Politics Reconsidered*, 6.

16. Baldwin, *Price of the Ticket*, 329.

17. Alcoff et al., *Identity Politics Reconsidered*, 6.

18. Patricia Hill Collins reminds us, for example, that "literature by U.S. Black women writers provides one comprehensive view of Black women's struggles to form positive self-

definitions in the face of derogated images of Black womanhood" (*Black Feminist Thought*, 102). In other words, literature serves a crucial epistemic function in that it provides access to the subjective realities that are systematically subjugated or distorted. Catrióna Rueda Esquibel reflects similarly on the crucial role literature has played in Chicana lesbian struggles to trace a history of their existence against the prevailing reality of homophobia and racism: "Lacking historical proof of Chicana lesbian existence, Chicana writers have created one" (*With Her Machete*, 6). Esquibel helps us to understand the ways that Chicana writers resist tangible epistemic violence by decolonizing their imaginations and creating genealogies to which they can belong and through which they can resist previous erasures. This is strikingly close to what Alice Walker, drawing on Toni Morrison, means when she states, "I write all the things *I should have been able to* read" (*In Search*, 13). On the importance of minority cultural production for epistemic decolonization, see L. Pérez, *Chicana Art*, 4, 17–49; La Fountain-Stokes, *Queer Ricans*, xiii; and Smith, *Decolonizing*, 34–35.

19. Mignolo, "Epistemic Disobedience."
20. See Quijano, "Coloniality of Power"; Tlostanova, *Gender Epistemologies*, 19–60.
21. Hames-García, "Can Queer Theory Be Critical Theory?" Hames-García has expanded this argument in a revised version of this essay entitled "Queer Theory, Revisited" (Hames-García and Martínez, *Gay Latino Studies*, 19–45).
22. Moraga and Hollibaugh, "What We're Rolling Around"; Moraga and Anzaldúa, *This Bridge*; Rubin, "Thinking Sex."
23. Hull, Scott, and Smith, *All the Women*; Lorde, *Sister Outsider*; Fuss, *Essentially Speaking*.
24. Garber, *Identity Poetics*.
25. Holland, "(White) Lesbian Studies"; Johnson, "'Quare' Studies"; Pellegrini, "Mind the Gap?"; Halberstam, "Shame"; H. Perez, "You Can Have."
26. E. Pérez, "Irigaray's Female Symbolic," 105.
27. Patton and Sánchez-Eppler, *Queer Diasporas*, 2.
28. Lima, *Latino Body*, 9.
29. For a good example of how this functions in Chicana feminist theory, see Moya's discussion of Norma Alarcón and Chela Sandoval (Moya, *Learning*, 78–95).
30. Alcoff, "Who's Afraid," 323.
31. Moya, "What's Identity Got to Do with It," 97.
32. My argument here is not intended as an out-of-hand dismissal of all postmodernist and poststructuralist projects. For example, I have found Sandra Soto's queer reading of Cherríe Moraga to be nothing short of brilliant (*Reading*, 15–38). Soto's essay is groundbreaking and inspiring, and this has everything to do with the kind of queer theoretical reading practice that she implements. My concern with scholarship that overly valorizes "instability" as both reading practice and ontological claim, then, is more aligned with what Michael Sneideker has recently articulated through his theory of "queer optimism," as a need for options against queer theory's insistent, normative bias toward pessimism and incoherence. He writes, "Queer theory, for all its contributions to our thinking about affect, has had far more to say about negative affects than positive ones. Furthermore . . . , queer theory's suspicious relation to persons has itself become suspiciously routinized, if not taken for granted in its own right. . . . Queer theory's habitation of this pessimistic field is cause for real concern. Melancholy, self-shattering, the death drive, shame: these, within queer theory, are categories to conjure with. . . . However, these terms have dominated queer-theoretical discourse, and they have often seemed immune to queer theory's own perspicacities" (*Queer Optimism*, 4).
33. Fricker, *Epistemic Injustice*, 1.
34. Sandra Soto, for example, writes, "It seems to me that one way to negotiate the

challenges I have outlined thus far is to use the best of the tools that queer theory has to offer. My qualification in that sentence ('the best of the tools') is meant to acknowledge that queer theory itself presents its own set of challenges. For queer theory has been slow to learn from the important work of scholars like José Quiroga, Juana María Rodríguez, José Esteban Muñoz, and Yvonne Yarbro-Bejarano—to name a few of the people who have staged imaginative interventions over the past dozen or so years against the heteronormativity of Latin@ studies and the racialized blind spots of queer theory. Too often queer theory continues to render race, ethnicity, and nation as niches within a broader, and unremarked, white erotics" (*Reading*, 4).

35. See H. Perez, "You Can Have"; Halberstam, "Shame"; and Hames-García, "Queer Theory, Revisited."

36. Sandra Soto refers to this as the "see-for-instance" endnote: "Queer theorists' engagement with queers of color, or with racial formation more broadly, is still to often contained in the tiny-font endnotes at the back of books. These usually refer back to acknowledgments of 'intersectionality' that often go something like this: 'thanks to women of color we now know that we have to address the *intersectionality* of race, class, gender, sexuality, and nation'" (*Reading*, 4).

37. Ortega, "Being Lovingly," 56.

38. Ibid.

39. For similar critiques, see Spelman, "Theories of Race and Gender"; Schueller, "Analogy"; Moya, *Learning*.

40. Holland, *Erotic Life*, 67.

41. Tinsley, *Thiefing Sugar*, 28.

42. H. Perez, "You Can Have," 180.

43. Deborah McDowell reminds us, for example, that there is no need to attribute maliciousness to the antirealism that dominated literary studies in the 1980s to nonetheless observe its impact on how black feminist criticism would be able to justify its decolonizing politics. She writes:

(1) While black feminist criticism was asserting the significance of black women's experience, poststructuralism was dismantling the authority of experience.

(2) While black feminist criticism was calling for non-hostile interpretations of black women's writing, poststructuralism was calling interpretation into question.

(3) While black feminist criticism required that these interpretations be grounded in historical context, deconstruction denied history any authoritative value or truth claims and read context as just another text.

(4) While the black woman as author was central to black feminist writers' efforts to construct a canon of new as well as unknown black women writers, poststructuralism had already rendered such efforts naïve by asking, post-Foucault, "What is an Author?" (1969) and trumpeting post-Barthes, "The Death of the Author" (1968). (*Changing Same*, 168)

McDowell is clear to note that her summary elides some convergences between black feminist criticism and poststructuralism. Still, her deliberately paired down sketch captures the tension (still present in today's academy) between intellectual projects that take race and coloniality as central to knowledge production, and those that don't. More than capture a tension or a failure of communication between competing knowledge paradigms, McDowell reminds us of the coloniality of the encounter. Here were two paradigms of critical thinking, each offering tools of analysis toward progressive criticism. Due to the coloniality of power, what we might also want to call a profound lack of attention to the geopolitics of knowledge, one body of knowledge was forced to dialogue with the other, was forced to translate and justify itself through the other's paradigms. The opposite was not true, and we are still dealing with the epistemic consequences of that profound lack of reciprocity today.

44. Mohanty, "Realist Theory," 97.

45. On the epistemological differences between realism and postmodernism, see Alcoff, *Visible Identities*, 71–81; Alcoff et al., *Identity Politics Reconsidered*, 98–100; Mohanty, *Literary Theory*, xi–xiii, 10–24, 129–31, 142–48, 202–9; Moya, *Learning*, 12–17, 27, 37–38, 61, 213–14; Moya and Hames-García, *Reclaiming Identity*, 57–58, 68–69, 115–18, 147–52, 322–25; Siebers, *Disability in Theory*, 82–83, 89–93, 126–27; Teuton, *Red Land*, 28–33, 86–88.

46. Chow, *Ethics After Idealism*, xxi; Champagne, *Ethics*, xxvi–xxvii.

47. Moya, *Learning*, 43.

48. Ibid., 38.

49. Colonialism and racism, for example, have historically distorted people of color (to themselves and to others), constructing them as incompetent or ugly, criminal or hypersexual. These constructions, still operative today, certainly influence the types of experiences people of color actually have and, as such, impact what people of color can known about the social world that others who are not similarly situated *might not know in the same way*.

50. Mohanty, *Literary Theory*, 213–15.

51. Ibid., 213.

52. According to Michael Hames-García, this question of the constraints that reality places on knowledge is not a question motivated by naive humanism or by unsophisticated empiricism, but more precisely motivated by a desire to develop a sophisticated account of social reference, one that "replaces the quest for direct, or *immediate*, knowledge with an acknowledgment that all knowledge is subject to influence, or *mediation*" (*Identity Complex*, 17). Hames-García goes on to explain: "If I have a theory that water boils at 100 degrees Celsius, I might attempt to verify that theory. If the water does not boil, something independent of my theory (for example, altitude) has acted on my experiment. I would therefore revise my theory to take altitude into account. If altitude were not a theory-independent *causal* feature of the world (something that acts on other things, causing observable effects), I could not be forced to revise my theory to improve its accuracy and reliability" (17). Hames-García reminds us that even though this is a "simplified example" of what realists mean by "gaining epistemic access to reality," similar processes and questions arise in theorizing reference to the seemingly more complex social phenomena of "identity" and "oppression." He goes on to provide another example:

Consider an intangible social force, like homophobia. I might sense that something acts on my life as I move through the world, but I cannot simply touch it and say, "This is homophobia." Rather, I must often infer its existence from cryptic comments by others, from hostile glances and words directed at my lovers and me as we hold hands in public, and so forth. (I am here leaving aside such tangible things as antigay legislation and physical violence.) Now, I could theorize that I am simply a paranoid person, distrustful of strangers. This theory of the world attempts to explain my experiences. However, another theory might claim that a social force called homophobia exists, so structuring my world as to bring about observable effects (glances and comments, as well as legislation and violence). Positing the existence of homophobia allows me to explain more reliably (and therefore, more accurately) my movement through the world and the kinds of responses I encounter. Importantly, it need not explain everything with complete certainty all the time in order to be a useful theory that refers to a real feature of the social world. (17)

Hames-García's realism, then, does not separate hard facts from the realm of ideology and values, since all knowledge is subject to causal constraints by the social and natural world.

CHAPTER I

1. In his book *The Ethics of Marginality*, John Champagne argues that people of color rely on unearned authority by white liberals to make claims about racism based on their experiences without being challenged as to their legitimacy (58–59). Champagne's argument is refuted by the African American performance studies scholar E. Patrick Johnson, who refers to Champagne's reading as a illustrative of the ways in which too many queer theorists "(mis)read" the lives and cultural production of queers of color in order to "minimize" their value ("'Quare,'" 131). For a critique of ethnocentrism in the work of Mary Daly, see Lorde's "Open Letter." While Champagne outwardly discredits queers of color drawing on experience and Daly chooses to remain silent about her ethnocentrism, other critics like Jane Gallop are accused of disingenuously performing hyperbolic feelings of inadequacy with regard to black feminist intellectuals, critiqued for making a mockery of genuine engagement with women of color. For an analysis of Jane Gallop's portrayal of black feminists as "monstrous" authorities (on questions of race) from which white feminists should seek approval, see duCille ("Occult of True Black Womanhood," 607–12). DuCille writes, "While she clearly desired McDowell's approval, like the white child who insults its mammy one moment and demands a hug from her the next, Gallop seemed to expect that approval without having to do the thing most like to win it: include McDowell and other black women scholars in the category of feminist theorists or treat black feminist critics as colleagues to be respected for the quality of their scholarship rather than as monsters to be feared for the quantity of their difference" (608–9).

2. Schueller, "Analogy," 64.

3. As described in the Introduction, antirealist schools of thought were first advanced and popularized in the late 1980s and 1990s by poststructuralist and postmodernist theory. Their most recognizable claims include, but are not limited to, the following: identities are fictions, normative claims are violent, linguistic reference is indeterminate, subjecthood is only and always a form of subjection, intelligibility (if desired) is a normative yearning to be recognized as a legitimate subject. Antirealist frameworks share a propensity for skepticism toward identity categories. They also endorse suspicion regarding the possibility of accurately referencing an objective reality.

4. Moya, *Learning*, 26.

5. Ibid., 26.

6. Stone-Mediatore, *Reading Across Borders*.

7. Halley, *Split Decisions*, 224. José Esteban Muñoz further reminds us that even in Scott's last attempt to reread Delany, an attempt that is meant to partly recant her previous interpretations, "she ultimately fails to comprehend [Delany's] project" (*Cruising*, 52).

8. Johnson, "'Quare.'"

9. Moya, *Learning*.

10. Here, Linda Martín Alcoff's observations regarding the unwitting similarities between classical liberalism and poststructuralism are pertinent. She notes, "Poststructuralism's negation of the authority of the subject . . . colludes with classical liberalism's view that human particularities are irrelevant. For liberalism, particularities are irrelevant because 'underneath we are all the same'; for the poststructuralist, race, class, and gender are all constructs and therefore incapable of decisively validating conceptions of justice and truth because underneath there is nothing—hence once again underneath we are all the same" (*Visible Identities*, 143).

11. Morrison, *Nobel Prize Lecture*, 7.

12. Ibid., 9–10.

13. Ibid., 10.
14. Ibid.
15. Ibid., 11.
16. Ibid., 12.
17. Ibid., 13.
18. Ibid., 14–18.
19. Ibid., 16–17.
20. Ibid., 22–23.
21. On "dialogic," see Bakhtin, *Dialogic Imagination*.
22. Morrison, *Nobel Prize Lecture*, 22.
23. Ibid., 19.
24. Ibid., 15.
25. My use of the term "indexical" is shorthand for "social reference," a concept more frequently used by literary theorists and philosophers, and one that I discuss further through the work of James Baldwin in Chapter 2.
26. Morrison, *Nobel Prize Lecture*, 27.
27. Ibid., 29.
28. Ibid., 30.
29. Butler, *Excitable Speech*, 1–41.
30. Ibid., 9.
31. Ibid., 1, 33.
32. Ibid., 9.
33. Morrison, *Nobel Prize Lecture*, 16.
34. Butler, *Excitable Speech*, 9; citations omitted.
35. Ibid., 9.
36. Ibid.
37. Quoted in Butler, *Excitable Speech*, 9.
38. Morrison, *Nobel Prize Lecture*, 12.
39. Ibid., 7.
40. To hear the recorded version, see http://nobelprize.org/nobel_prizes/literature/laureates/1993/morrison-lecture.html.
41. To speak of literature or literariness is, of course, a complicated venture. After all, literariness has less to do with an objective set of practices and more to do with institutional power to define certain conventions. Also, literariness can often be achieved through practices of reading rather than through the intentions and talents of an author. Finally, literariness comes into a definitional crisis of sorts, since all uses of language are constructed and rhetorical (making the province of the literary seem less specific and special).
42. See Chow's discussion of Karl Marx and Friedrich Engels (*Ethics After Idealism*, 174–75).
43. Ibid., 174.
44. Ibid., 175.
45. Morrison, *Nobel Prize Lecture*, 20–21.
46. Baldwin, *Price of the Ticket*, 238.
47. Morrison, *Nobel Prize Lecture*, 28.
48. Ibid., 16.
49. Ibid., 16–17.
50. Butler, *Excitable Speech*, 23.
51. INCITE! Women of Color against Violence and Critical Resistance, "Statement on

Gender Violence and the Prison Industrial Complex," 2001. http://www.incite-national.org/index.php?sp92.

52. Schwartzman, "Hate Speech."

53. Ibid., 429.

54. "In order to characterize the total situation of the speech act, one would need to provide an account of exactly what conventions were invoked at the moment of utterance, as well as an account of the 'rituals' that were at work. Because conventions and rituals are not fixed, but must be repeated in time, Butler suggests that attempts to delineate this 'total speech situation' will always, in some ways, fail. She explains that there is simply 'no easy way to decide on how best to delimit that totality.' Thus, she concludes that Austin's demand that we must first delineate this total speech situation before we can know the force of an illocution is 'beset by a constitutive difficulty'" (Schwartzman, "Hate Speech," 429).

55. Ibid., 429.

56. Ibid., 430.

57. Ibid.

58. Ibid., 434, 432.

59. Ibid., 432.

60. Reflecting on Butler's *Bodies that Matter*, for example, Moya details the rhetorical process through which Cherríe Moraga's insights are distorted and, subsequently, found useful: "Butler extracts one sentence from Moraga, buries it in a footnote, and then misreads it in order to justify her own inability in that text to account for the complex interrelations that structure various forms of human identity" (Moya, *Learning*, 35). Moya goes on to note the shockingly acontextual character of the misreading: "To read Moraga the way Butler reads her is to ignore the italicized statement that immediately follows . . . as well as to ignore the statement that immediately follows that one" (*Learning*, 35). Moraga, as Moya notes, is not simply employed as instrumental proof of Butler's ideas, but in fact Moraga and her ideas need to first be distorted (in fact, parts of her writing must actually be ignored) in order to function in this manner—the distortion and instrumentality coming together to form a disturbing portrait, much like that of Butler's use of Morrison, of the strategic and perfunctory presence of writers of color in postmodernist feminist theory.

61. Morrison, *Nobel Prize Lecture*, 22.

CHAPTER 2

1. Set primarily in New York City, *Another Country* follows the racially strained and sexually intertwined lives of a group of bohemian artists. Early in the novel, one of them—Rufus, an African American jazz drummer with an ambiguous sexual orientation—unexpectedly commits suicide, initiating a crisis among those who surround him. After Rufus's death, his sister, Ida, begins a relationship with one of his closest friends, a struggling Italian American writer named Vivaldo. Ida loves Vivaldo but resents his privileges and holds him responsible for Rufus's untimely death. Vivaldo loves Ida but is encumbered by his own identity and haunted by a fear that he could have done more to save Rufus. Toward the end of the novel, Vivaldo has a soul-searching sexual encounter with Eric, another member of this group of friends. Eric is an actor recently returned from France and one of Rufus's former lovers. These relationships, in turn, are entangled with those of other characters in the circle of friends, and the racial and sexual tensions remain unresolved at the novel's foreboding end.

2. See, for example, Bone, "Novels," 236; Cleaver, "Notes," 122–37; Kazin, *Bright Book*, 223–24; Hyman, *Standards*, 27. For a summary of critical responses to *Another Country*, see Cohen, "Liberalism," 201–22.

3. On this tendency, see Ohi, "'I'm Not the Boy,'" 261–81.

4. Baldwin's commitment to documenting the contradictions of living in an age of heightened social unrest and racial conflict is one reason critics experience difficulty reading him. However, Baldwin was also subject to pressures that necessarily impacted his writing and ideas. For biographical details regarding Baldwin's own formative existential crisis during the writing of *Another Country*, see Campbell, *Talking*, 128–32; Kenan, *James Baldwin*; Baldwin, "Art," 51. For an analysis of Baldwin's seemingly wavering public support of sexual identity politics, see McBride ("Can the Queen Speak?", 363–79), on the pressures of being a racial spokesperson. For an analysis of the anticommunist climate that saturated public discourse and impacted Baldwin's writing, see Corber, *Homosexuality*, 160–90; Murphy, "Subversive Anti-Stalinism," 1021–46.

5. For other readings of suicide, see Cleaver, "Notes," 122–37; Fryer, "Retreat," 21–28; Ohi, "'I'm Not the Boy,'" 261–81; Ross, "White Fantasies," 13–55; Rowden, "Play of Abstractions," 41–50; Ryan, "Falling," 95–119.

6. For a discussion of incoherence and white liberalism, see Baldwin, "White Man's Guilt," 409–14; Aanerud, "Now More than Ever," 64–65.

7. My argument recalls two recent studies of death and black identity. Its resemblances to Abdul JanMohamed's *The Death-Bound Subject* have less to do with his insightful theorization of the "imminent threat of death" that encompasses black subjectivity than with the attention JanMohamed gives to how black subjects "might 'free' themselves by overcoming their fear of death and redeploying it as a ground for their struggle" (291–300). My argument shares with Sharon Holland's *Raising the Dead* a cautionary approach to the ostensibly liberating process of ending certain pernicious identities and assimilating "better" ones (124–48).

8. This understanding of Baldwin on identity differs from the early 1990s work of Henry Louis Gates Jr. and William Cohen. As Robert Corber notes, Gates and Cohen mistakenly interpret Baldwin's distress over the narrowly defined identity categories available in his lifetime "as evidence that he thought the classification of individuals by their race, class, gender, and sexuality was [in and of itself] dehumanizing" ("Everybody," 167).

9. For a discussion of realism, see my Introduction and Chapter 1.

10. Baldwin's novel may be an important mediating text for scholars like LaCapra ("Identity and Experience," 228–45) and Saldívar ("Multicultural Politics," 849–54), who, although largely in agreement with realists, feel that experience and identity are more illusive than realists have so far theorized.

11. The epigraph to *Another Country* emphasizes the conceptual centrality of confusion: "They strike one, above all, as giving no account of themselves in any terms already consecrated by human use; to this inarticulate state they probably form, collectively, the most unprecedented of monuments; abysmal the mystery of what they think, what they feel, what they want, what they suppose themselves to be saying."

12. Babbitt, "Moral Risk," 235–54; Mohanty, *Literary Theory*, 198–254.

13. Baldwin, *Another Country*, 344.

14. Ibid., 347.

15. Susan Feldman writes, "The conventional approach among scholars has been to read Baldwin's treatment of love and sexuality as evidence of the novelist's faith in the promise of liberal individualism, and to thus maintain that in Baldwin's fiction the sexual and the political, the private and the public, are bipolar opposites" ("Another Look at *Another Country*," 101).

16. This emphasis on adjudication and the epistemic value of identity is based on a corollary claim that identities have the power to motivate or impinge on resistance to oppressive networks of power. "Some identities," writes Moya, "because they can more ad-

equately account for the social categories constituting an individual's social location, have greater epistemic value than some others that the same individual might claim" (*Learning*, 85).

17. Babbitt, "Moral Risk," 236–42.
18. Baldwin, *Another Country*, 6.
19. Ibid., 12.
20. Ibid., 20.
21. Ibid., 5.
22. Ibid.
23. Ibid., 10.
24. Ibid., 52.
25. Ibid., 29.
26. Ibid., 30.
27. Ibid.
28. Ibid.
29. Ibid., 32.
30. Ibid., 32–33.
31. When Ida angrily communicates to Cass the difference that racial identities make to how one perceives and is perceived in the world, she offers us insight into the complexity of taking responsibility for one's identity in oppressive contexts: "You don't know, and there's no way in the world for you to find out, what it's like to be a black girl in this world, and the way white men, and black men, too, baby, treat you. You've never decided that the whole world was just one big whorehouse and so the only way for you to make it was to decide to be the biggest, coolest, hardest whore around, and make the world pay you back that way" (347).
32. Baldwin, *Another Country*, 3.
33. Ibid., 211.
34. Ibid., 43.
35. Ibid., 42.
36. Ibid., 41.
37. Online *Oxford English Dictionary*.
38. Ibid.
39. Ibid.
40. A further investigation into the misogyny of the novel would need to account for two very important scenarios—Rufus's violent sexual relationship with Leona and Yves's (Eric's boyfriend) hatred of his female patrons (209–10). These two disturbing moments suggest how anger arising from racism and homophobia manifests itself as misogyny.
41. For more on the "geographic discontinuities" of queers of color, see Lugones (*Pilgrimages*, 167–80).
42. For a discussion of misogyny and sexual identity in *Another Country*, see Toombs ("Black-Gay-Man Chaos," 105–27).
43. "The chronotope is where the knots of narrative are tied and untied. . . . Time becomes, in effect, palpable and visible; the chronotope makes narrative events concrete, makes them take on flesh, causes blood to flow in their veins. . . . Thus the chronotope, functioning as the primary means for materializing time in space, emerges as a center for concretizing representation, as a force giving body to the entire novel" (Bakhtin, *Dialogic Imagination*, 250).
44. See Chapter 3, "Queer Migrant Labor" for a more detailed discussion of queer migration.

45. Baldwin, *Another Country*, 11.
46. For a critique of "cultural" explanations for gay Chicano men, see Cantú, "Entre Hombres/Between Men," 147–67.
47. Babbitt, "Feminism."
48. Rufus rapes Leona on a balcony during a cocktail party, on the first night that they meet: "He wanted her to remember him the longest day she lived. And, shortly, nothing could have stopped him, not the white God himself nor a lynch mob arriving on wings. Under his breath he cursed the milk-white bitch and groaned and rode his weapon between her thighs. She began to cry. *I told you*, he moaned, *I'd give you something to cry about*, and, at once, he felt himself strangling, about to explode or die. A moan and a curse tore through him while he beat her with all the strength he had and felt the venom shoot out of him, enough or a hundred black-white babies" (22).
49. Baldwin, *Another Country*, 193–94.
50. In this respect, Ida and Cass are seemingly counterexamples, as they both risk a great deal when they confess to having sexual affairs with other men. Nothing about this process is easy for them. Indeed, they suffer a great deal as a consequence of their confessions. Still, Baldwin seems to be making an interesting observation about gender, and gendered scripts, that helps us to understand that the reason for the difference between how the men and women in his novel deal with sexual affairs is not, strictly speaking, about the ability to take responsibility, but more to do with how different groups are taught to value different forms of disclosure and communication.
51. Baldwin, *Another Country*, 263. Ohi writes, "*Another Country* speaks repeatedly of 'revelation' and of the revelation of secrets, but the content of the secrets revealed is nowhere specified; the secret seems to occupy a purely structural place in the novel" ("'I'm Not the Boy,'" 264).
52. Baldwin, *Another Country*, 264.
53. Ibid., 683.
54. Ibid., 210–11.
55. Baldwin, "Notes," 238.
56. Baldwin, *Another Country*, 335.
57. Ibid., 336.
58. Ibid.
59. Babbitt, "Feminism," 254.
60. Baldwin, *Another Country*, 337.
61. Ibid.
62. Ibid., 301–3.
63. Ibid., 302.
64. McNay writes, "If, following Michel Foucault, the process of subjectification is understood as a dialectic of freedom and constraint—'the subject is constituted through practices of subjection, or, in a more autonomous way, through practices of liberation, of liberty'—then it is the negative moment of subjection that has been accorded theoretical privilege in much work on identity construction" (*Gender and Agency*, 2–3).
65. On epistemological denial, see Alcoff, "Politics," 5–27; Moya, *Learning*, 84–85; Roof, "Lesbians and Lyotard," 59; Creech, *Closet Writing*, 13; Mohanty, *Literary Theory*, 10–18.
66. Mohanty, "Dynamics," 233–34; see also Mohanty, *Literary Theory*, 198–253; and Mohanty, "Can Our Values?"
67. Mohanty, "Dynamics," 231.
68. Mohanty, *Literary Theory*, 2.

69. These questions are raised in the work of the realist theorists Hames-García, Mohanty, and Moya. While not the first to seek answers for these questions, these scholars are unique in their collective attempt to make this line of inquiry speak to the theoretical weaknesses of some of the most referenced and theoretically dominant approaches in literary and cultural criticism.

70. For realist accounts of representation, see, among others, Alcoff, "Problem," 5–32; Hames-García, "Which America?" 19–53; Hau, "On Representing Others," 133–204; Mohanty, *Literary Theory*, 198–253; Moya, *Learning*, 23–57.

71. Babbitt, "Moral Risk," 240.

72. Baldwin, "No Name," 386.

CHAPTER 3

1. For more on "queer migration" and "queer diaspora," see Luibheid and Cantú, *Queer Migrations*; and Luibheid, *Queer/Migration*; Patton and Sánchez-Eppler, *Queer Diasporas*; Cant, "Introduction," 1–28; Eng, *Racial Castration*, 204–28; Fortier, "'Coming Home,'" 405–24; Gorman-Murray, "Rethinking Queer Migration," 105–21; Puar, "Queer Tourism."

2. Gorman-Murray, "Rethinking Queer Migration," 105–21.

3. Fortier, *Queer Diaspora*, 183–98; Massad, *Desiring Arabs*, 160–90.

4. Queer exodus—that is, queer banishment or flight from "home"—is one way of capturing the implicit logic in studies of rural to urban migration among LGBTQ communities. There have been many critiques of this logic, as well as many studies that implicitly rely on it as a tool of analysis. For more on queer exodus, rural-to-urban migrations, and their broader significance to twentieth-century queer social formations and identity politics, see Brown, *Space*; Cant, "Introduction"; Chauncey, *Gay New York*; D'Emilio, "Capitalism"; Gorman-Murray, "Rethinking Queer Migration"; Gray, *Out in the Country*; Herring, *Another Country*; La Fountain-Stokes, "Gay Shame"; Patton and Sánchez-Eppler, *Queer Diasporas*; Preston, *Hometowns*; Weston, *Families We Choose*.

5. Anzaldúa, *Borderlands*, 44.

6. Ibid., 43.

7. Anzaldúa draws on the emblematic Aztec serpent goddess of creation, Coatlicue, in order to theorize the queer mestiza's self-assessment in a decolonial vein, as serpentine movement that makes possible an alternative cosmology and political landscape, one through which the queer mestiza moves, creating a new sense of introspection through distance:

Every time she makes "sense" of something, she has to "crossover," kicking a hole out of the old boundaries of the self and slipping under or over, dragging the old skin along, stumbling over it. . . . It is only when she is on the other side and the shell cracks open and the lid from her eyes lifts that she sees things in a different perspective. It is only then that she makes the connections, formulates the insights. (*Borderlands*, 49)

As this passage suggests, making "sense" for the queer mestiza is a decolonizing effort that involves, in some form or another, distance ("crossing over"), metamorphosis (a shedding of skin), and a remapping of older boundaries. In hopes of making sense of her social world and circumstances, the queer mestiza must first distance herself from those ideological frameworks that mark that process as impossible, so that, in the course of making sense for herself in this new cognitive territory, she may continue problematizing her subject position and questioning herself in those places that she sometimes learns to inhabit complacently. It is in this decolonizing act of critical movement that the queer mestiza enacts, not so much a "truer" self or a "liberated" consciousness, but a resistant practice—a process, to be more exact, that is gradual, transformational, but not teleological, one where "her consciousness expands a tiny notch, another rattle appears on the rattlesnake's tale, and the added growth slightly alters the sounds she makes" (*Borderlands*, 49).

8. Danielson, *Homecoming*, 4.

9. Esquibel writes, "Lacking historical proof of Chicana lesbian existence, Chicana writers have created one, indeed, created many, through . . . [images of] women in the histories of conquest . . . , [like] La Llorona and the Aztec Princess . . . , [and through] narrative strategies that create Chicana lesbian histories in colonial New Spain, in the rural Southwest, and in the coming-of-age story (*With Her Machete*, 6).

10. See Decena, *Tacit Subjects*; Romero, "When Something Goes Queer"; Lugones, *Pilgrimages*; Gopinath, *Impossible Desires;* La Fountain-Stokes, "Gay Shame."

11. Gopinath, *Impossible Desires*, 15.

12. Ibid.

13. My argument, here, shares a great deal of resonance with two recent twenty-first-century studies in Chicana/o literature and cultural studies: Mary Pat Brady's *Extinct Lands, Temporal Geographies* and Raúl Homero Villa's *Barrio-Logos*. What these two studies share in common is not simply an attentiveness to spatial analysis in Chicana/o cultural production, but an enhanced awareness—a historicization and theorization—of how such spatialized insight is cultivated as Chicana/o subjects are living out their lives in resistance to colonialism and capitalism, heteronormativity and racist structures of power. Brady makes the point explicitly when she writes, "Chicana/os have been considering space, taking it seriously, not simply as something to produce, but as something to understand, since, as it were, our inception. The turn by Chicanas to space can be traced to any number of causes beyond individual writers' critical acumen and skills of observation. As Norma Alarcón reminds us, 'displacement and dislocation are at the core of the invention the Americas'. . . . In this sense, the colonization process, an obviously spatial process, has had ongoing ramifications, and Chicano/as have felt and observed them to this day" (*Extinct Lands*, 9).

14. Echoing her migratory inclinations a decade after the writing of *Loving in the War Years*, Cherríe Moraga writes in *Waiting in the Wings: A Portrait of a Queer Motherhood*: "Although I did not keep my sexuality secret from the closest members of my family, I knew it could never be fully expressed there. So, the search for a *we* that could embrace all the parts of myself took me far beyond the confines of heterosexual family ties. I soon found myself spinning outside the orbit of that familial embrace, separated by thousands of miles of geography and experience" (18).

15. Moraga, *Loving*, x.

16. Moraga's statement, which associates better knowledge with distance and estrangement, is strikingly similar to what Anzaldúa articulates in *Borderlands/La Frontera* ("I had to leave home so I could find myself" [x]) as well as what Juanita Díaz (who published this work using the pseudonym Juanita Ramos) argues in her introduction to *Compañeras*, one of the first Latina Lesbian anthologies ("On the whole, to be a lesbian we have to leave the fold of our family, and seek support within the mainstream white lesbian community" [x]).

17. Romero, "When Something Goes," 127.

18. Ibid., 129.

19. Ibid., 136.

20. Moraga, *Loving*, 122.

21. See "Introducción" and "Voices of the Fallers," in *Loving* (i–1). Also, see Yvonne Yarbro-Bejarano's essay "De-constructing the Lesbian Body," for a description of how bodily

dismemberment plays a role in other works by Moraga, such as *The Shadow of Man* and *Heroes and Saints*.

22. Moraga, *Loving*, ii.

23. Ibid.

24. See "A Long Line of Vendidas," in *Loving* for a critique of those social networks of power in Chicana/o communities that demand the invisibility, loyalty, and sexual silence of its women. In this essay, Moraga offers a critique of these cultural "standards," while still maintaining a strong commitment to a revised Chicana/o political agenda.

25. In *Loving*, Moraga's empathy extends to individuals who have either physically or psychologically lost part or all of themselves. A brief list of these occasions includes "Introducción" (iv), "Voice of the Fallers" (1), "La Güera" (52–59), "What Does it Take" (65), "You Call It, AMPUTATION" (82), "For Amber" (83), and "Traitor Begets Traitor" (98).

26. Moraga, *Last Generation*, 41.

27. While Lugones agrees that movement toward the queer bar scene is a partial departure from the Latina/o community (latent with epistemic consequences) and full of potential for the development of strategic resistance, her vision in "Enticements and Dangers of Community and Home for a Radical Politics" is to propose a break with the logic that situates Latina/o communities as politically stagnant and never changing.

28. "Cachapera" and "tortillera" are names some Latina/o communities use to reference queer Latinas, often in a derogatory manner. They are also terms of self-reference that have been reclaimed by queer Latinas/os.

29. Lugones, *Pilgrimages*, 174.

30. Ibid., 174.

31. Moraga, *Last Generation*, 7.

32. Moraga, *Hungry Woman*, 46.

33. Lugones, *Pilgrimages*, 173.

34. Ibid., 172.

35. The work of Michael Warner in *The Trouble with Normal* is useful here in further understanding the importance of alternative social relations. As a challenge to sexual normativity in US culture, Warner argues for the nurturing of sexual diversity through an emphasis on sexual autonomy. By sexual autonomy Warner means not simply the ability of individuals to experience "freedom of choice, tolerance, and the liberalization of sex laws," but more importantly the ability of cultures to nurture and create access to "pleasures and possibilities, since people commonly do not know their desires until they find them" (*Trouble with Normal*, 7). Warner's emphasis, then, is on the crucial importance of nurturing activities, practices, sensibilities whereby sexualities are practiced, learned, and experimented with.

36. Babbitt, "Feminism," 247.

37. Ibid., 251.

38. Ibid., 249.

39. Ibid., 247.

40. Ibid., 250.

41. Ibid., 255.

42. Lugones, *Pilgrimages*, 185.

43. Scholarship in the social sciences suggests that migration away from family and nation for gay Latino men specifically has not always proven beneficial psychologically or emotionally. In his study of US gay Latino culture and sexuality, *Latino Gay Men and HIV*, social scientist Rafael Díaz finds that many of the queer Latino immigrants to the United States that he interviewed still exhibited a strong sense of internalized homophobia even

after relocation. "Once in the U.S.," Díaz writes, "they may remain in the closet with co-workers and friends, see the gay community as 'them,' and still live their sexual lives in the context of silent, anonymous encounters" (*Latino Gay Men,* 103). Terming it the "geographic pseudo-cure," Díaz concludes migration to the United States has failed to prove an adequate vehicle, in and of itself, for psychological change in queer Latino immigrants. Diaz's work further suggests that even "acculturated" gay Latinos, men whom he describes as "highly identified with and integrated to the non-Hispanic White gay culture," experience exodus as a pseudo-cure. He writes, "Many Latino gay men may be quite competent in dealing and functioning within the mainstream gay culture, but affectively and emotionally they feel quite disconnected and ill-at-ease within it for a number of different reasons, ranging from non-standard physical appearance to institutionalized class and race discrimination practices" (*Latino Gay Men,* 131).

44. Critics of the film, like Larry La Fountain-Stokes, have cautioned that its representational politics merit further scrutiny, not the least because expulsion narratives have been sensationalized through misleading "stereotypes of working-class intolerance" ("Gay Shame," 104).

45. Morgan, "Pages of Whiteness," 280.

46. Negrón-Muntaner, in *Brincando el Charco,* is not, by any means, articulating through her film some archaic phobia about interracial desire. In fact, through the brief portrayal of two of Claudia's friends (one Korean American and the other black) the film humorously suggests that interracial desire does not have to evacuate political interrogation.

47. Lugones, *Pilgrimages,* 175.

48. Ibid., 77–102.

49. Cuadros, *City of God,* 56.

50. Ibid., 58.

51. Villa, *Barrio-Logos,* 139–41.

52. Ibid., 139–40.

53. For a realist theory of emotions and knowledge, see Mohanty, *Literary Theory,* 206–11, 216–29, 236–39.

54. Moraga, *Loving,* 54–55.

55. Alcoff, "Politics," 17.

56. Anzaldúa, "La Herencia Coatlicue," 66.

57. See Anzaldúa's short story entitled "La historia de una marimacho," in *Sexuality of Latinas,* 64–68.

58. See Alarcon, "Chicana Feminism."

59. Anzaldúa, *Borderlands,* 43.

60. Ibid.

61. Moraga, *Loving,* 125.

62. Ibid., 126.

63. Anzaldúa, *Borderlands,* 16.

64. Ibid., 88.

65. Ibid.

66. Ibid., 89.

67. Ibid., 82.

68. Ibid., 91.

69. Moraga, *Loving,* 82.

70. Lugones, *Pilgrimages,* 178.

71. Ibid., 171.

72. Lugones describes Latina Lesbian activism outside of communities of origin in the following manner: "*Busy, together, articulate, proud, flamboyant, Latina emphasized in the tone, the style, the direction of the Lesbian politics. Brazen, self-confident, radical. Influential in the movement, quick to point out the racism, the ethnocentrism, the classism. Fun, intense, warm, no nonsense, fiery, red hot angry presence among lesbians. Planning and risking. Way out,* bien asumida, en la sociedad grande, *far away from the barrio*" (*Pilgrimages*, 172; emphasis added).

73. Ibid., 186.

74. Ibid., 185–86.

75. Moraga, *Loving*, 126.

76. Ibid., 137.

77. Ibid., 126.

78. Ibid., 195.

79. Elaborating on this thesis through the work of Cherríe Moraga, Mary Pat Brady writes, "Moraga's turn to Aztlán brings into focus Chicano nationalism's alternative cartographic practice. . . . For Moraga, however, the turn to Aztlán clearly does not just function as yet another iteration of alternative cartographies. Instead, Moraga actively suggests an anticartography—one that does not conceive of space as a thing to be possessed or a set of rationalized relations to be mapped. Moraga offers a different concept of spatiality, in which land and bodies blend in both metaphysical and real senses, in which perception and living cannot be distinguished so easily" (*Extinct Lands*, 139).

80. J. Muñoz, *Disidentifications*, 11–12.

81. Ibid., 162.

82. Cited in ibid., 14.

83. "Cholo/Salvatrucho" was first published in the National Association for Chicana and Chicano Studies Proceedings for 1996, in an issue dedicated to the analyses of intersectionality and multiple oppressions. See Roque-Ramírez, *Mapping Strategies*.

84. Roque-Ramírez, "Cholo/Salvatrucho," 198–99.

85. Ibid., 199.

86. Ibid.

87. Ibid., 200.

88. Ibid.

89. Horacio Roque-Ramírez, through his creative work and historical scholarship, frequently reflects on queer Latino identity and space. For instance, in his short story "El Sereno," Roque-Ramírez elaborates on horizontal visibility and sociality among closeted queer Latinos well before they adopt, or are labeled in relationship to, a homosexual identity. In "El Sereno," the young narrator and his best friend George are visible (in their queer schoolground rompings) to some of their queer teachers at the middle school. Ms. Guzman "an obviously lesbian P.E. teacher" is described as "peeking at the not-so-obvious lovers' private time together" ("Cholo/Salvatrucho," 9). Mr. Miranda, the Argentinean homeroom teacher, also takes note of them: "He knew you'd assigned yourself the task of giving me campus tours during second period, but smirked and lifted his thick eyebrows when he saw you standing too close to me, leading me out of the classroom, grabbing my hand firmly. . . . I'm sure he wanted to know more about us" ("Cholo/Salvatrucho," 7). The pressures of remaining closeted perhaps restricts the teachers and the students from becoming role models and a community of support for each other, but this does not stop the two young boys from manipulating their circumstances to achieve a sociality—a familiarity with community codes of male conduct that allows for the expression of self. For the two boys who are exploring their sexuality, it is the taking up of "rough housing" with each other that allows them a moment of public privacy.

"I knew that you wanted to play too," the narrator writes, "that those painful two-seconds-too-long bear hugs you gave me let your sweet sweat mix on purpose with mine. Both of our bodies in quick friction with just enough force to bring that nice pain; I just knew you were smiling. I'd always break out in sweat from being too close to him in public" ("Cholo/Salvatrucho," 9). For more on Roque-Ramírez's scholarly work on queer Latino culture and space, see "'That's *My* Place': Negotiating Racial, Sexual, and Gender Politics in San Francisco's Gay Latino Alliance, 1975–1983."

CHAPTER 4

1. The Chicana feminist critic Yvonne Yarbro-Bejarano succinctly describes the impact of this practice when she reflects on the work of Cherríe Moraga that it "enacts an impossible scenario: to give voice and visibility to that which has been erased and silenced" (*Wounded Heart*, 3). We should be careful to note, along the lines of what Ramón Saldívar has argued about Chicano narrative, that giving "voice and visibility" is not always a desire to "simply illustrate, represent, or translate a particular exotic reality," but that it can be an intervention of a less essentialist order, working to "shape modes of perception in order to effect new ways of interpreting social reality and to produce in turn a general . . . revaluation of values" (*Chicano Narrative*, 6–7). Karen Christian echoes and extends Saldívar's and Yarbro-Bejarano's reflections when she writes that gay and lesbian Chicano/a writers intervene culturally and politically by narrating "subject positions that operate as counternarratives to essentialist gender norms" (*Show and Tell*, 25). Christian argues that this body of work challenges the homophobic and misogynist "unintelligibility" often ascribed to gays and lesbians by actively representing the seemingly unrepresentable, that is, by representing homosexuality in its "multifaceted and ever-changing character" (27–31).

2. Leyva, "Listening."

3. As Paula Moya has noted, examples of this modern concept of agency are evident in the way the minority neocons Shelby Steele, Richard Rodriguez, and Linda Chávez promote "individual" success and "individual" agency against the collective problems faced by minority groups in the United States. For more details of this discussion, see Moya, "Cultural Particularity vs. Universal Humanity."

4. Lugones writes:

All one has to do is try to move with people against oppression, to understand oneself as not able to intend in this sense. What I am proposing is a viable sense of intentionality for moving against the interlocking of oppressions that animates oppressions as intermeshed. As I unveil the collectivity backing up the individual, I am pointing not just to the illusory quality of the individual, but to the need of an alternative sociality for resistant intentionality. Intending may "feel" as arising in a subject, but surely the production of intentions is itself a haphazard and dispersed social production. Subjects participate in intending, but intentions acquire life to the extent that they exist between subjects. (*Pilgrimages*, 216–17)

5. Lugones writes, "The understanding of agency that I propose, which I call 'active subjectivity' and which I contrast with the influential understanding of agency of late modernity, is highly attenuated. It does not presuppose the individual subject and it does not presuppose collective intentionality of collectives of the same. It is adumbrated to consciousness by a moving with people, by the difficulties as well as the concrete possibilities of such movings. It is a sense of intentionality that we can reinforce and sense as lively in paying attention to people and to the enormously variegated ways of connection among people without privileging the word or a monological understanding of sense" (*Pilgrimages*, 6).

6. Gerard Genette's distinction in *Narrative Discourse* between heterodiegetic and homodiegetic narratives is useful for the theoretical argument I am developing about the narrative situations in Muñoz's short stories. I do not use the terminology *third-person narration* for the reasons that the narratologist Mieke Bal offers: "By definition, a 'third-person' narrator does not exist: any time there is narrating, there is a narrating subject, one that to all intents and purposes is always in the 'first person.' The 'person' of the narrator . . . can be distinguished only in terms of his presence or absence in the narrative at the level in question" ("Narrating," 237).

7. Consider, as a contrasting example, Achy Obejas's novel *Memory Mambo*. Written from the perspective of a Latina lesbian, it conveys an intimate first-person account of queer Latina experience. However, because of this first-person narrative structure, it is restricted in the type of information it can provide, especially as it pertains to foregrounding of queer experience as shared and social.

8. Consider, as just one other example, Achy Obejas's short story, "Above All, a Family Man," which is written from the first-person perspective of a white man living with AIDS, about his relationship with a married, heterosexually identified Latino man. This *homodiegetic* narrative explores queer experience at a highly self-conscious and explicit level. It feels appropriate as a narrative strategy to have the white man speak in the first person, given that the white man speaking has an unproblematized sense of self and a fetishistic relationship with Rogelio's racialized sexuality in the United States. Furthermore by narrating this story in the first person and from the perspective of the white man, his Latino lover remains an enigma (what Rogelio feels and thinks cannot be foregrounded), and hence he becomes reified as the impenetrable Latino man.

9. M. Muñoz, *Zigzagger*, 126.

10. Ibid. I think this is an important point to emphasize, particularly because the narrative also provides a sense of Vero as someone who has always taken care of her little brother. We see this in scenes where she remembers childhood car trips with her family. She remembers Nicky fearlessly peering out of a moving car window, over a ravine, and she remembers instinctively locking the car door for safety—all of this happening without the parents knowing or sharing any of her anxiety about her brother's safety.

11. "To witness faithfully," María Lugones writes, is to witness "against the grain of power, on the side of resistance. To witness faithfully, one must be able to sense resistance, to interpret behavior as resistant even when it is dangerous, when that interpretation places one psychologically against common sense, or when one is moved to act in collision with common sense, with oppression" (*Pilgrimages*, 7).

12. M. Muñoz, *Zigzagger*, 141.

13. Vero is particularly conflicted about her brother's gender nonconformity. The way that Nicky chooses to inhabit his body, effeminately, bothers her ("She hates to see his hand extended out like that, his exaggerations, his boldness at sixteen" [122]). She often scolds him for acting effeminately in public and is concerned that he has developed friendships with other effeminate boys. At the same time she is very attentive to her younger brother and more frequently than not restrains herself when she thinks she should chastise him. She marks the moment when she started to feel this *ethical* self-restraint as being coterminous with the day her brother was assaulted—the day so much was articulated and so much was left unspoken.

14. "Vero remembers how Julián came on the inside of her thigh: he pushed at her so he could rub himself clean on her skin. . . . Sometimes she can't help thinking about what Julián and her younger brother did at the drive-in. She is ashamed to think of Julián com-

ing on the inside of her younger brother's thigh. She is embarrassed to think of one, then two fingers" (M. Muñoz, *Zigzagger*, 150).

15. "She tells herself that she is doing the right thing, that she can ignore her own humiliation at having her younger brother carry on like this with someone she had known so intimately. She tells herself that she is stronger, that ultimately she has more options than someone like Nicky will ever have in a place like this" (M. Muñoz, *Zigzagger*, 144–45).

16. M. Muñoz, *Zigzagger*, 122–23.

17. Ibid., 123.

18. Ibid., 123–24; emphasis added.

19. That the narrative refers to the queer subject's parents as "the man" and "the wife" further emphasizes the patriarchal imaginary that so fundamentally constitutes life in this small town. More important, however, this ascription gestures toward a *generalizability* of this particular story to other contexts. In other words what transpires is being gestured toward as fundamentally relevant to various other situations and circumstances, particularly as married men and women indiscriminately adopt and internalize rigid heteronormative ways of being that truncate their interpretive horizons.

20. M. Muñoz, *Zigzagger*, 39, 40.

21. Ibid., 41.

22. Foucault, "Of Other Spaces," 181.

23. M. Muñoz, *Zigzagger*, 17.

24. Arturo Islas's protagonist in *The Rain God*, Miguel Chico, is similarly situated within a community stifled by religious dogma. In such a context his nascent desire to rebel against cultural mores becomes manifest in his interest in hearing stories describing "Satan's pride."

25. M. Muñoz, *Zigzagger*, 18.

26. Ibid., 6, 7.

27. Through various other narrative perspectives we also come to understand the role that secrecy plays for the young man, as well as for his mother. Unlike the secrecy in "The Unimportant Lila Parr," the secrecy in this story is given a more tangible presence in being acknowledged by the mother as something to self-consciously maintain. Toward the end of the story the mother makes every attempt to keep her son from naming what has transpired, and this need to reproduce silence around taboo subjects is made evident as an extension of her desire to keep quiet about certain aspects of her own life: "The mother sees him, the look in his eye, and she wants to say nothing at all. She believes, as she always has, that talking aloud brings moments to light, and she has refused to speak of her mother's death, of her husband's cheating, of the hatred of her brothers and sisters. She sees her son at the doorway and wants to tell him not to speak" (M. Muñoz, *Zigzagger*, 18).

28. Two of Baldwin's novels, *Another Country* and *Just Above My Head*, are powerful examples of early experimentations with shifting the site of queer enunciation. These two novels begin in the most provocative of manners, by killing off the queer protagonist and leaving the rest of the characters to make sense of it all.

29. La Fountain-Stokes, *Queer Ricans*, 2.

30. As a way to problematize the generally positive connotation I have been attributing to this tradition, we could also include the controversial short story "Whose Song?" by the Jamaican American writer Thomas Glave. There the shift in queer enunciation occurs as readers inhabit the perspectives of three young men who rape a young black lesbian. The entire perspectival shift is disturbing, but what is gained in the process is an intimately disturbing understanding of how violence against women, and women of color in particular, functions symbolically for some of the young men as their own (dis)avowal of their homo-

sexual and racial fantasies. Here it might prove useful to ask ourselves, if in fact something of political and emotional importance is gained in the process of shifting from the perspective of the young woman to the perspective of the men who rape her, what if anything is lost? What type of violence is redone by inhabiting this perspective? An interesting contrast to Glave's narrative approach would be Junot Díaz's short story "Drown." In that story a young, heterosexually identified man recalls his close friendship with a young queer man. Importantly, the narrative perspective fostered in this story allows readers to see firsthand the negotiations of masculinity and social class that eventually fracture their close bond of friendship and camaraderie. The narrator in Díaz's "Drown," in contrast to the narrative perspectives in Glave's story, bears a certain kind of witness to the homophobia that so permeates relationships between young men. In his own way the narrator takes some responsibility for the ideological investments in class and masculinity that often get in the way of true affection, queer desire, and solidarity between men.

31. McKoy, "Rescuing," 18.
32. Ibid., 20.
33. Holland, *Raising the Dead*, 114.
34. Kenan, *Visitation*, 57.
35. Ibid., 60–61.
36. Ibid., 56.
37. Ibid., 63.

CHAPTER 5

1. Cho is a well-known advocate for the gay and lesbian community. Her performance material not only draws on gays and lesbians for inspiration, but her advocacy and activism has often centered on gay and lesbian civil rights. In 2000, she won the GLAAD award for "making a significant difference in promoting equal rights for all, regardless of sexual orientation or gender identity." In 2007, she performed in the True Colors Tour benefiting the Human Rights Campaign. In 2008, she hosted benefits like the "Equalipalooza" concert benefiting the campaign to defeat proposition 8 on the California ballot.

2. Cho speaks openly about her involvement in heterosexual and homosexual relationships, but in an interview for the *New York Times Magazine*, she clarifies: "I refer to myself as gay, but I am married to a man. Of course, I've had relationships with women, but my politics are more queer than my lifestyle" (Lewine, "Margaret Cho").

3. From the early comedy of Eddy Murphy to the contemporary stand-up comedy "mas puto" routines of George Lopez, homophobic jokes about effeminate men and same-sex desire have been central to articulating racialized masculinities on stage. See, for example, Johnson, *Appropriating Blackness*, 48–75.

4. For more on camp as a gay form, see Miller, "Sontag's Urbanity" (particularly his critique of Sontag's "Notes on Camp"); Newton, *Mother Camp*; Bergman, *Camp Grounds*; Bérubé, *Coming Out Under Fire*, 86–91; Altman, *Homosexualization of America*, 152–55.

5. Chauncey, *Gay New York*, 290.
6. Bergman, *Camp Grounds*, 9.
7. Robertson, *Guilty Pleasures*, 9.
8. Robertson, for example, points out the frequent analogies made between camp and blackness in critical discourse: "Denise Altman, for instance, says, 'Camp is to gay what soul is to black.' Describing post-Stonewall attitudes towards camp, Andrew Ross refers to camp falling into disrepute 'as a kind of black face,' and George Melly dubs camp 'the Stepin Fetchit of the leather bars, the Auntie Tom of the denim discos'" (20). Most impor-

tantly, Robertson notes that the "white feminist" camp tradition gains as much from black cultural references as it does from it's appropriation and engagement with gay male subculture: "Mae West and Madonna, for example, both foreground their affinity with African American culture as much as gay male culture. Similarly, as Patricia Juliana Smith argues, Dusty Springfield's camp masquerade simultaneously transforms her into a black woman and a femme gay man. . . . In a different vein, Joan Crawford's status as a grotesque is reaffirmed by her blackface performance in *Torch Song*" (20–21).

9. J. Muñoz, *Disidentifications*, 128.

10. "I never saw Asian people on television or in movies, so my dreams were somewhat limited. I would dream: 'maybe someday, I can be an extra on M.A.S.H. Maybe someday I could play Arnold's girlfriend on *Happy Days*. Maybe I can play a hooker in something.' I'd be looking in the mirror: 'Sucky-fucky –two-dollar. Me-love-you-long-time'" (*Notorious*).

11. "I met with an agent who told me that Asian people would never be successful in entertainment and that I should just quit and stop wasting my life. And I probably would have if it weren't for my two best friends from high school—Allen and Jeremy. And Allen and Jeremy were tough; they were teenage drag queens. You have to be tough to be a drag queen. Drag queens have to fight everything: they have to fight homophobia, they have to fight sexism, they have to fight pink eye. Allen and Jeremy would get in fights at school every day and they would kick ass. It was like crouching drag queen, hidden faggot."

12. In an essay theorizing multiculturalism in the United States, María Lugones and Joshua Price explain the dangers of ornamentalization, reminding us that the process of "accepting difference" can become an *expression* of domination, rather than resistance to it. They write, "It is one thing for a society to be multicultural in the sense of having restaurants that offer 'ethnic foods' or places for entertainment where the music, art, and literature of different cultures is showcased. In such a society people may appreciate these differences without being deeply affected by then. It is another thing for a society's institutions, such as its courts, the different organized ways of producing material life, the practices that comprise government, and the institutions of education, to be multicultural. In this latter case, society can be considered multicultural *structurally*. . . . Drawing the contrast between *structure* and *ornament* is central to the understanding of cultural domination. Ornamental cultural pluralism not only is compatible with cultural domination, but is its product" ("Dominant Culture," 103). Lugones and Price go on to explain, "As ornamental, non-dominant cultures are necessary to the perpetuation of the dominant culture in two ways. They lend the dominant culture a sense of its own importance and originality. Practitioners within the non-dominant culture who are reduced to ornaments are perceived as persons who use values and norms that are both socially irrelevant and exotic. . . . But at the same time as they are judged inferior, their presence is also socially valuable because it highlights the requirement to use a certain set of values, norms, and meanings in order to be accorded full agency, personhood, and interiority; that is, in order to be understood as a full subject. As lacking full personhood, agency, autonomy, and the ability to make judgments, they are justifiably devalued from the dominant culture's standpoint" ("Dominant Culture," 104).

13. For more on sexual-racial shame, see Lee's discussion of Cho and stand-up comedy, especially her discussion of John Limons, "'Where's My Parade?'", 110–13. Also see H. Perez, "You Can Have," 171–91; Halberstam, "Shame," 219–23; La Fountain-Stokes, "Gay Shame," 55–80; García, "Comment," 81–85.

14. J. Muñoz, *Disidentifications*, 11.

15. This understanding of "disidentification" and the "world-making" possibilities of performance art are key insights in the early work of Muñoz.

16. As noted by Robertson, "The fag hag stereotype presumes a failed object choice.... [T]he fag hag chooses gay men because she 'can't get a man' (she is stereotypically unattractive) and/or because she desires a man who doesn't want her (she is stereotypically secretly, desperately attracted to gay men)" (*Guilty Pleasures*, 8).

17. Lee, "'Where's My Parade?'", 117.

18. This claim of critiquing heterosexuality *from within* relies on the ways that Cho came across, early on in her career, as primarily heterosexual, rather than on her own self-understanding as queer (see Lewine, "Margaret Cho"). In *I'm the One,* Cho talks about same-sex experiences, but she never claims a lesbian or bisexual identity. She explains, "I went through this whole thing. Am I gay? Am I straight? And I realized I'm just slutty." Bacalzo notes, "While it's clear from the rest of *I'm the One that I Want* that Cho usually dates men, this early acknowledgment of an alternative to heterosexuality is important in the way Cho fashions her image" (44).

19. Lee, "'Where's My Parade?'", 122.

20. Bond Stockton, *Beautiful Bottom*, 5.

21. Johnson, *Appropriating Blackness*, 6.

22. The 1970s predecessors to Bonquiqui and Shanaynay include "Florence" the housekeeper in *The Jeffersons* and "Willona" on *Good Times*.

23. See Cho, "Dick O'Clock," 24.

24. For more on Knipp's controversial performances, see the following blogs:
http://www.pamshouseblend.com/diary/16112/
http://banshirleyqliquor.typepad.com/my_weblog/
http://www.rupaul.com/news/2002/11/these-folks-is-just-plain-ignunt-last.shtml
article in *Rolling Stone*
http://sfbayview.com/2010/shirley-q-liquor-freedom-of-speech-or-hate-speech/

25. Johnson, *Appropriating Blackness*, 8.

26. Reddy, "Asian Diasporas," 101–19. See also the Audre Lorde Project.

BIBLIOGRAPHY

Aanerud, Rebecca. "Now More than Ever: James Baldwin and the Critique of White Liberalism." In *James Baldwin Now*, edited by Dwight McBride, 56–74. New York: New York University Press, 1999.
Ahmed, Sara. *The Cultural Politics of Emotion*. New York: Routledge, 2004.
Alarcón, Norma. "Chicana Feminism: In the Tracks of 'the' Native Woman." In *Cultural Studies* 4.3 (1990): 248–56.
Alcoff, Linda Martín. "The Politics of Postmodern Feminism, Revisited." *Cultural Critique* 36 (spring 1997): 5–27.
———. "The Problem of Speaking for Others." *Cultural Critique* 20 (winter 1991–92): 5–32.
———. *Visible Identities: Race, Gender, and the Self*. Oxford: Oxford University Press, 2006.
———. "Who's Afraid of Identity Politics?" In *Reclaiming Identity: Realist Theory and the Predicament of Postmodernism*, edited by Paula M. L. Moya and Michael R. Hames-García, 312–44. Berkeley: University of California Press, 2000.
Alcoff, Linda Martín, Michael Hames-García, Paula M. L. Moya, and Satya P. Mohanty, eds. *Identity Politics Reconsidered*. New York: Palgrave, 2006.
Aldama, Arturo J., and Naomi Quiñonez, eds. *Decolonial Voices: Chicana and Chicano Cultural Studies in the 21st Century*. Bloomington: Indiana University Press, 2002.
Alexander, M. Jacqui. *Pedagogies of Crossing: Meditations on Feminism, Sexual Politics, Memory, and the Sacred*. Durham, NC: Duke University Press, 2005.
Alexander, M. Jacqui, and Chandra Talpade Mohanty, eds. *Feminist Genealogies, Colonial Legacies, Democratic Futures*. New York: Routledge, 1997.
Altman, Dennis. *The Homosexualization of America: The Americanization of the Homosexual*. New York: St. Martin's Press, 1982.
Anzaldúa, Gloria. *Borderlands/La Frontera: The New Mestiza*. San Francisco, CA: Aunt Lute, 1987.

———. "Del Otro Lado." In *Compañeras: Latina Lesbians*, edited by Juanita Ramos. New York: Latina Lesbian History Project, 1987.

———. "La historia de una marimacho." In *Third Woman: The Sexuality of Latinas*, edited by Norma Alarcón, Cherríe Moraga, and Ana Castillo, 64–68. Berkeley, CA: Third Woman Press, 1993.

Audre Lorde Project. *Community at a Crossroads: US Right Wing Policies and Lesbian, Gay, Bisexual, Two Spirit, and Transgender Immigrants of Color in New York City.* New York: Audre Lorde Project, 2004.

Ayala, George. "Foreward." In *Corpus: An HIV Prevention Publication*, edited by Jaime Cortez, v–ix. Los Angeles, CA: AIDS Project Los Angeles, 2003.

Babbitt, Susan E. "Feminism and Objective Interests: The Role of Transformational Experiences in Rational Deliberation." In *Feminist Epistemologies*, edited by Linda Alcoff and Elizabeth Potter, 245–64. New York: Routledge, 1993.

———. "Moral Risk and Dark Waters." In *Racism and Philosophy*, edited by Susan E. Babbitt and Sue Campbell, 235–54. Ithaca, NY: Cornell University Press, 1999.

Bacalzo, Dan. "The One She Wants: Margaret Cho, Mediatization, and Autobiographical Performance." In *Embodying Asian/American Sexualities*, edited by Gina Masequesmay and Sean Metzger, 43–50. Plymouth, UK: Rowman and Littlefield, 2009.

Bakhtin, M. M. *The Dialogic Imagination: Four Essays.* Edited by Michael Holquist. Translated by Caryl Emerson and Michael Holquist. Austin: University of Texas Press, 1981.

Bal, Mieke. "The Narrating and the Focalizing: A Theory of the Agents in Narrative." Translated by Jane E. Lewin. *Style* 17 (1983): 234–69.

Baldwin, James. *Another Country.* New York: Vintage, 1992.

———. "The Art of Fiction LXXVIII." *Paris Review* (spring 1984): 51.

———. "The Devil Finds Work." In *The Price of the Ticket*, 557–636. New York: St. Martin's Press, 1985.

———. "Here Be Dragons." In *The Price of the Ticket*, 677–90. New York: St. Martin's Press, 1985.

———. *Just Above My Head.* New York: The Dial Press, 1979.

———. "The Male Prison." In *The Price of the Ticket*, 101–6. New York: St. Martin's Press, 1985.

———. "Notes for a Hypothetical Novel." In *The Price of the Ticket*, 237–44. New York: St. Martin's Press, 1985.

———. *The Price of the Ticket.* New York: St. Martin's Press, 1985.

———. "White Man's Guilt." In *The Price of the Ticket*, 409–14. New York: St. Martin's Press, 1985.

Bergman, David. *Camp Grounds: Style and Homosexuality.* Amherst: University of Massachusetts Press, 1993.

———. *Gaiety Transfigured: Gay Self-Representation in American Literature.* Madison: University of Wisconsin Press, 1991.

Bérubé, Allan. *Coming Out Under Fire: The History of Gay Men and Women in World War Two.* New York: Free Press, 1990.

Bond Stockton, Kathryn. *Beautiful Bottom, Beautiful Shame: Where "Black" Meets "Queer."* Durham, NC: Duke University Press, 2006.

Bone, Robert A. "The Novels of James Baldwin." In *The Negro Novel in America*, 215–39. New Haven, CT: Yale University Press, 1965.

Brady, Mary Pat. *Extinct Lands, Temporal Geographies: Chicana Literature and the Urgency of Space.* Durham, NC: Duke University Press, 2002.

Brown, Michael P. *The Space of the Closet: Geographies of Metaphor from the Body to the Globe.* New York: Routledge, 2000.
Butler, Judith. *Excitable Speech: A Politics of the Performative.* Routledge: New York, 1997.
Campbell, James. *Talking at the Gates: A Life of James Baldwin.* Berkeley: University of California Press, 2002.
Cant, Bob. "Introduction." In *Invented Identities? Lesbians and Gays Talk About Migration,* 1–28. London: Celtic Press, 1997.
Cantú, Lionel. "Entre Hombres/Between Men: Latino Masculinities and Homosexualities." In *Gay Latino Studies: A Critical Reader,* edited by Michael Hames-García and Ernesto Javier Martínez, 147–67. Durham, NC: Duke University Press, 2011.
Champagne, John. *The Ethics of Marginality: A New Approach to Gay Studies.* Minneapolis: University of Minnesota Press, 1995.
Chauncey, George. *Gay New York: Gender, Urban Culture, and the Making of the Gay Male World, 1890-1940.* New York: Basic Books, 1994.
Cho, Margaret. "Dick O'Clock." *Advocate* 1012 (August 12, 2008): 24.
———. *I'm the One that I Want.* Windstar, 2001.
———. *Notorious C.H.O.* Windstar, 2002.
Chow, Rey. *Ethics After Idealism: Theory-Culture-Ethnicity-Reading.* Bloomington: Indiana University Press, 1998.
———. "The Interruption of Referentiality: Poststructuralism and the Conundrum of Critical Multiculturalism." *South Atlantic Quarterly* 101.1 (2002): 171–86.
Christian, Barbara. "The Race for Theory." *Cultural Critique* 6 (spring 1987): 51–63.
Christian, Karen. *Show and Tell: Identity as Performance in U.S. Latina/o Fiction.* Albuquerque: University of New Mexico Press, 1997.
Cleaver, Eldridge. "Notes on a Native Son." In *Soul On Ice,* 122–37. New York: McGraw Hill, 1968.
Cohen, William A. "Liberalism, Libido, and Liberation: Baldwin's *Another Country.*" In *The Queer Sixties,* edited by Patricia Juliana Smith, 201–22. New York: Routledge, 1999.
Collins, Patricia Hill. *Black Feminist Thought: Knowledge, Consciousness, and the Politics of Empowerment.* New York: Routledge Press, 2008.
Corber, Robert J. "Everybody Knew His Names: Reassessing James Baldwin." *Contemporary Literature* 42.1 (2001): 166–75.
———. *Homosexuality in Cold War America: Resistance and the Crisis of Masculinity.* Durham, NC: Duke University Press, 1997.
Cortez, Jaime, ed. *Corpus: An HIV Prevention Publication.* Vol. 1.1. 2003.
———. *Corpus: An HIV Prevention Publication.* Vol. 2.1. 2004.
Creech, James. *Closet Writing/Gay Reading: The Case of Melville's* Pierre. Chicago: University of Chicago Press, 1993.
Crenshaw, Kimberlé, Neil Gotanda, Garry Peller, and Kendall Thomas, eds. *Critical Race Theory: The Key Writings that Formed the Movement.* New York: The New Press, 1995.
Cuadros, Gil. *City of God.* San Francisco, CA: City Lights, 1994.
Danielson, Marivel T. *Homecoming Queers: Desire and Difference in Chicana Latina Cultural Production.* New Brunswick, NJ: Rutgers University Press, 2009.
D'Emilio, John. "Capitalism and Gay Identity." In *The Lesbian and Gay Studies Reader,* edited by Henry Abelove, Michèle Aina Barale, and David M. Halperin, 467–76. New York: Routledge, 1993.
Decena, Carlos. *Tacit Subjects: Belonging and Same-Sex Desire Among Dominican Immigrant Men.* Durham, NC: Duke University Press, 2011.

Delany, Samuel. *The Motion of Light in Water: Sex and Science Fiction Writing in the East Village*. New York: Arbor House, 1988.
Delgadillo, Theresa. *Spiritual Mestizaje: Religion, Gender, Race, and Nation in Contemporary Chicana Narrative*. Durham, NC: Duke University Press, 2011.
Díaz, Junot. *Drown*. New York: Riverhead Books, 1997.
Díaz, Rafael. *Latino Gay Men and HIV: Culture Sexuality, and Risk Behavior*. New York: Routledge, 1998.
duCille, Ann. "The Occult of True Black Womanhood: Critical Demeanor and Black Feminist Studies." *Signs: Journal of Women in Culture and Society* 19.3 (1994): 591–629.
Eng, David L. *Racial Castration: Managing Masculinity in Asian America*. Durham, NC: Duke University Press, 2001.
Esquibel, Catrióna Rueda. *With Her Machete in Her Hand: Reading Chicana Lesbians*. Austin: University of Texas Press, 2006.
Feldman, Susan. "Another Look at *Another Country*: Reconciling Baldwin's Racial and Sexual Politics." In *Re-viewing James Baldwin: Things Not Seen*, edited by D. Quentin Miller, 88–104. Philadelphia, PA: Temple University Press, 2000.
Ferguson, Roderick A. *Aberrations in Black: Toward a Queer of Color Critique*. Minneapolis: University of Minnesota, 2004.
Foley, Barbara. "Review of *Reclaiming Identity: Realist Theory and the Predicaments of Postmodernism*." *Cultural Logic: An Electronic Journal of Marxist Theory and Practice* 4.2 (2001).
Fortier, Ann Marie. "'Coming Home': Queer Migrations and Multiple Evocations of Home." *European Journal of Cultural Studies* 4.4 (2001): 405–24.
———. "Queer Diasporas." In *Handbook of Lesbian and Gay Studies*, edited by Diane Richardson and Steven Seidman, 183–98. London: Sage, 2002.
Foucault, Michel. "Of Other Spaces." Translated by Jay Miskowiec. http://foucault.info/documents/heteroTopia/foucault.heteroTopia.en.html. September 13, 2004.
Freire, Paulo. *Pedagogy of the Oppressed*. 30th anniversary ed. Translated by Myra Bergman Ramos. New York: Continuum, 2000.
Fricker, Miranda. *Epistemic Injustice. Power and the Ethics of Knowing*. Oxford: Oxford University Press, 2007.
Fryer, Sarah Beebe. "Retreat from Experience: Despair and Suicide in James Baldwin's Novels." *The Journal of the Midwest Modern Language Association* 19.1 (1986): 21–28.
Fusco, Coco. *English Is Broken Here: Notes on Cultural Fusion in the Americas*. New York: New Press, 1995.
Fuss, Diana. *Essentially Speaking: Feminism, Nature and Difference*. New York: Routledge, 1989.
Garber, Linda. *Identity Poetics: Race, Class, and the Lesbian-Feminist Roots of Queer Theory*. New York: Columbia University Press, 2001.
García, Ramón. "Comment: Lawrence La Fountain-Stokes's 'Gay Shame, Latina-and Latino-Style: A Critique of White Queer Performativity." In *Gay Latino Studies: A Critical Reader*, edited by Michael Hames-García and Ernesto Javier Martínez, 81–85. Durham, NC: Duke University Press, 2011.
Gates, Henry Louis, Jr. "The Welcome Table." In *English Inside and Out: The Places of Literary Criticism*, edited by Susan Gubar and Jonathan Kamholtz, 47–60. New York: Routledge, 1993.
Genette, Gerard. *Narrative Discourse: An Essay in Method*. Translated by Jane E. Lewin. Ithaca, NY: Cornell University Press, 1972.
Gopinath, Gayatri. *Impossible Desires: Queer Diasporas and South Asian Public Cultures*. Durham, NC: Duke University Press, 2005.

Gorman-Murray, Andrew. "Rethinking Queer Migration Through the Body." *Social & Cultural Geography* 8.1 (February 2007): 105–21.
Gray, Mary L. *Out in the Country: Youth, Media, and Queer Visibility in Rural America.* New York: New York University Press, 2009.
Grosfoguel, Ramón, "Colonial Difference, Geopolitics of Knowledge, and Global Coloniality in the Modern/Colonial Capitalist World-System." *Review* 25.3 (2002): 203–24.
Halberstam, Judith. "Shame and White Gay Masculinity." *Social Text* 84–85/23.3–4 (2005): 219–23.
Halley, Janet. *Split Decisions: How and Why to Take a Break from Feminism.* Princeton, NJ: Princeton University Press, 2008.
Hames-García, Michael. "Can Queer Theory Be Critical Theory?" In *New Critical Theory: Essays on Liberation*, edited by William S. Wilkerson and Jeffery Paris, 201–22. Lanham, MD: Rowman & Littlefield, 2001.
———. *Fugitive Thought: Prison Movements, Race, and the Meaning of Justice.* Minneapolis: University of Minnesota Press, 2004.
———. *Identity Complex: Making the Case for Multiplicity.* Minneapolis: University of Minnesota Press, 2011.
———. "Queer Theory, Revisited." In *Gay Latino Studies: A Critical Reader*, edited by Michael Hames-García and Ernesto Javier Martínez, 19–45. Durham, NC: Duke University Press, 2011.
———. "Which America Is Ours? Martí's 'Truth' and the Foundations of 'American Literature.'" *Modern Fiction Studies* 49.1 (2003): 19–53.
———. "'Who Are Our Own People?' Challenges for a Theory of Social Identity." In *Reclaiming Identity: Realist Theory and the Predicament of Postmodernism*, edited by Paula M. L. Moya and Michael R. Hames-García, 102–32. Berkeley: University of California Press, 2000.
Hames-García, Michael, and Ernesto Javier Martínez, eds. *Gay Latino Studies: A Critical Reader.* Duke, NC: Duke University Press, 2011.
Hanson, Ellis. "Teaching Shame," In *Gay Shame*, edited by David M. Halperin and Valerie Traub, 132–64. Chicago: University of Chicago Press, 2009.
Harris, Trudier. *Black Women in the Fiction of James Baldwin.* Knoxville: University of Tennessee Press, 1987.
Hau, Caroline S. "On Representing Others: Intellectuals, Pedagogy, and the Uses of Error." In *Reclaiming Identity: Realist Theory and the Predicament of Postmodernism*, edited by Paula M. L. Moya and Michael R. Hames-García, 133–204. Berkeley: University of California Press, 2000.
Hennessey, Rosemary. *Profit and Pleasure: Sexual Identities in Late Capitalism.* New York: Routledge, 2000.
Herring, Scott. *Another Country: Queer Anti-Urbanism.* New York: New York University Press, 2010.
Hinojosa, Rolando. *Estampas del valle.* Berkeley, CA: Quinto Sol, 1973.
Holland, Sharon. *The Erotic Life of Racism.* Durham, NC: Duke University Press, 2012.
———. *Raising the Dead: Readings of Death and (Black) Subjectivity.* Durham, NC: Duke University Press, 2000.
———. "[White] Lesbian Studies." In *The New Lesbian Studies: Into the Twenty-First Century*, edited by Bonnie Zimmerman and Toni A. H. McNaron, 247–55. New York: Feminist Press, 1996.
Hull, Gloria T., Patricia Bell Scott, and Barbara Smith, eds. *All the Women Are White, All*

the Blacks Are Men, But Some of Us Are Brave: Black Women's Studies*. Old Westbury, NY: Feminist Press, 1982.
Hyman, Stanley Edgar. *Standards: A Chronicle of Books for Our Time*. New York: Horizon Press, 1966.
Islas, Arturo. *The Rain God: A Desert Tale*. New York: Avon Books, 1991.
JanMohamed, Abdul. *The Death-Bound Subject: Richard Wright's Archaeology of Death*. Durham, NC: Duke University Press, 2005.
Johnson, E. Patrick. *Appropriating Blackness: Performance and the Politics of Authenticity*. Durham, NC: Duke University Press, 2003.
———. "'Quare' Studies, or (Almost) Everything I Know about Queer Studies I Learned from My Grandmother." *Callaloo* 23.1 (2000): 120–21.
Kazin, Alfred. *Bright Book of Life: American Novelists and Storytellers from Hemingway to Mailer*. Notre Dame, IN: University of Notre Dame Press, 1980.
Kenan, Randall. *James Baldwin*. New York: Chelsea House, 1994.
———. *Let the Dead Bury Their Dead*. New York: Harcourt Brace Jovanovich, 1992.
———. *A Visitation of Spirits*. New York: Vintage, 2000.
Kusch, Rodolfo. *Indigenous and Popular Thinking in América*. Translated by María Lugones and Joshua M. Price. Durham, NC: Duke University Press, 2010.
LaCapra, Dominick. "Identity and Experience." In *Identity Politics Reconsidered*, edited by L. Alcoff et al., 228–45. New York: Palgrave, 2006.
La Fountain-Stokes, Lawrence. "Gay Shame, Latina/o Style: A Critique of White Queer Performativity." In *Gay Latino Studies: A Critical Reader*, edited by Michael Hames-García and Ernesto Javier Martínez, 55–80. Durham, NC: Duke University Press, 2011.
———. *Queer Ricans: Cultures and Sexualities in the Diaspora*. Minneapolis: University of Minnesota Press, 2009.
Lee, Rachel. "'Where's My Parade?' Margaret Cho and the Asian American Body in Space." *TDR: The Drama Review* 48.2 (2004): 108–32.
Lewine, Edward. "Margaret Cho: Comedy Clubhouse." *The New York Times Magazine* (March 26, 2009).
Leyva, Yolanda Chávez. "Listening to the Silences in Latina/Chicana Lesbian History." In *Living Chicana Theory*, edited by Carla Trujillo, 429–34. Berkeley, CA: Third Woman Press, 1998.
Lima, Lazaro. *The Latino Body: Crisis Identities in American Literary and Cultural Theory*. New York: New York University Press, 2007.
Lorde, Audre. "An Open Letter to Mary Daly." In *Sister Outsider*, 66–71. Trumansburg, NY: Crossing Press, 1984.
Lugones, María. "El Pasar Discontinuo de la Cachapera/Tortillera del Barrio a la Barra al Movimiento/The Discontinuous Passing of the Cachapera/Tortillera from the Barrio to the Bar to the Movement." In *Daring to be Good: Essays in Feminist Ethico-Politics*, edited by Bat-Ami Bar On, 156–67. New York: Routledge, 1998.
———. *Pilgrimages/Peregrinajes: Theorizing Coalition Against Multiple Oppressions*. New York: Roman and Littlefield, 2003.
Lugones, María, and Joshua Price. "Dominant Culture: *El Deseo por un Alma Pobre* (The Desire for an Impoverished Soul)." In *Multiculturalism from the Margins: Non-Dominant Voices on Difference and Diversity*, edited by Dean A. Harris, 103–28. Westport, CT: Greenwood, 1995.
Luibheid, Eithne, ed. *Queer/Migration: Journal of Lesbian and Gay Studies*. Durham, NC: Duke University Press, 2008.

Luibheid, Eithne, and Lionel Cantú, eds. *Queer Migrations: Sexuality U.S. Citizenship, and Border Crossings.* Minneapolis: University of Minnesota Press, 2005.

Macdonald, Amy, and Susan Sánchez-Casal. "Identity, Realist Pedagogy, and Racial Democracy in Higher Education." In *Identity in Education*, edited by Amy Macdonald and Susan Sánchez-Casal, 16–28. New York: Palgrave Macmillan Press, 2009.

Manalansan, Martin F. *Global Divas: Filipino Gay Men in the Diaspora.* Durham, NC: Duke University Press, 2003.

Massad, Joseph. *Desiring Arabs.* Chicago: University of Chicago Press, 2007.

McBride, Dwight A. "Can the Queen Speak? Racial Essentialism, Sexuality, and the Problem of Authority." *Callaloo* 21.2 (1998): 363–79.

McDowell, Deborah. *The Changing Same: Black Women's Literature, Criticism, and Theory.* Bloomington: Indiana University Press, 1995.

McKoy, Sheila Smith. "Rescuing the Black Homosexual Lambs: Randall Kenan and the Reconstruction of Southern Gay Masculinity." In *Contemporary Black Men's Fiction and Drama*, edited by Keith Clark, 15–36. Urbana: University of Illinois Press, 2001.

McNay, Lois. *Gender and Agency: Reconfiguring the Subject in Feminist and Social Theory.* Malden, MA: Blackwell, 2000.

Mignolo, Walter. "Delinking: Rhetoric of Modernity, Logic of Coloniality, and Grammar of Decoloniality." *Cultural Studies* 21.2-3 (2007): 449–514.

———. "Epistemic Disobedience, Independent Thought and Decolonial Freedom." *Theory, Culture & Society* 26.7-8 (December 2009): 159–81.

———. "The Geopolitics of Knowledge and the Colonial Difference." *South Atlantic Quarterly* 101.1 (2002): 57–96.

———. "Globalization and the Geopolitics of Knowledge: The Role of the Humanities in the Corporate University." *Nepantla: Views from South* 4.1 (2003): 97–119.

Miller, D. A. "Sontag's Urbanity." *October* 49 (1989): 91–101.

Mohanty, Satya P. "Can Our Values Be Objective? On Ethics, Aesthetics, and Progressive Politics." *New Literary History* 32.4 (2001): 803–33.

———. "The Dynamics of Literary Reference: Narrative Discourse and Social Ideology in Two 19th-Century Indian Novels." In *Thematology: Literary Studies in India*, edited by Sibaji Bandyopadhyay, 230–48. Calcutta, India: Jadavpur University, 2004.

———. "The Epistemic Status of Cultural Identity: On Beloved and the Postcolonial Condition." In *Reclaiming Identity: Realist Theory and the Predicaments of Postmodernism*, edited by Paula Moya and Michael Hames-García, 29–66. Berkeley: University of California Press, 2000. Rpt. from *Cultural Critique* 24 (1993): 41–80.

———. *Literary Theory and the Claims of History: Postmodernism, Objectivity, Multicultural Politics.* Ithaca, NY: Cornell University Press, 1997

———. "Realist Theory." In *International Encyclopedia of the Social Sciences*, 2d ed., edited by William Darity, Jr., 97–100. New York: McMillan Reference Books, 2007.

Moraga, Cherríe. *Heroes and Saints and Other Plays.* New York: West End Press, 1994.

———. *The Hungry Woman/Heart of the Earth.* New York: West End Press, 2001.

———. *The Last Generation: Prose and Poetry.* Boston, MA: South End Press, 1993.

———. *Loving in the War Years: Lo que nunca pasó por sus labios.* Boston, MA: South End Press, 1983.

———. *Waiting in the Wings: A Portrait of a Queer Motherhood.* Ithaca, NY: Firebrand Press, 1997.

Moraga, Cherríe, and Gloria Anzaldúa, eds. *This Bridge Called My Back: Writings by Radical Women of Color.* New York: Kitchen Table Press, 1983.

Moraga, Cherríe, and Amber Hollibaugh. "What We're Rolling Around in Bed With: Sexual Silences in Feminism." *Heresies* 3.4 (1981): 58–62.
Morgan, Tracy. "Pages of Whiteness: Race, Physique Magazines, and the Emergence of Public Gay Culture." In *Queer Studies: A Lesbian, Gay, Bisexual, and Transgender Anthology*, edited by Brett Beemyn and Mickey Eliason, 280–97. New York: New York University Press, 1996.
Morrison, Toni. *The Nobel Prize Lecture in Literature*. New York: Alfred A. Knopf, 1999.
Moya, Paula M. L. "Introduction: Reclaiming Identity." In *Reclaiming Identity: Realist Theory and the Predicament of Postmodernism*, edited by Paula M. L. Moya and Michael Hames-García, 1–28. Berkeley: University of California Press, 2000.
———. *Learning from Experience: Minority Perspectives, Multicultural Struggles*. Berkeley: University of California Press, 2002.
———. "Postmodernism, 'Realism,' and the Politics of Identity: Cherríe Moraga and Chicana Feminism." In *Feminist Genealogies, Colonial Legacies, Democratic Futures*, edited by M. Jacqui Alexander and Chandra Talpade Mohanty, 125–50. New York: Routledge Press, 1997.
———. "What's Identity Got to Do with It: Mobilizing Identities in the Multicultural Classroom." *Identity Politics Reconsidered*, edited by L. Alcoff et al., 96–117. New York: Palgrave, 2006.
Moya, Paula M. L., and Michael R. Hames-García. *Reclaiming Identity: Realist Theory and the Predicament of Postmodernism*. Berkeley: University of California Press, 2000.
Muñoz, José Esteban. *Cruising Utopia: The Then and There of Queer Futurity*. New York: New York University Press, 2009.
———. *Disidentifications: Queers of Color and the Performance of Politics*. Minneapolis: University of Minnesota Press, 1998.
Muñoz, Manuel. *Zigzagger*. Evanston, IL: Northwestern University Press, 2003.
Muñoz, Miguel Elías. *The Greatest Performance*. Houston, TX: Arte Público Press, 1991.
Murphy, Geraldine. "Subversive Anti-Stalinism: Race and Sexuality in the Early Essays of James Baldwin." *English Literary History* 63.4 (1996): 1021–46.
Negrón-Muntaner, Frances. *Brincando el Charco: A Portrait of a Puerto Rican*. New York: Women Make Movies, 1994.
Newton, Esther. *Mother Camp: Female Impersonators in America*. Chicago: University of Chicago Press, 1979.
Obejas, Achy. *We Came All the Way from Cuba So You Could Dress Like This?* San Francisco, CA: Cleis, 1994.
Ohi, Kevin. "'I'm Not the Boy You Want': Sexuality, 'Race,' and Thwarted Revelation in Baldwin's *Another Country*." *African American Review* 33.2 (1999): 261–81.
Ortega, Mariana. "Being Lovingly, Knowingly Ignorant: White Feminism and Women of Color." *Hypatia* 21.3 (2006): 56–74.
Patton, Cindy, and Benigno Sánchez-Eppler. *Queer Diasporas*. Durham, NC: Duke University Press, 2000.
Pellegrini, Ann. "Mind the Gap?" *GLQ: A Journal of Lesbian and Gay Studies* 10.4 (2004): 637–39.
Pérez, Emma. *The Decolonial Imaginary: Writing Chicanas into History*. Bloomington: Indiana University Press, 1999.
———. "Irigaray's Female Symbolic in the Making of Chicana Lesbian *Sitios y Lenguas (Sites and Languages)*." In *The Lesbian Postmodern*, edited by Laura Doan, 104–17. New York: Columbia University Press, 1994.

Perez, Hiram. "You Can Have My Brown Body and Eat It, Too!" *Social Text* 84–85/23.3–4 (2005): 171–91.
Pérez, Laura E. *Chicana Art: The Politics of Spiritual and Aesthetic Altarities*. Durham, NC: Duke University Press, 2007.
Preston, John. *Hometowns: Gay Men Write About Where They Belong*. New York: Penguin, 1992.
Puar, Jasbir, ed. *Queer Tourism: Geographies of Globalization*. A special issue of *GLQ: A Journal of Lesbian and Gay Studies* 8.1–2 (2002).
———. *Terrorist Assemblages: Homonationalism in Queer Times*. Durham, NC: Duke University Press, 2007.
Quijano, Aníbal. "Coloniality of Power, Knowledge, and Latin America." *Nepantla: Views from South* no. 1: 533–80.
Ramos, Juanita (pseudonym for Juanita Díaz), ed. *Compañeras: Latina Lesbians*. New York: Latina Lesbian History Project, 1987. Rpt. New York: Routledge, 1994.
Reddy, Chandan. "Asian Diasporas, Neoliberalism and Family: Reviewing the Case for Homosexual Asylum in the Context of Family Rights." *Social Text* 84–85/23.3–4 (2005): 101–19.
Reid-Pharr, Robert. *Black Gay Man: Essays*. New York: New York University Press, 2001.
Rivera, Thomás. *Y no se lo tragó la tierra*. Houston, TX: Arte Público Press, 1995.
Robertson, Pamela. *Guilty Pleasures: Feminist Camp from Mae West to Madonna*. Durham, NC: Duke University Press, 1996.
Robles, Augie. *Cholo/Joto*. 1993. Director's private collection.
Rodriguez, Richard. *Hunger of Memory: The Education of Richard Rodriguez*. New York: Bantam, 1983.
Romero, Lora. "When Something Goes Queer: Familiarity, Formalism, and Minority Intellectuals in the 1980's." *The Yale Journal of Criticism* 6.1 (1993): 121–41.
Romo, Ito. *The Bridge*. Albuquerque: University of New Mexico Press, 2000.
Roque-Ramírez, Horacio. "Cholo/Salvatrucho." *Mapping Strategies: NACCS and the Challenge of Multiple (Re)Oppressions: Selected Proceedings of the National Association for Chicana and Chicano Studies*. Phoenix, AZ: Orbix Press, 1999.
———. "'That's *My* Place': Negotiating Racial, Sexual, and Gender Politics in San Francisco's Gay Latino Alliance, 1975–1983." *Journal of the History of Sexuality* 12.2 (2003): 224–58.
Roof, Judith. "Lesbians and Lyotard: Legitimation and the Politics of the Name." *The Lesbian Postmodern*, edited by Laura Doan, 47–66. New York: Columbia University Press, 1994.
Ross, Marlon. "White Fantasies of Desire: Baldwin and the Racial Identities of Sexuality." In *James Baldwin Now*, edited by Dwight McBride, 13–55. New York: New York University Press, 1999.
Rowden, Terry. "A Play of Abstractions: Race, Sexuality, and Community in James Baldwin's *Another Country*." *Southern Review* 29.1 (1993): 41–50.
Rubin, Gayle. "Thinking Sex: Notes for a Radical Theory of the Politics of Sexuality." In *Pleasure and Danger: Exploring Female Sexuality*, edited by Carole S. Vance, 267–319. Boston, MA: Routledge & Kegan Paul, 1984.
Rusk, Lauren. "Selfhood and Strategy in *Notes of a Native Son*." In *James Baldwin Now*, edited by Dwight McBride, 360–92. New York: New York University Press, 1999.
Ryan, Katy. "Falling in Public: Larsen's *Passing*, McCarthy's *The Group*, and Baldwin's *Another Country*." *Studies in the Novel* 36 (2004): 95–119.
Saldívar, Ramón. *Chicano Narrative: Dialectics of Difference*. Madison: University of Wisconsin Press, 1990.
———. "Multicultural Politics, Aesthetics, and the Realist Theory of Identity: A Response to Satya Mohanty." *New Literary History* 32.4 (2001): 849–54.

Sánchez, Luis Rafael. "¡Jum!" In *En Cuerpo de Camisa*. Rio Piedras: Editorial Cultural, 1990 [1996]. Translated by Rose M. Sevillano as "Hum!" *Grand Street* 61 (summer 1997): 130–35.

Schueller, Malini Johar. "Analogy and (White) Feminist Theory: Thinking Race and the Color of the Cyborg Body." *Signs: Journal of Women in Culture and Society* 31.1 (2005): 63–92.

Schwartzman, Lisa H. "Hate Speech, Illocution, and Social Context: A Critique of Judith Butler." *Journal of Social Philosophy* 33.3 (2002): 421–41.

Scott, Joan W. "The Evidence of Experience." *Critical Inquiry* 17.4 (1991): 773–97.

Sedgwick, Eve. *Epistemology of the Closet*. Berkeley: University of California Press, 1990.

Seidman, Steven. *Beyond the Closet: The Transformation of Gay and Lesbian Life*. New York: Routledge, 2002.

Shimizu-Parreñas, Celine. *The Hypersexuality of Race: Performing Asian/American Women on Screen and Scene*. Durham, NC: Duke University Press, 2007.

Siebers, Tobin. "Disability in Theory: From Social Constructionism to the New Realism of the Body." *American Literary History* 13.4 (2001): 737–54.

Smith, Linda Tuhiwai. *Decolonizing Methodologies: Research and Indigenous Peoples*. New York: Zed Books, 1999.

Sneideker, Michael. *Queer Optimism: Lyric Personhood and Other Felicitous Persuasions*. Minneapolis: University of Minnesota Press, 2008.

Sommer, Doris. *Proceed with Caution, When Engaged by Minority Writing in the Americas*. Cambridge, MA: Harvard University Press, 1999.

Soto, Sandra K. *Reading Chican@ Like a Queer: The De-Mastery of Desire*. Austin: University of Texas Press, 2010.

Spelman, Elizabeth V. "Theories of Race and Gender: The Social Construction of Whiteness." *Quest: A Feminist Quarterly* 5.4 (1982): 36–62.

Spurlin, William. "Culture, Rhetoric, and Queer Identity: James Baldwin and the Identity Politics of Race and Sexuality." In *James Baldwin Now*, edited by Dwight McBride, 103–21. New York: New York University Press, 1999.

Stone-Mediatore, Shari. *Reading Across Borders: Storytelling and Knowledges of Resistance*. New York: Palgrave, 2003.

Teuton, Sean. *Red Land, Red Power: Grounding Knowledge in the American Indian Novel*. Durham, NC: Duke University Press, 2008.

Tinsley, Omise'eke Natasha. *Thiefing Sugar: Eroticism Between Women in Caribbean Literature*. Durham, NC: Duke University Press, 2010.

Tlostanova, Madina. *Gender Epistemologies and Eurasian Borderlands*. New York: Palgrove MacMillan, 2010.

Toombs, Charles P. "Black-Gay-Man Chaos in *Another Country*." In *Re-viewing James Baldwin: Things Not Seen*, edited by D. Quentin Miller, 105–27. Philadelphia, PA: Temple University Press, 2000.

Trujillo, Carla, ed. *Chicana Lesbians: The Girls Our Mothers Warned Us About*. Berkeley, CA: Third Woman Press, 1991.

Villa, Raúl Homero. *Barrio-Logos: Space and Place in Urban Chicano Literature and Culture*. Austin: University of Texas Press, 2000.

Waldrep, Shelton. "'Being Bridges': Cleaver/Baldwin/Lorde and African-American Sexism and Sexuality." In *Critical Essays: Gay and Lesbian Writers of Color*, edited by Emmanuel S. Nelson, 167–80. Binghamton, NY: Harrington Park Press, 1994.

Walker, Alice. *In Search of Our Mothers' Gardens: Womanist Prose*. New York: Mariner Books, 2003.

Warner, Michael. *The Trouble with Normal: Sex, Politics, and the Ethics of Queer Life.* Cambridge, MA: Harvard University Press, 2000.
Weston, Kath. *Families We Choose: Lesbians, Gays, Kinship.* New York: Columbia University Press, 1991.
Williams, Patricia J. *The Alchemy of Race and Rights: Diary of a Law Professor.* Cambridge, MA: Harvard University Press, 1991.
Womack, Craig S. *Red on Red: Native American Literary Separatism.* Minneapolis: University of Minnesota Press, 1999.
Yarbro-Bejarano, Yvonne. "De-constructing the Lesbian Body: Cherríe Moraga's *Loving in the War Years.*" In *Chicana Lesbians: The Girls Our Mothers Warned Us About,* edited by Carla Trujillo, 143–55. Berkeley, CA: Third Woman Press, 1991.
———. *The Wounded Heart: Writing on Cherríe Moraga.* Austin: University of Texas Press, 2001.

INDEX

Active subjectivity, 114, 177*n*5
Agency, 114, 140–41, 177*n*3, 177*n*5
AIDS Project Los Angeles (APLA), 1–3
Aiken, Susanne, and Carlos Aparicio: *The Salt Mines*, 106; *Transformation*, 106
Alarcón, Norma, 173*n*13
Alcoff, Linda, 6–7, 25, 95, 166*n*10
Alexander, M. Jacqui, 25
All the Women Are White, All the Blacks Are Men, But Some of Us Are Brave (Hull, Bell-Scott, and Smith), 10
Altman, Denise, 180*n*8
Antirealism: Baldwin's *Another Country* and, 18–19; decolonizing theory vs., 5; hegemony of, 19; identity- and experience-based epistemology criticized from standpoint of, 9–12, 25–27, 42, 164*n*43; principal claims of, 9; writers of color and, 18
Anzaldúa, Gloria, 4, 10, 77, 79, 112, 172*n*7, 173*n*16; *Borderlands/La Frontera*, 96–100
Aparicio, Carlos. *See* Aiken, Susanne, and Carlos Aparicio
Asian Americans. *See* Korean Americans/Asian Americans
Assimilation, 105–6
Austin, J. L., 38
Ayala, George, 1–2, 6

Babbitt, Susan, 45, 48, 61, 68, 74–75, 86–89, 94, 98
Bal, Mieke, 178*n*6
Baldwin, James, vii, 3–4, 7, 37, 65, 132; *Another Country*, 18–19, 45–71, 74–78, 168*n*1, 179*n*28; *Just Above My Head*, 179*n*28
Bergman, David, 139
Black feminists, 10, 164*n*43
Bond Stockton, Kathryn, 22, 141, 151
Boyd, Richard, 20, 73
Bracho, Ricardo, 112
Brady, Mary Pat, 104–5, 173*n*13, 176*n*79
Butler, Judith, 18, 23–25, 28, 34–43, 168*n*60; *Excitable Speech*, 18, 25

Cachaperas, 85, 174*n*28
Camp, 139–45, 148, 150, 157, 180*n*8
Cant, Bob, 60–61, 90
Cantú, Lionel, 90–91
Card, Claudia, 50
Certainty, 6, 7, 10, 13, 40–41, 73
Champagne, John, 24, 26, 166*n*1
Charo, 140
Chauncey, George, 139
Chávez, Linda, 177*n*3
Cho, Margaret, 21–22, 137–59, 180*n*1, 180*n*2; *I'm the One that I Want*, 141–58; *Notorious C.H.O.*, 141–58

Chow, Rey, 36
Christian, Barbara, 25
Christian, Karen, 177n1
Cleaver, Eldridge, 74–75
Closeted Latinas, 101–3
Coatlicue, 79, 96, 97, 172n7
Cohen, William, 64, 169n8
Collins, Patricia Hill, 162n18
Comedy. *See* Humor, gay male subculture and
Community, queer Latina/o migrant labor and, 80–91, 93–94, 96–105
Constructivism: identity and, 6–8, 12, 71–76; revised, 19–20, 161n9. *See also* Social construction
Corpus (journal), 1–3, 6
Cortez, Jaime, 1
Counteridentification with dominant ideology, 105–6
Crawford, Joan, 181n8
Critical race theory, 5, 19, 28, 38, 40–41
Cuadros, Gil, 90, 93–94; "My Aztlán: White Place," 94
Cultural production. *See* Literature and cultural production

Daly, Mary, 24, 166n1
Danielson, Marivel, 80
Decolonization: of the academy, 17; Anzaldúa and, 96–100, 172n7; of knowledge, 4–5; of one's mind, 97; realism and, 5, 13
Deconstruction, 73. *See also* Poststructuralism
Deferential Wife, 87–89
Delany, Samuel, *The Motion of Light in Water*, 26, 74–75
De la Peña, Terri, 90
de la tierra, tatiana, 90
Díaz, Juanita, 173n16
Díaz, Junot, "Drown," 180n30
Díaz, Rafael, 174n43
Disidentifications, 105–11, 141, 148–51
Du Bois, W.E.B., 57
duCille, Ann, 166n1

Easy riders, 59–60
Emotion, epistemic possibilities of, 94–100
Empathy, 83–84
Empiricism, 1–4
Epistemic access, 73–74
Epistemic injustice, 14
Epistemology: confusion and incoherence in relation to, 46–47, 63–71, 169n11; Eurocentric, 9; experience and, 6, 19–20, 25–26, 95; foundationalism in, 73; identity and, 6–7, 10–12, 19–20, 25–26, 47, 51; injustice related to, 14; literature and, 3–4, 8, 28, 159, 162n18; from the position of the suppressed, 4, 6, 13, 20, 162n10. *See also* Knowledge
Esquibel, Catrióna Rueda, 80, 163n18, 173n9
Essentialism, strategic, 11–12
Ethics and responsibility: Baldwin's *Another Country* and, 47–48, 50–51, 62–63, 66–71; Kenan's "The Foundations of the Earth" and, 134–35; language and, 33, 43
Eurocentrism: lack of reflexiveness in, 4, 9, 17; in queer theory, 16–17; theorizing of people of color criticized from standpoint of, 11, 18, 27
Existential distance, 124–28
Experience, epistemological role of, 6, 19–20, 25–26, 95

Fag hags, 146, 182n16
Family: narrative perspective and, 115–31; of oppressed peoples, 61; queer Latina/o migrant labor and, 80–91, 93, 96–105
Fear, epistemic possibilities of, 96–100
Feldman, Susan, 169n15
Feminism: and camp, 139–40, 181n8; and race, 10, 139–40. *See also* Black feminists; Women's movement
Ferguson, Roderick, 4, 16, 25
Fortier, Anne Marie, 78
Foundationalism, epistemological, 73
Freedman, Marilyn, 103
Freire, Paolo, 4
Fricker, Miranda, 14
Frye, Marilyn, 17
Fuss, Diana, 10

Gallop, Jane, 166n1
Garber, Linda, 10
Gates, Henry Louis, Jr., 169n8
Gay male subculture, Cho's comedy and, 138–59
Gay sex: journal devoted to, 1; meanings of, 1–2
Genette, Gerard, 178n6
Glave, Thomas, "Whose Song?," 179n30
Goldman, Julie, 155
Goldsby, Jackie, 91
Gonzalez, Rigoberto, 90
Gopinath, Gayatri, 81
Gorman-Murray, Andrew, 78
Grosfoguel, Ramón, 27
Guevara, Ernesto "Ché," 107–8

Halberstam, Judith, 11
Halley, Janet, 26
Hames-García, Michael, 10, 165n52, 172n69
Handy, W. C., 59
Haraway, Donna, 25

Harding, Sandra, 20
Hate speech, 38, 40
Hebert, Patrick "Pato," 1
Hemphill, Essex, 112
Heterodiegetic narratives, 115–16, 124, 131, 178n6
Heteronormativity: in Baldwin's *Another Country*, 70; in immigrant communities, 155–57; in Latina/o culture, 101–5; privilege associated with, 107; resistance to, 137, 141; and social stigma, 79
Heterosexuality: critique of, 22; disidentification with, 141–42, 148–51
Hill, Thomas, 87
Hinojosa, Rolando, 115
HIV prevention, 1–2
Hoagland, Sara, 85
Holland, Sharon, 11, 17, 133, 169n7
Hollibaugh, Amber, 10
Home, 80, 99–100
Homero, Raúl, 173n13
Homodiegetic narratives, 116, 178n6, 178n8
Homophobia: in Baldwin's *Another Country*, 51, 52, 57, 62; in Cho's comedy act, 145–48; and coercion/intimidation, 144; directed at queers of color, 14; "humanity" as inadequate defense against, 21; in immigrant communities, 157–58; in Latina/o culture, 80, 82, 86, 93, 102, 107–8, 174n43; nonqueer resistance to, 16, 113–14; and social stigma, 117, 119–20, 123, 133–35, 138; in United States, 3, 45; and violence, 118
hooks, bell, 25
Humor, gay male subculture and, 138–59
Hustling, 57–58

I Ching, 99
Identification with dominant ideology, 105–6
Identity: in Baldwin's *Another Country*, 52–63, 66–71; epistemological role of, 6–7, 10–12, 19–20, 25–26, 47, 51; realism and, 47–48, 71–72, 87–88; as social construct, 6–8, 12, 71–76; and social relations, 51; as spatial praxis, 105–11
Identity politics, 9, 11, 17, 19–20
INCITE! Women of Color against Violence and Critical Resistance, 39
Indexicality of language, 31–32, 167n25
Intelligibility, 13–14
Intentionality, 114, 177n4
Interracial relationships, 49–50, 53–56, 93, 175n46
Islas, Arturo, 90, 115; *The Rain God*, 179n24

JanMohamed, Abdul, 169n7
Johnson, E. Patrick, 11, 151, 155, 166n1

Kenan, Randall, 15, 113, 115, 132–36, 137; "The Foundations of the Earth," 133–36; *A Visitation of Spirits*, 132–33
Kitt, Eartha, 140
Knipp, Charles, 154–55
Knowledge: decolonization of, 4–5; emotion and, 94–100; about gay men, 1–3; literature and, 74–75; migration as means to, 15; nonpropositional, 61–62, 94–100; queer Latina/o migrant labor and, 81; realism and, 165n52. *See also* Epistemology; Self-knowledge
Korean Americans/Asian Americans, 140–41, 147–48, 154–58
Kusch, Rodolfo, 4

Lacan, Jacques, 95
LaCapra, Dominick, 169n10
La Fountain-Stokes, Larry, 132, 175n44
Lagerfeld, Karl, 143–45
Language: Butler on violence of, 34–43; conduct in relation to, 38–39; ethical character of, 33, 43; generative power of, 31–32; indeterminacy of, 18–19, 25, 41, 72–73; indexicality of, 31–32, 167n25; literary, 35–37, 167n41; misuse of, 29; Morrison on, 28–33; relational character of, 30–31, 43; and representation, 34–37
Latina/os. *See* Queer Latina/o migrant labor
Lee, Rachel, 148, 149
Lemus, Felicia Luna, 90
Lesbian bar culture, 101–3
Leyva, Yolanda Chávez, 112, 113
Liberalism, 87–88
Lima, Lázaro, 11
Lincoln, Abraham, 36
Literature and cultural production: disidentifications practiced in, 105–11; epistemological role of, 3–4, 8, 28, 74–75, 159, 162n18; peculiar linguistic character of, 35–37, 167n41; and representation, 75–76; sociopolitical role of, 3
Lopez, George, 180n3
Lorde, Audre, 10, 112, 113, 166n1
Lugones, María, 4, 17, 25, 77, 84–86, 89, 92–93, 101–4, 113, 114, 174n27, 176n72, 177n3, 177n5, 178n11, 181n12; "The Hungry Woman: A Mexican Medea," 86; *The Last Generation*, 85–86
Lynch, Michael, 64

Madonna (singer), 139, 181n8
Mann, Thomas, *Death in Venice*, 66–67
McDowell, Deborah, 25, 164n43
McKoy, Sheila Smith, 133

McNay, Lois, 71–72
Melly, George, 180n8
Menchú, Rigoberta, 162n10
Midler, Bette, 147
Mignolo, Walter, 4, 9, 27
Migration: in Baldwin's *Another Country*, 59–60; and knowledge acquisition, 15; queer, 60–63, 78. *See also* Queer Latina/o migrant labor; Spatiality
Miranda, Carmen, 140
Mohanty, Chandra, 25
Mohanty, Satya, 6–7, 19, 20, 48, 73, 172n69
Moraga, Cherríe, 4, 10, 25, 95, 100, 103–4, 163n32, 168n60, 173n14, 173n16, 173n24, 176n79, 177n1; *Loving in the War Years*, 81–84, 98–99
Morgan, Tracy, 92
Morrison, Toni, 18, 23–25, 27–39, 41–43; *Nobel Prize Lecture in Literature*, 28–33
Moya, Paula, 20, 25–27, 50, 168n60, 169n16, 172n69, 177n3
Muñoz, José Esteban, 81, 105–7, 139–40, 141, 164n34, 166n7
Muñoz, Manuel, 15, 93, 113, 115–32, 137; "Good as Yesterday," 115, 116–24, 128–29; "The Unimportant Lila Parr," 115, 124–29; "Zigzagger," 115; *Zigzagger*, 115; "Zigzagger," 129–31
Muñoz, Miguel Elías, *The Greatest Performance*, 132
Murphy, Eddie, 180n3

Narrative perspective, 14–16, 112–13. *See also* Queer enunciation, shifting sites of
Negrón-Muntaner, Frances, *Brincando el Charco*, 91–92, 175n46
Nelson, Emmanuel, 64
Nonpropositional knowledge, 61–62, 94–100

Obejas, Achy, 90, 93; "Above All, a Family Man," 178n8; *Memory Mambo*, 178n7
Objectivity: defense of, 5–6; defined, 6; realism and, 20–21, 73–74, 161n9; social practice and, 20–22
Ohi, Kevin, 64–65, 72
Oppression: agency and, 114; epistemology from position of victims of, 4, 6, 13, 20, 162n10; knowledge available to victims of, 61–62; knowledge of, 48–49, 68, 99; of queers of color, 48
Ornamentalization, 140, 181n12
Ortega, Mariana, 17

Parables, 31–32
Patton, Cindy, 11
Peirce, Charles Sanders, 73

Pelligrini, Ann, 11
People for the Ethical Treatment of Animals (PETA), 143
Pérez, Emma, 11, 136
Pérez, Hiram, 11, 17, 23–24
Pérez, Laura, 4
Performance art, 105–11
PETA. *See* People for the Ethical Treatment of Animals
Place. *See* Spatiality
Postmodernism, 9, 25, 163n32
Poststructuralism, 9, 25, 163n32, 164n43. *See also* Deconstruction
Price, Joshua, 181n12

Queer diaspora, 78–79
Queer diasporic imaginary, 81
Queer enunciation, shifting sites of, 113–36; epistemic significance of, 115–16; in Kenan's work, 132–36; in Muñoz's work, 115–31; sociopolitical implications of, 114; themes revealed by, 15–16, 113–14
Queer exodus, 79–105; and community/family, 80–91, 93–94, 96–105; crisis in, 89–105; and rural to urban migration, 172n4; tensions in, 101–3
Queer Latina/o migrant labor, 77–111; and community/family, 80–91, 93–94, 96–105; crisis in, 89–105; and fear, 96–100; and freedom, 80–81; of gay men, 174n43; and identity as spatial praxis, 105–11; and knowledge, 81; and lesbianism, 81–86, 101–4, 173n9, 176n72; practices of, 79–80; tensions in, 101–3
Queer of color critique, 4–5, 16–17, 25
Queers of color: bearing witness to experience of, 16, 114–17, 120, 121, 123, 132, 134, 136–38, 178n11; disidentifications of, 105–11; epistemic injustice toward, 14; epistemology of, 5, 9; oppression of, 14; social context of, 16; sociality of, 16, 113, 116, 123–24, 129–33, 136; solidarity with, 138–39, 142, 145, 146, 148, 151, 152, 158; white gays/lesbians and, 91–94
Queer theory, criticisms of, 10–11, 16–18, 163n32, 163n34, 164n36, 166n1
Quintanales, Mirtha, 103–4
Quiroga, José, 164n34

Race and racism: in Baldwin's *Another Country*, 52–57; Cho's comedy act and, 148, 151–58; directed at queers of color, 14; feminism and, 10, 139–40; in scholarship, 26–27; stereotypes, 152–55; in United States, 3, 45; white gays/lesbians and, 91–94

Race fatigue, 23–24
Racialized conduits, 22, 141. *See also*
   Switchpoints
Rational choice, 87
Realism: Baldwin and, 7, 47–48; benefits of, 13; decolonial, 5, 13; defined, 161*n*9; and identity, 47–48, 71–72, 87–88; and objectivity, 20–21, 161*n*9; perspectival view of, 75; return to, 19; as revised constructivism, 19–20, 161*n*9; role of knowledge in, 165*n*52
Rechy, John, 90
Reddy, Chandan, 155
Reference, 73–74
Relativism, 5
Representation: language and, 34–37; literature and, 75–76
Responsibility. *See* Ethics and responsibility
Rivera, Tomas, 115
Robertson, Pamela, 139–40, 180*n*8, 182*n*16
Robles, Augie, *Cholo/Joto*, 107–8
Rodríguez, Juana María, 164*n*34
Rodriguez, Richard, 177*n*3; *Hunger of Memory*, 89–90
Romero, Lora, 82, 84
Romo, Ito, 115
Romo-Carmona, Mariana, *Conversaciones*, 132
Roque-Ramírez, Horacio, "Cholo/Salvatrucho," 108–10, 176*n*89
Ross, Andrew, 180*n*8
Rowden, Terry, 64
Rubin, Gayle, 10
Ru Paul, 155

Saldívar, Ramón, 169*n*10, 177*n*1
Sánchez, Juanita, 93
Sanchez, Luis Rafael, "¡Jum!," 132
Sánchez-Eppler, Benigno, 11
Sara/Ricardo, 106–7
Schwartzman, Lisa, 39–41
Science. *See* Social sciences
Scott, Joan W., 26, 166*n*7
Self-knowledge, 19, 46–47, 66–71
Shame, 141–42, 148, 155
Shimizu, Celine Parreñas, 141
Skepticism, limitations of, 5, 25–26, 39–42, 73, 75
Smith, Jack, 106
Smith, Patricia Juliana, 181*n*8

Sneideker, Michael, 163*n*32
Social construction: Baldwin and, 7; identity as, 6–8. *See also* Constructivism
Sociality of queerness, 16, 113, 116, 123–24, 129–33, 136
Social sciences, 1–4
Solidarity, Cho's comedy as expression of, 138–39, 142, 145, 146, 148, 151, 152, 158
Sommer, Doris, 162*n*10
Soto, Sandra, 163*n*32, 163*n*34, 164*n*36
Spatiality: Chicana/os and, 173*n*13; homosexuality and, 57; identity and, 105–11; queer identity and, 79. *See also* Migration; Queer Latina/o migrant labor
Spivak, Gayatri, 11
Springfield, Dusty, 181*n*8
Steele, Shelby, 177*n*3
Stereotypes, racial, 152–55
Stone-Mediatore, Shari, 25–26
Strategic essentialism, 11–12
Subjecthood, 72. *See also* Identity
Subjectivism, 5
Suicide, 46–48, 50
Switchpoints, 22, 141, 142, 151, 155, 157

Tinsley, Omise'eke Natasha, 17
Tortilleras, 85, 86, 102, 174*n*28
Tower of Babel, 31
Transformational experiences, 87–88, 98
Tropicana, Carmelita, 106, 140

Utopian practice, 105–6

Villa, Raúl, 93–94
Virgen de Guadalupe, 83

Walker, Alice, 163*n*18
Warner, Michael, 174*n*35
West, Mae, 139, 181*n*8
Williams, Patricia, 155
Witnessing to queerness, 16, 114–17, 120, 121, 123, 132, 134, 136–38, 178*n*11
Women's movement, 98
World-making, 105, 106
Writers of color: and knowledge acquisition, 18; reading, 162*n*10

Yarbro-Bejarano, Yvonne, 164*n*34, 177*n*1

Stanford Studies in
COMPARATIVE RACE AND ETHNICITY

Published in collaboration with the Center for Comparative Studies in Race and Ethnicity, Stanford University

SERIES EDITORS

  Hazel Rose Markus
  Paula M.L. Moya

EDITORIAL BOARD

  H. Samy Alim
  Gordon Chang
  Gary Segura
  C. Matthew Snipp

This series publishes outstanding scholarship that focuses centrally on comparative studies of race and ethnicity. Rather than exploring the experiences and conditions of a single racial or ethnic group, this series looks across racial and ethnic groups in order to take a more complex, dynamic, and interactive approach to understanding these social categories. By comparative, we mean a serious engagement with two or more groups or possibly one ancestry group studied across large geographic boundaries. Our definition is meant to be broad and capacious, not limiting, and we invite new ways of thinking about the comparative study of race and ethnicity.